D1333266

GREEN SHOOTS

IRISH FOOTBALL HISTORIES

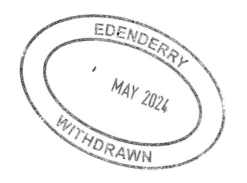

GREEN SHOOTS

IRISH FOOTBALL
HISTORIES

MICHAEL WALKER

deCoubertin
BOOKS

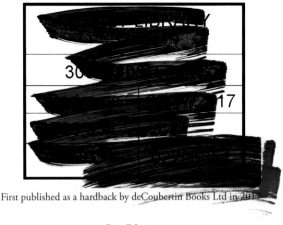

First published as a hardback by deCoubertin Books Ltd in 2017

First Edition

deCoubertin Books, Studio I, Baltic Creative Campus, Liverpool, L1 OAH
www.decoubertin.co.uk

ISBN: 978-1909245501

A CIP catalogue record for this book is available from the British Library.

Cover design by Zoran Lucić

Printed and bound by Jellyfish

FOR

The Browns of Lecumpher Street, Belfast
The Walkers of Roslyn Street, Belfast
The Pattersons of Distillery Street, Belfast

And for Alastair Bruce (1962-2015) of Kirkcaldy,
Fife.

CONTENTS

INTRODUCTION

THE OLD JOKE ABOUT SEEKING DIRECTIONS FROM AN IRISHMAN AND receiving the reply: 'Well, I wouldn't start from here if I were you,' is one of those that keeps on giving.

It has been present throughout the researching and writing of this book, whether at the end walking down the Newtownards Road in east Belfast looking at a portrait of Derek Dougan; or on the way hearing tales of early years in rural Galway from Paddy Mulligan; or wading through edition after edition of the *Ipswich Evening Football Star* from the 1950s in the British Library in London.

If literally lost in the hills above Castlerock in search of Harry Gregg, there have also been other moments of metaphorical dislocation. Irish football, in an organized sense, is almost 140 years old. It has had a border driven through it, it has not had a linear development; trying to find a pathway through it has meant wrong turns and dead ends.

Therefore, while it may sound peculiarly Irish, it seems necessary, like the old joke, to start with what this is not. It was re-assuring that on returning to Dave Hannigan's book on Irish football from 1998, *The Garrison Game,* he began with a similar declaration. In Hannigan's case it was about a chapter on Northern Ireland. There wasn't one.

Here there is much Northern Ireland football – and Northern Ireland – but the book is 32-county in approach, even if quite a few counties go unmentioned. That is because this is not an encyclopedia of Irish football, nor is it an attempt at a definitive history of the sport on this island, a chronological re-telling of goals and games. As far as the Republic of Ireland is concerned, Sean Ryan has done that with *Boys In*

Green, while Malcom Brodie wrote his first history of the game in the North in 1963.

It is, rather, a history of sorts, a compendium of stories and opinions and interviews that, hopefully, amounts to an overall impression of football, or soccer, in Ireland.

Its 32-county nature stems from the fact Irish football pre-dated the Irish border by 40 years and someone like William McCrum grew up playing football – and shaping it forever – in a united Ireland. It stems from meeting men such as Con Martin, a Dubliner who wore the green jersey of both northern and southern Ireland.

The lower case 'n' and 's' are deliberate and cases are interchanged in the text, which should be self-explanatory. Con Martin did not play for Northern Ireland when they were called that, he played for them when they were simply called 'Ireland', even though they represented the northern, Irish Football Association (IFA), and the southern, Football Association of Ireland (FAI), bitterly resented them using the name.

Johnny Brown, from our family, did the same as Martin but in the opposite direction. It has been revealing and educational to revisit their lives and times, why it was possible to play for two Irelands and how that division – The Split – was sustained and maintained.

It meant that at the most recent international tournament Irish football sent two teams to France for Euro 2016.

The island of Ireland has a population of approximately 6.5 million; the Republic of Ireland's first opponents in France – Sweden – has a population of 10 million. Sweden sent over only one team to France.

Ireland is a crowded sporting country. It contains an organization of unique cultural significance and sporting scale, the Gaelic Athletic Association, while rugby has attracted growing modern popularity and sponsorship and media followings. And there is, of course, always the horse.

Football, soccer, has long had to battle for its place in Irish society and that position remains unchanged despite the huge contribution of Irish footballers to Irish life.

In France, both Irelands produced memorable moments, against Ukraine and Italy, and both made it through to the knock-out stage. But both finished third in their group – in previous tournaments there would not have been progression.

Within Ireland the two-team status was remarked upon rarely in 2016, but in France there was consternation from a local journalist at Northern Ireland's squad base north of Lyon.

The IFA had decorated the sports hall beside the team hotel with squad portraits, celebratory photographs of the qualification campaign and some biographical details of the players.

It was Shane Ferguson who prompted French curiosity as below his picture his place of birth was described as: 'Derry/Londonderry'. Ferguson not only comes from a city and county where people still cannot agree on its name, he was thought to be another of those players from Derry, which is in Northern Ireland, who would choose to play for the Republic of Ireland. As it turned out, Ferguson was capped by Northern Ireland.

The local journalist pointed at Ferguson and asked the Irish reporters about 'Derry/ Londonderry', why there were two names for one place.

If the Frenchman was bemused, the Irishmen were equally unsure as to how to begin an answer. If accurate, they knew it would be long, controversial and include many detours through Irish history. And they also knew that it was most likely to feature the words: 'Well, I wouldn't start from here if I were you.'

Michael Walker
Belfast, July 2017

PART I

SOME HISTORY
SOME IDENTITY

FRANKIE KERR'S BALL

FRANKIE KERR'S KNOWING YOUNG FINGERTIPS SMOOTHED THEIR WAY across the leather skin panels of the freshly-made football. Frankie had threaded a yellow lace through five pairs of holes running along a seam of the brown ball. He had checked the weight, minimum 12oz. It was ready.

The enlarged knuckle on Frankie's right hand brushed against the ball. The knuckle was a small dislocation from birth that became useful when Frankie started boxing – and at 16 he was amateur Flyweight champion of Ireland.

On this day, that title was a year away. On this day – 1 February 1930 – 15 year-old Frank Kerr had to focus on his Saturday job. It was as a racquet-stringer and ball-lacer at the Athletic Stores sports shop on Bridge Street in the middle of Belfast. On this particular Saturday, though, there was more to do than string tennis racquets and tie up footballs.

Young Frankie had an extra errand. It entailed leaving the shop in the city centre and walking west, away from York Lane where he and his seven brothers were born, towards the Falls Road and a place known locally as 'Paradise'.

That was the name given to Celtic Park, home of Belfast Celtic Football Club, a unique institution in the history of Irish football, whose team had won the previous four Irish League titles. Belfast Celtic were the strongest, most talented team in Ireland.

In Kerr's gifted hands were two balls he had prepared that morning. One was a matchball, the other a replacement, and Kerr was to hand them over to Irish Football Association (IFA) officials who that afternoon were staging an Ireland-Wales international in the British Home Championships. The balls were branded: 'Special Victory'.

The game had been overshadowed by withdrawals from players based in England, such as the great Irish goalkeeper Elisha Scott, who was told to play for his club Liverpool that afternoon. Wintry rain was also a concern to the IFA. They thought it might affect the pitch and the attendance. It poured all Friday in Belfast.

Nevertheless, there was still anticipation. The *Belfast Telegraph* reported in its preview: 'Everything is in readiness to house a big crowd.' It said there would be 'over 20 turnstiles in operation' and that 'there will be the usual special tram service via both Donegall and Falls Roads.' At Celtic Park, it added, 'the RUC Band will be in attendance.'

The Wales team had arrived on the boat from Liverpool. The visitors spent Friday at Carlingford Lough on the Irish border, which had been established nine years earlier.

It was the first-ever such match at Celtic Park. From 1910 most Ireland home games had been played at Windsor Park, home of Linfield, Belfast Celtic's fierce rivals – politically as well as sporting. So, locally, the game was already historic. By its end, there was an international dimension to the history. The final score was Ireland 7-0 Wales. It was a record victory – just like the ball, a special victory.

The pitch had indeed cut up but as the *Ireland's Saturday Night* newspaper put it, 'the representatives of Erin' held firm. Their kit was blue, St. Patrick's blue and the headlines read: 'Welsh Soccer Rout'; '7-0 at Paradise'; 'Tallest Score in International for Forty Years'; 'Bambrick's Amazing Achievement'.

The last of those referred to Joe Bambrick, a 24 year-old striker from Linfield who was winning his fifth cap. Bambrick scored the opening goal in the twelfth minute and the second just before half-time. He then got a third, a fourth, a fifth and a sixth. It was 6-0 and Joe Bambrick had scored them all.

His captain, Andy McCluggage, made it seven late on. The Welsh goalkeeper, Dick Finnigan, once of Manchester City, received some praise, but this was to be his first and last cap. It was Bambrick who was shooting and heading his way into history.

As the *Irish News* began its report:

> 'Ireland seven, Wales nil; Joe had six of the goals.' This copy of a telegram handed over the Post Office counter by a delighted Linfield enthusiast on Saturday evening tells crisply the story of the game. But what a theme for the novelist is suggested by this message of ten words. All that is required is a little padding. The material is there for a sixty thousand words thriller. Joe Bambrick, of course, would be the hero of the story.'

A prolific centre forward with Linfield in the Irish League, Bambrick would go on to join Chelsea to replace Hughie Gallacher. No-one in Irish or British international football had scored six before in an international, or since.

Bambrick was born and bred on Roden Street, close enough to Celtic Park for the six roars he provoked from the 18,000 crowd who braved the cold – no rain – to be heard in his family's back yard. Well-known in Irish League football, Bambrick became a sensation beyond the game. Within a week Belfast soft drinks company, Cantrell & Cochrane, had a new product called 'Joe Six', while a terrace catchphrase moved from local football's vocabulary into broader Irish culture:

'Head, heel or toe
Slip it to Joe.'

Bambrick was famous. Repeatedly described as 'modest' and 'quiet-spoken', fans loved relaying Bambrick's laconic and uncharacteristic exchange with Fred Keenor, the fearsome Wales captain and the man who had lifted the 1927 FA Cup for Cardiff City.

'Six kicks of the ball and you get six goals!' said Keenor, with a few expletives inserted.

'Ah, wait a minute Taffy,' replied Bambrick, 'one of them was a header.'

Poems were written in Bambrick's honour, and when he was hospitalised by a severed nerve in his hand ten months later, Joe's progress was the subject of daily bulletins. The legend of Joe Bambrick grew and grew and on the fiftieth anniversary of his six strikes he was taken back to the dilapidated Celtic Park – by then a dog track – to rekindle memories of the day in 1930 against Wales.

'It was always a great pitch,' Bambrick said with a professional's knowledge, 'never heavy, though it was a bit soggy that day. I hit two in the first half at the Donegall Road end, then four at the other end in the second half.' There were few oratorical flourishes, that was not Bambrick's style. Anyway, those had come half a century before, *Ireland's Saturday Night* describing Bambrick's second goal thus:

Just before the interval, Bambrick got a real old-timer. He succes-
sively beat Keenor, Lawrence, Hugh and Jones, carried the ball
to within half-a-dozen yards of goal and scored well out of reach,
Finnigan and his colleagues seeming to be electrified by this sud-
den and unexpected turn of events.

Old-timer, all-timer, to Joe Bambrick it came naturally. At Glentoran aged 20, he had also scored six in one match; thereafter at Linfield he scored 539 goals in seven-and-a-half seasons.

The Irish League hosted five additional competitions then, besides the league itself and the Irish Cup, and the change in the offside law in 1925 – caused by another west Belfast man, Bill McCracken, while playing for Newcastle United – made it easier for strikers. Even so, Bambrick was a phenomenon.

In the season of the Wales game, he scored 96 goals, including the six at Celtic Park. He returned to the same venue for the Irish Cup final, where Linfield won 4-3 against Ballymena: Joe Bambrick scored all four.

Observing this from afar was a man who had the misfortune to be Arsenal manager immediately before Herbert Chapman – Leslie Knighton. In 1933 Knighton was managing Chelsea, a young, trophyless club then with a reputation for large crowds and showmanship.

Chelsea were ambitious and, back in England's First Division in 1930, demonstrated intent by signing the great Gallacher from Newcastle for £10,000, not far short of a world record transfer fee. The idea was that Gallacher would propel the newly-promoted side into title contenders. But although he scored goals, Chelsea flat-lined and in November 1934 Gallacher was sold to Derby County. Knighton, as he said in his memoirs, was quickly on the boat to Ireland:

> Before very long I was making that frightful sea crossing to Belfast once again. I have done it so often, and I swear that each time has consistently been worse than the last. But I would cross the Bay of Biscay in a fishing-smack to get the best sort of players that Ireland breeds!

A month after Gallacher left, Joe Bambrick joined Chelsea. Linfield received £3,000 of which £750 went to Bambrick. He could have bought most of Roden Street.

Direct from the Irish League into the Chelsea first team, Bambrick's debut came on Christmas Day 1934 at home to Aston Villa. His second game was the next day at Villa Park. There Bambrick scored his first Chelsea goal and once settled in London, Bambrick soon scored four against Leeds United, part of a streak of 17 goals in 14 First Division matches. Chelsea were second-bottom when he was signed; they finished 12th.

Bambrick also scored on the October day in 1935 when Stamford Bridge recorded what was then the largest-ever attendance for a league match – 82,905 – against Arsenal. Chelsea had moved up to eighth, but they were far from champions and even being the club's top scorer in season 1935-36 did not make Bambrick a Chelsea hero. He is remembered as often for being part of the forward line on the afternoon in 1936 when Sunderland goalkeeper Jimmy Thorpe sustained injuries that killed him a week later. Bambrick scored twice at Roker Park.

Bambrick's Ireland career also turned curious. While he played in the match after that 7-0 Wales result, he was then omitted for 22 months. Returning to the Ireland team in late 1931, he did not play again until 1935. After three more caps, he was out until 1938. His eleventh and final appearance came in a 1-0 victory over Wales at Windsor Park. Ireland's scorer: Joe Bambrick.

*

THE 'IRELAND' TEAM THEN REPRESENTED THE IFA. THIS WAS FORMED in Belfast in 1880 and selected players from all 32 counties of a country then unified. After the Partition of Ireland in 1921, a Dublin-based body, the Football Association of Ireland (FAI) was formed. It organised an 'Ireland' team which represented the 26 counties of the just-declared Irish Republic, or Irish Free State.

This is how it remains, so that at the European Championships of 2016 in France, the island of Ireland sent two teams, the Republic of Ireland and Northern Ireland.

Back in the 1920s and 30s both Associations insisted they could select players from across the island and more than 30 did so, men such as Billy Lacey and Johnny Carey. The northern IFA 'Ireland' continued to pick players who had been born beyond the new Irish border which separated the six counties of Northern Ireland from the 26 counties of the Irish Republic. This explains why, when Bambrick was overlooked by the erratic committee which made decisions then, the player often replacing him was a Dubliner from a very different background, Jimmy Dunne.

Like Bambrick, Dunne was born in 1905. From Ringsend in inner Dublin on the south bank of the River Liffey, Dunne left for English football in 1925, for New Brighton, then in Division Three North with clubs such as Grimsby Town and Rochdale.

Dunne did not stay long. After just eight matches (six goals) Sheffield United offered £800. The Bramall Lane club were about to finish fifth in the First Division – England's top tier – and this was a considerable sum for a novice.

If United knew about Dunne's recent past, it was not off-putting. It had included a period of internment at the Curragh and at Portlaoise prison. In a brief obituary in the Irish Press, Dunne was described as 'a former member of 'D' Company IRA' who had, during incarceration, 'spent a term on hunger strike'.

It has since been said that Dunne, from a Republican family, was interned by the new Free State government because of the IRA activities of his brother, Christy. It is also said Dunne practiced soccer while behind bars and got a nickname, 'Snowy', due to his fair hair.

Jimmy Dunne had been a talented Gaelic footballer but once he had played soccer in England, he was no longer welcomed by the GAA, the Gaelic Athletic Association. He was playing a game 'foreign' to the Gaelic ideal.

He played it well. It took time to break through at Sheffield United but once Dunne did he scored with Bambrick frequency. There was a debut against Arsenal in 1926 before his 21st birthday and a first cap for the northern, IFA Ireland came in 1928 – eight months before Bambrick. But it was not until 1929 that Dunne bloomed.

Bramall Lane was a three-sided stadium, which doubled as a cricket ground for Yorkshire and England, and Dunne started running up cricket scores. Turning 24, there were 42 goals in 43 games in 1929/30, 50 in 47 the next season, then 35 in 40 and 32 in 43 in 1932/33. It says everything about Dunne's calibre that it was another 63 years before his top-flight record of scoring more than 30 goals in three consecutive seasons was equalled – by Alan Shearer at Blackburn Rovers.

Dunne's goals in season 1931/32 prompt further modern comparison. In 2015/16 Leicester City's Jamie Vardy scored in 11 consecutive Premier League games. That took him past the post-1992 Premier League record set by Ruud van Nistelrooy.

But it did not take Vardy past Jimmy Dunne's top division record. Between 24 October 1931 and New Year's Day 1932 Dunne scored in 12 consecutive Sheffield United games. Unmatched.

Dunne's unbeaten run began at Grimsby. Like Belfast, like every other English town, Sheffield had a Saturday night sports paper. Printed on green paper, thus known as the *Green Un*, it was published immediately after the final whistle and was hugely popular. Its report from Grimsby said: 'It was good to see Jimmy Dunne scoring goals again, and playing with something of his old dash.'

Liverpool were then beaten at Bramall Lane, Dunne scoring the opener. He scored against Leicester and Bolton Wanderers were next, when Dunne's heading prowess was compared to Dixie Dean's, the *Green Un's* 'Big Blades' column declaring: 'Last Saturday it was hard to conceive that anyone, I don't care who it is, can be better than Jimmy. I must dispute the claim that Dean is better. Jimmy's two goals and the one he made for Oswald were masterpieces.'

A Sheffield derby followed – Wednesday had been League champions in 1930 – and Dunne scored another header. Chelsea were then beaten.

Having played in four of the previous five Ireland (IFA) matches – and scored in each of them – Dunne was called up again to face Wales at Windsor Park on 5 December. He declined. 'Jimmy has nothing to say by way of explanation and no one can blame him for that,' commented the *Green Un*.

In Belfast there was dismay but Dunne could do little wrong in Sheffield, though there was one criticism of the Irishman leading United up the table – his lack of hat-tricks. It was mentioned before the Blades' next game, at Middlesbrough. On the afternoon he could have been playing in Belfast for Ireland, Dunne was with United at Ayresome Park. The Blades lost 4-3, this despite a hat-trick from Jimmy Dunne.

A detail from the match report was the presence in the crowd of Alf Common. Common was the first-ever £1,000 footballer – in 1905 he moved from Sunderland to Middlesbrough for that fee having previously played for Sheffield United. The history man was watching another history man.

When Dunne scored against Aston Villa his run was noted for the first time in the local press: 'Jimmy Dunne has scored in his last eight games.' Sheffield United were fourth in the table. They lost to Newcastle United – Dunne scored of course – and Christmas 1931 brought a double-header against Arsenal. Christmas Day's 4-1 home win at Bramall Lane was followed by a 2-0 victory at Highbury 24 hours later.

'The scoring power of Jimmy Dunne has been maintained,' boasted the *Green Un*. 'Today is the eleventh successive Saturday in which Sheffield United's centre-forward has found the net, in league or international football. It's fine going.'

What had been noticed is that the Saturday before the Sheffield sequence, Dunne had scored for Ireland against England at Windsor Park. So when Dunne then scored against Blackburn on New Year's Day 1932 it was his 12th consecutive league game scoring but his 13th match overall. The run had taken Sheffield United to second in the table, behind Dean's Everton.

It ended the day after the Blackburn game, at Fratton Park. Portsmouth won 2-1 and though the *Sheffield Telegraph* acknowledged 'an end to Jimmy Dunne's scoring sequence,' it said there was 'no anxiety'. As proof, Dunne scored in the next game, a strike so good the paper produced a diagram of it complete with arrows, a forerunner of graphics used today.

Sheffield United were top of the League and Dunne's goals had taken them there. This prompted Herbert Chapman to act. Chapman was a Yorkshireman and a former Sheffield United player, but the Arsenal manager's bid for Dunne was rebuffed. He would have to wait, but wait he did and 18 months after Dunne's record run, the *Green Un* reported breathlessly:

> *Jimmy Dunne, darling of the Bramall Lane crowd, was trans-*
> *ferred to Arsenal this morning in a lightning operation. When*
> *United sent to his lodgings, Jimmy was in bed. Once he had*

reached Bramall Lane, however, things went forward in very quick time, and almost the next thing was that he was an Arsenal player, catching the 11.05 train to London in order to assist his new club against Middlesbrough.

Arsenal won 6-0 and the headline was: 'Dunne Soon Shines'.

It was late September 1933. Four months later, Herbert Chapman died suddenly. Dunne turned out to be the great manager's last signing. He cost £8,250.

Perhaps in tribute to Chapman, Arsenal won the league title that season. Sheffield United were relegated.

Arsenal won the league the next season, too, but the club had bought Ted Drake from Southampton to replace Dunne, who was downgraded to Highbury's reserves. Sheffield United tried to buy back their star but Arsenal sold Dunne to Drake's former club, Southampton, instead.

Dunne passed his 31st birthday at the Dell and helped the Saints stay in the Second Division, the Championship today. By his 32nd birthday he was back in Dublin as player-manager of Shamrock Rovers.

All the while he continued to be selected for international football, but having started out with the northern, Belfast version of Ireland in 1928, Dunne finished with the southern, Dublin version of Ireland in 1939. In total he won 22 caps, the last coming in the last international before the Second World War. It was controversial – against Germany in Bremen in May 1939. Adolf Hitler's armies had already annexed Austria and the Sudetenland in Czechoslovakia by then but the FAI had agreed to go.

The Irish were on an end of season tour and had played Hungary in Budapest five days earlier. Hungary's government was sympathetic to Nazi Germany but the southern version of Ireland was only 28 games old and opponents were hard to come by. The Republic of Ireland, as the team would come to be known, did not play England until 1946, Wales until 1960 and Scotland until 1961. Hungary and Germany, in football terms, offered early recognition and revenue.

In Bremen, the Irish were also offered the chance to make a Nazi salute before kick-off. As with England in Berlin twelve months before, there was official pressure on the players to make the raised arm gesture. The England players did not enjoy being forced to do it and, as captain of Ireland, neither did Dunne. The story re-told from the dressing-room is that as the Irish players were about to salute, Dunne shouted 'Remember 1916! Remember Aughrim!'

The latter was a lost Irish battle from 1691 and is celebrated in the second line of the Protestant anthem, 'The Sash My Father Wore'. The photograph of the Irish

XI is grainy but several players can be seen giving the Nazi salute. On Dunne it is inconclusive.

The game, for what it is worth, ended 1-1, Germany's scorer being a 23 year-old from Dresden, Helmut Schoen. He, of course, became manager of post-war West Germany and won the World Cup in 1974.

Dunne had played 15 times for the FAI's Ireland and scored 13 goals. His record would not be beaten until 1967, by Noel Cantwell. Sadly, aged 44, Dunne died in Dublin the day after watching his Irish successors face Sweden at Dalymount Park. He saw Con Martin score but he did not see his sons, Tommy or Jimmy junior, begin their careers. Tommy won two caps, Jimmy joined Leicester City, where Vardy would later chase down his father's record, unsuccessfully.

Vardy is from Sheffield. News of Dunne's death made the front pages there, the *Sheffield Star* paying this tribute:

> *His passing will come as a great shock to Sheffielders with whom*
> *he was unfailingly popular … Dunne's leadership often possessed*
> *the quality of genius.*

*

JIMMY DUNNE AND JOE BAMBRICK WERE NEVER TOGETHER ON THE same Irish team. Bambrick did not play for the southern FAI Ireland, while Dunne stopped playing for the northern IFA Ireland in 1932.

This remained a new, fluid era for the two Irelands, however. Players continued to be selected for both countries – 20 in total, from the start of the FAI team in a friendly in Italy in 1926, until 1939.

It made for odd overlaps, one example being Coventry City's Johnny Brown, who played alongside Bambrick for the north in 1938 against Wales, ten months after playing alongside Dunne for the south in Paris against France. In all Brown would play ten games for Ireland – the northern version based in his home town of Belfast – and two, both in 1937, for the FAI team when it was known as 'Eire'.

Brown is not a celebrated dual-national like Jimmy Dunne or, later, Con Martin or Peter Farrell, but he has some personal importance: he was my father's uncle. With just over eight years between them, their relationship was brotherly. Johnny Brown is the man on the cover of this book.

That photograph of Brown in his Ireland schoolboy kit lived in an album in our house in east Belfast. Occasionally it would come out, as would one of Brown's velvet

Irish caps and a thick cotton, green Irish schoolboy jersey. It might have been that jersey Brown was wearing in the picture.

Sadly there are no markings or dates on the back of the photograph, which is printed on a postcard. Brown was born in 1914 so the photograph probably dates from 1929 or 1930 when he was 15 and attracting the attention of Belfast Celtic.

Johnny Brown came from 37 Lecumpher Street, off the Beersbridge Road in east Belfast. The Walker side of the family lived initially around the corner in Glenvarlock Street, then on Roslyn Street off the Woodstock Road.

East Belfast was industrial then, dominated by the shipyards which built the Titanic. There was a huge ropeworks too – where Danny Blanchflower's mother worked – plus many heavy engineering factories such as the Sirocco Works where my father, Tommy, was employed for three decades.

In an intensely political and often violent era, east Belfast was almost exclusively Protestant in religion and Orange in outlook, though those local conditions did not prevent Johnny Brown crossing the city to join Belfast Celtic. The club's fanbase was largely Catholic and Irish nationalist, but by the 1930s their recruitment policy was talent-based, apolitical. When Elisha Scott became manager and was challenged by fans who wanted more Catholics in the team, and by fellow Protestants who criticised his position at the club, he replied: 'I don't play good Protestants or good Catholics, I just play good players.'

Belfast Celtic will not have found it difficult to sign Brown. The now deceased club had a glamour and a pull that few, if any, other Irish club could touch. In his 1963 *History of Irish Soccer*, Malcolm Brodie reserved the last chapter for Celtic and began:

> *Belfast Celtic were more than an ordinary soccer team. They were an institution: a club which excited the attention of everyone; a club whose name never fails to create nostalgia. Many contended they were unquestionably the greatest team Ireland has ever known. Certainly I am filled with rapturous thoughts.*

Belfast Celtic were formed in 1891 by a group of eight businessmen at No. 88 Falls Road. There was from the beginning a desire to be what is today called a community club, a desire to be like Glasgow Celtic, who made a donation to the new club in Belfast. Without premises, in their first season in the Irish League in 1896/97 Belfast Celtic finished bottom. The lack of a home meant all games were played away, which helps explain results.

On a militarized island, the North Staffordshire Regiment were in the Irish League then and later the Royal Scots Guards would be members. This is how football – or soccer – came to be labelled the 'Garrison Game', a view expressed by Irish Republican leader Michael Collins who decried what he saw as the cultural "penetration of Ireland". Collins said there should be "no soccer for Gaels".

From their earliest days in the Irish League, Belfast Celtic and their supporters found themselves enmeshed in the discontent and politics of the era. This was to manifest itself at government level, but more frequently on the streets. Belfast Celtic were often most unwelcome visitors to city rivals, particularly Glentoran and Linfield, who were based in Protestant areas. On their first League visit to Glentoran at the Oval, adjacent to the shipyards, Belfast Celtic's travelling fans were involved in a riot with the locals. In 1899 a cup semi-final with the same opponents at Distillery's ground, Grosvenor Park, had to be abandoned due to crowd trouble. The matchball was taken and sliced apart by some knife-wielding fans.

Belfast was a city enduring daily political turmoil. The 1899/00 season consisted of so few games, Belfast Celtic became champions for the first time after playing only nine times. The Royal Scots played seven games before being called to the Boer War.

Two years later Belfast Celtic bought a plot of land that would become Celtic Park – 'Paradise' – where Frankie Kerr walked to. While it would later attract Bambrick's goals and Brodie's eulogies, there was crowd trouble there early on.

In what was a united Ireland, a part of the United Kingdom, Dublin clubs gradually joined the Irish League and in 1910 Bohemians went to Belfast Celtic for an Irish Cup-tie. It too was abandoned following a pitch invasion, the Dubliners having gone ahead through Harold Sloan, who seven years later would die in northern France in World War I.

A culture of street violence was embedded in Belfast and Irish League football came from the streets of the city. Meanwhile in London, in the House of Commons, in 1912 came the Home Rule Bill. Its aim was to give Ireland some governmental autonomy and it was once again on Belfast's streets where the chief resistance to this was found.

One high-profile English politician who pushed against this resistance, who supported Home Rule, was Winston Churchill. It was Churchill's father Randolph who had coined the phrase: 'Ulster will fight and Ulster will be right', but his son took a different view.

Randolph Churchill's slogan had been made in 1886 in the Ulster Hall in Belfast and 26 years later, in February 1912, son Winston planned a trip of his own to Belfast to speak *for* Home Rule. Churchill junior also chose the Ulster Hall as his venue until Ulster Unionists discovered this and scuppered the plan.

When Churchill heard, he wrote frankly to his wife Clementine about an alternative arrangement on the Falls Road, which he said would mean: 'The Orange faction will be left to brood morosely over their illegal and uncontested possession of the Ulster Hall. Dirty dogs. Chained like suffragettes to the railings . . .'

Churchill needed another venue and the West Belfast MP Joe Devlin offered him the use of Celtic Park. The club agreed. And so, on the Falls Road, Winston Churchill, with Clementine alongside, gave a speech in favour of Home Rule to 5,000 inside a giant marquee erected on Celtic Park, with Irish Nationalist leader John Redmond there too.

Clementine had overcome worries about the threat of being rendered disfigured by what had become known as 'Belfast confetti' – it was reported that 'great quantities of bolts and nuts' had been looted from the shipyard. The Churchills' visit was notorious and provocative and their convoy was jostled as it headed towards the Falls. But the Churchills came and went, Belfast Celtic remained and as Barry Flynn writes in *Political Football: The Life & Death of Belfast Celtic*: 'Celtic Park as a venue had become politicised and associated with the Nationalist cause.'

As sectarian tensions rose that summer, Catholic workers were expelled from the Harland & Wolff shipyard and when the 1912/13 Irish League kicked off, 14 September brought Linfield to Celtic Park. Reports say 20,000 were there and it was peaceful until half-time. But rival political colours – orange and green – were in evidence: Irish League football had become the theatre for Irish sectarian division.

A fist-fight broke out. Then another. Matters escalated quickly and violently. A shot was fired, then another, guns having joined knives as items to take to a football match in Belfast. A full-scale riot developed and lasted an hour, spreading from the terraces to the pitch.

In the midst of it the Celtic and Linfield players wanted to start the second half. 'The sound of more gunfire and the sight of four policemen laid out on stretchers soon put an end to any such notions,' writes Flynn, who adds that much Belfast confetti was 'exchanged'.

Following 'a further burst of twenty shots', the police began to evacuate Celtic Park. But the mayhem continued through the streets and through the night. Dozens of injured spectators were left on the terraces and turf and were eventually treated by medics. Fifty-four men were taken to hospital, five with gunshot wounds.

One witness to this was Ina Heron, daughter of James Connolly, executed by the British Army four years later for his leading role in the Easter Rising.

Belfast was suffering the disfigurement Clementine Churchill had feared and all its citizens knew that two Saturdays later the Unionist firebrand leader Sir Edward

Carson had scheduled 'Ulster Day'. This was the day when over 450,000 men and women signed the Ulster Covenant to oppose Home Rule. It was a defining moment in the history of Ireland and was followed three months later by the establishment of the Ulster Volunteer Force (UVF). Unionism now had a 90,000-strong dedicated militia. Serious incidents were piling up.

All local football was cancelled on Ulster Day, bar one match – Distillery versus Belfast Celtic at Grosvenor Park, in between the City Hall where Unionism had gathered, and the Falls Road where Celtic fans came from.

The Irish Football Association had reacted to the Celtic Park shooting with a statement declaring 'that under no circumstances will any [political] flag, banner or other emblems of any kind be permitted inside our respective grounds.' It was the first of many such pleas.

A year later Glentoran issued one saying it had been instructed by the IFA to point out it was 'unsportsmanlike' for crowd behavior to reach a stage 'whereby the field of play is invaded after the game and revolvers and explosive material used to intimidate players and referee.'

The sound of gunfire at games became sufficiently common for the terms 'revolver music' and 'revolver idiot' to enter local press coverage of matches.

*

WHILE BELFAST WAS THE CENTRE OF POLITICAL – AND FOOTBALL – violence, Ireland was a united country and so was its football team. Internationals were held in Dublin as well as Belfast and the Scottish FA complained about the rough treatment it received at a match at Dalymount Park in March 1913. The SFA indicated it might boycott Ireland, a threat it followed through on during the 1970s.

As civil war approached Ireland, the First World War began in the summer of 1914. This diverted some attention from the sectarian strife scarring Belfast. The Irish League played on and the league champions for season 1914/15 were Belfast Celtic, their second title – although the season is recalled as much for Redmond returning to Celtic Park to drill the Irish Volunteers.

That was October 1914. One month later Johnny Brown was born across the increasingly divided city. By the time he started to kick a ball around, the Ireland Brown had been born into had experienced the Easter Rising, the loss of 5,000 men of the 36th Ulster Division in two days at the Battle of the Somme and, in May 1921, the enacting of the Government of Ireland Act bringing Partition to the island.

Two states were now in existence – the Irish Republic of 26 counties and Northern

Ireland, of six counties. In Brown's future line of work, that would mean two Ireland football teams.

Belfast Celtic continued. So did Belfast violence. When the Irish League resumed after WWI Belfast Celtic won a 14-game league which included Bohemians and Shelbourne from Dublin, an indication of the 32-county nature of the game then.

But the bigger headlines were for two meetings with Glentoran in two cup-ties – in March 1919 and St. Patrick's Day 1920 – at Cliftonville's ground, Solitude. On both occasions there was major trouble and at the latter match a man with a gun emerged from the Belfast Celtic fans invading the pitch. He fired into the Glentoran supporters. No-one was killed, five were wounded.

This was the semi-final of the Irish Cup. The IFA responded by kicking out both clubs which meant that the winners of the other semi-final won the Cup without a final. That club was Shelbourne, from Dublin.

But with the Anglo-Irish War, which had led to the agreement to partition Ireland, followed by the Irish Civil War, the entire island was gripped by a long, vicious spasm of suffering and division. And soon there would be no more 32-county football in Ireland.

As author Barry Flynn writes:

> One of the most violent episodes – and one of the most overlooked – was the frenzy of sectarian murder that gripped Belfast from the summer of 1920 until 1922. Compared to the troubles from 1969 to 1994, the disorders of the early 1920s plumbed depths of hatred that, in hindsight, seem incredible. The football team known as Belfast Celtic would not partake in the local game during that period . . that would have been an impossible task which would, in all probability, have ended in a bloodbath for the team and its supporters.

Flynn notes that some of the worst sectarian excesses were in the Ballymacarrett area of east Belfast, close to where Brown was growing up. The ugly expulsion of Catholic workers from the shipyards fuelled other conflicts. Neighbourhoods changed, the atmosphere changed, Belfast Celtic withdrew from the Irish League as the city underwent its own partition and sowed the seeds of later troubles.

Disturbingly, one of those who suffered in the shipyard was Harry Buckle. Buckle was an Ireland international who played in England with Sunderland and Portsmouth before, at 27, becoming player-manager of Coventry City. He returned to his home town in 1911 to play for Belfast Celtic and to work at Harland & Wolff, where the

Titanic was in the last phase of construction. It was a workplace of frequent intimidation and Buckle's past as an international was deemed less important than his Catholic background. He was once hit by a bolt and was also thrown in the deep dock water.

Somehow there was still some football played in the city. The great England international Charles Buchan recalled visiting in October 1921 for an Irish League versus English League match. The English players were offered the chance to decline the trip but 'all agreed' to travel, according to Buchan. He asked his former Sunderland teammate, English McConnell, who lived in Belfast, to show him the local sights.

'We went by tram,' Buchan said. 'As we passed the end of one street the conductor shouted: 'Down on the floor!' Without any question we fell flat on our faces. Luckily for us no bullets passed our way.'

A true professional, Buchan added: 'We won 1-0.'

By 1924 Belfast Celtic began to consider a return to an altered local football landscape. The establishment of an Irish Republic begat a new Irish association and a new Irish league. In 1922 St. James's Gate became the first winners of the League of Ireland, a new eight-team division administered by a Dublin body, the Football Association of Ireland.

In August 1924 Belfast Celtic were back in the Irish League. They finished third, but the team under manager Austin Donnelly was getting into a stride that saw Belfast Celtic win the Irish League for the next four seasons. In 1926 they also won the Irish Cup, 'Blind' Sammy Curran scoring a hat-trick against Linfield. Curran was blind, apparently, because he only had 'eyes for goal'.

There were still outbreaks of sectarian hooliganism at matches but Celtic had become the dominant football club in the Irish League by the start of the 1930s. For Johnny Brown, a schoolboy international, the club's football status will have meant more than its place in society, even if it must have provoked the odd questioning look where he lived.

He was coming from Glentoran territory, Protestant territory. In Lecumpher Street (now gone) there were 46 terraced houses and when the Ulster Covenant was signed, 44 of the signatories came from 29 addresses on Lecumpher Street. The house numbered 37 was not a signatory, though members of the extended family did sign the Covenant.

No. 37 was the home of Thomas and Susan Brown and their four children, one of whom was Johnny. Thomas Brown is registered as a joiner in the 1932 Belfast street directory. In 19 of the addresses the man of the house is listed as a labourer. There was an iron fitter, a yarn dresser and a smith's helper. This was working-class Belfast as the Depression hit.

*

FOR A TEENAGER LIKE BROWN, FOOTBALL WAS A HAPPY DIVERSION
and a way to earn money. Ultimately, it offered him an exit.

He must have been good. Belfast Celtic's records show that Brown was a given a
debut not long after his sixteenth birthday, January 1931.

Celtic won 4-1 against Ballymena (before they added 'United'). Rain had been
constant, reports said, and Celtic Park was like a bog – one headline was 'Paradise
Ploughing'. Playing on the right wing, Brown was described as 'altogether too fragile'
by the *Irish News*, though it also said: 'The youngster was clever in slipping his man,
but was beaten by the conditions underfoot.'

A football career had started. It was not professional, the teenage Brown spent
his days as an apprentice 'linen lapper' – a printer – at Ewart & Sons factory, but
there was progress on the pitch. Brown's debut was his one appearance that season
but even as a 16 year-old going on 17, there were 14 the next season. There was a
first goal, against Linfield. Joe Bambrick scored for Linfield.

Belfast Celtic reclaimed the Irish League title in 1933 and, passing his nineteenth
birthday in November, Brown was an established first-team player. He began season
1933-34 with 23 consecutive appearances and 11 goals. In form, English clubs were
beginning to notice Johnny Brown and one month after his 20th birthday, came his
last match for Belfast Celtic.

There was a ceremony before the game against Derry City. A recently-won trophy,
the Gold Cup, was paraded around Celtic Park by the former Belfast boxer Felix
Darragh, but Darragh was secondary to the presence of Wolverhampton Wanderers
manager, Major Frank Buckley. Brown was on Buckley's radar.

But at the centre of it was Davy 'Boy' Martin. An orphan born in Belfast nine
months before Brown, Martin joined the British Army as a youth – a drummer
boy – and had to buy his way out to join Cliftonville. From there, in 1932, he moved
to Belfast Celtic. A prolific and stylish striker, he became 'Boy Martin'.

The following year, on his Ireland debut, he scored two in a 2-1 win against
Scotland in Glasgow. One week later Sheffield United – Jimmy Dunne included –
visited Belfast Celtic for a friendly and lost 3-1 to a Martin hat-trick. He was 19 and
going places, most likely Everton.

Buckley intervened. Martin and Brown were bought for a combined £7,500.
Brown's valuation was £1,750. Martin's – £5,750 – was double what any club had
ever paid for an Irish footballer.

The *Irish News* reported that this was 'a terrible wrench' for Belfast Celtic, but also that: 'Cheques for £7,500 are not found on goosebury bushes.'

It was a big deal and for the players' departure to England, the pair were placed on a carriage and taken on a procession from Celtic Park to the docks accompanied by a band. An eye-witness was George Walker, the eldest of the six siblings in my father's family. Born in 1921, George was 13, seeing his uncle lauded.

'Oh yes, I went to watch Johnny play for Belfast Celtic,' George says. 'I'd take the tram up from outside the Hippodrome on Great Victoria Street. It would go up Divis Street. I saw him at Celtic Park, at Windsor Park, Glentoran, Cliftonville. He was sometimes a left winger, sometimes right, Boy Martin was in the middle. Then all of a sudden Major Buckley signed them.

'Joining Wolves was huge. I went down to the docks to see them off. I was 13 or 14, it was a really great procession, the club gave them such a send-off.'

Ireland's Saturday Night had the headline: 'Loss To Irish Game'. It said Brown's transfer had been 'a trifle overshadowed by the dazzle of the Celtic leader [Martin]'. In a lengthy editorial it went on to say Brown had gone from a schoolboy international match aged 15 in March 1930 to England's First Division in December 1934. 'This is climbing with a vengeance,' it said, 'but Brown has earned the step up. With splendid ball control and the ability to vary his methods he too should reach great heights in the game and the biggest cheque ever paid for a brace of Irishmen may yet prove to have been a rare bargain. [We] hope to see them bring glory to the 'Old Country'. Goodbye Davy; goodbye Jacky, and all success.'

John, Johnny, Jack and Jacky – Brown was accumulating names as well as praise and money.

Wolves needed the pair. They had just lost 7-1 at Arsenal, then at Portsmouth and were third-bottom, their top-division status under threat. That night's Wolverhampton *Sporting Star* reported the Portsmouth result but also on its front page: 'Wolves' Capture'. It said the transfer of Martin and Brown had been concluded and the tone was one of excitement, especially regarding Boy Martin: 'Everton and Arsenal were among other clubs interested in him.'

On 22 December 1934 Martin made his debut. It was at Molineux against Manchester City. Wolves won 5-0. The *Star* said: 'Martin did not score but he was the fastest man on the field and showed himself a fine leader.'

Three weeks later came Brown's debut. It was in the FA Cup against Notts County in front of 27,000. Wolves won 4-0 and Johnny scored, though he was being called Jack or Jackie. 'Brown, the Belfast Celtic player, made a splendid debut,' said the *Star*. One week on Tottenham Hotspur were the visitors to Molineux. Wolves, with Brown and Martin both playing, won 6-2, Brown 'dazzling the crowd' with his wing play.

The easing of Wolves' relegation fears was temporary. They lost the next six and Boy Martin and Johnny-Jackie Brown were dropped. Stan Cullis, who would go on to manage Wolves for 16 years, made his debut in this run. Wolves rallied and finished seventeenth.

There was no Brown headline until the opening day of the 1935/36 season. He scored in a 3-1 win over Birmingham – 'an exceptionally clean goal', according to the *Star*.

In November, though, Boy Martin was placed on the transfer list at the club's 'initiative'. It was less than a year since his move from Belfast Celtic. No explanation is given but Major Buckley liked to buy and sell and part of his legend surrounds the profits he made Wolves in the transfer market.

That said, one month on Boy Martin scored four for the reserves at Elland Road and he remained at Wolves for the season before being transferred to Nottingham Forest, then a division below, for £7,000.

Brown stayed. He began 1936/37 in the reserves but by September was back in the first team and winning at Preston. Then, on 19 September, Wolves beat Arsenal 2-0.

The attendance, over 53,000, was a new record for Molineux. Just as significant, it was the first time Wolves had beaten Arsenal there in 32 years. Johnny Brown scored the second after 19 minutes and his stern face stared out of the front page of the *Sporting Star* that evening. It must have been his best day at Wolverhampton. A month later he was sold.

As Brown scored at West Bromwich Albion the following week, the *Star* was reporting: 'Wolves have sold their fifth player of the season.'

It was Johnny Brown and he was joining Coventry City. The fee was £3,000, a new high for Coventry. It meant Major Buckley had bought two players from Belfast Celtic for £7,500 and sold them for £10,000 within two years.

*

IT MEANT A BIT MORE TO BROWN OF COURSE. IN ALL HE PLAYED 31 times for Wolves, scoring seven goals. His impact on an inconsistent team was not decisive but it was enough for him to earn international recognition. In February 1935, Brown made his IFA Ireland debut against England at Goodison Park in a 2-1 defeat. Arsenal's Cliff Bastin scored both England's goals; Alex Stevenson, the Dubliner who joined Glasgow Rangers, got Ireland's goal.

The game was significant for the Irish because Brown was one of three debutants.

His former colleague at Belfast Celtic, Drogheda-born Tommy Breen, was in goal – Breen would later move to Manchester United. And in attack was a player many have considered to be Ireland's greatest-ever, Peter Doherty.

Brown and Doherty also won their second caps together – a 3-1 loss to Wales in Wrexham in which Joe Bambrick scored – and their third, again against England. This was in Belfast in October 1935 and was another defeat. There must have been some pride in Lecumpher Street, though, as Johnny Brown gave the Irish the lead. The Irish goalkeeper that that day was Elisha Scott.

By the time Brown won his fourth cap – November 1936 against England at Stoke – he was at Coventry. City were then an ambitious Second Division club under the management of Harry Storer, a former England international who continued to play first-class cricket for Derbyshire. Coventry had won the Third Division South the previous season and were eager to reach the First Division for a first time.

The *Midland Daily Telegraph* of 22 October 1936 announced: 'City Secure International Winger: Jack Brown From Wolverhampton.'

It referred to 'a big fee'; in subsequent editions this would become 'a high price'. The paper said that Brown had stood out as a boy at Ledley Memorial school in Belfast and had been transferred with Boy Martin to Wolves. It said Belfast Celtic had presented each player with gold watches – 'and were escorted to the quay-side by a brass band.'

Brown was reported as being 5ft 7in, weighed 10st. 3lbs and was 25 years old – this was later corrected. He was 21. One other detail supplied was: 'Last season Manchester United made a bid for his services but Wolverhampton refused the offer.' United's manager was Scott Duncan, which was to be of relevance later.

Come Saturday, the *Midland Daily Telegraph* previewed Coventry's game with West Ham: 'If Brown proves himself the player he is reputed to be … [he] should be doubly valuable on account of his ability to play on either wing. Apart from his prowess as a winger, he possesses a powerful shot.'

One of the sub-headings read: 'Foundation Laid For Great Side.'

Coventry won 4-0 in front of 28,500 at Highfield Road and Monday's headlines were: 'Coventry City do the 'Hammering''; 'Brown the 'star' craftsman'; 'Best 'gate' of season'; 'Dazzling Display by International Winger.' The match report began:

> *There was only one subject of conversation in Coventry over the weekend and that was Brown, Coventry City's new right-winger. The ex-Wolverhampton Wanderers wing-man and Irish international re-vitalised not only the forward line but the whole team.*

His feet literally twinkled as he played ducks and drakes with the
West Ham defence … The City with this form are going to draw
bigger and bigger gates with Brown as a big attraction.

What a start for Johnny Brown. Coventry won 3-0 at Norwich the next Saturday and were on an unbeaten run that would see Brown score his first goals, against Barnsley, as Coventry moved to third in the table. He scored two at St. James' Park against Newcastle, one at White Hart Lane against Tottenham, plus the only goal in Coventry's win over Aston Villa in front of 40,000 at Highfield Road. By the end of the season, Brown was top scorer with 13, Coventry City were eighth and the *Midland Daily Telegraph* saluted: 'The Best Season Ever'.

The last game of the season had been at Fulham. Before it, the paper carried another headline about their popular winger: 'Jack Brown to tour with Irish Free State side.'

That was published on May Day 1937. Six weeks earlier Brown had won his fifth northern, Ireland cap. Now he had been called up by the southern FAI. In between, on 30 April, the future Taoiseach Eamon de Valera introduced a bill in the Irish Parliament regarding a new Irish constitution, one that altered the official name of the country from the Irish Free State to 'Ireland', or Eire in Irish.

On 13 May the statue of England's King George II in Dublin was blown up. On 17 May Johnny Brown, an east Belfast Protestant, lined up alongside Jimmy Dunne in a forward line in Switzerland representing De Valera's new 'Ireland'.

Tommy Breen, who like Brown had just played for the northern, IFA Ireland, was also selected. So too, Davy Jordan, who had begun his career with Glentoran before moving to Hull City. He was now with Wolves. Another new northerner requested by the Free State was Newry-born Johnny Feenan, who played for Sunderland.

It was the first time the FAI had picked players from beyond the 26 counties of their jurisdiction as dictated by Partition and FIFA. This was historic and, to some, inflammatory. De Valera's new constitution laid claim to 'the whole island of Ireland' and now the Football Association of Ireland was picking players from the North and the IFA. The FAI could respond that this is only what the IFA did in the opposite direction.

On the pitch, the new recruits made an impact. The first of two tour games was in Berne and after 30 minutes Davy Jordan found Dunne, who scored the only goal. Switzerland 0-1 Eire.

Six days later, Ireland met France in Paris. The French were warming up for the 1938 World Cup, which they were hosting, and the game was played at the venue of the 1938 final, Stade de Colombes. The committee who picked the Irish team named an unchanged side. It was under more pressure than it had been in Berne and France were awarded an early penalty when the Anglo-French forward Fred Aston had a shot handled. Tommy Breen saved it.

Then, seven minutes into the second half, Davy Jordan put the Irish ahead. It was a move started by Brown. Six minutes later it was 2-0 with those two players involved again. This time Jordan lobbed a pass to Brown, who scored with a volley past France goalkeeper Laurent Di Lorto.

It ended 2-0, the Irish Free State, Eire, the FAI Ireland team, however it was named, had triumphed over France in Paris thanks to goals from two men from east Belfast.

This was a landmark for Irish football domestically in terms of who was selected. Internationally, it was also a landmark: this is the only time Ireland, north or south, have beaten France in France. Although Robbie Keane's goal in 2009 gave the Republic of Ireland a 90-minute victory, that notorious game went to extra-time. Then Thierry Henry's hand-ball enabled William Gallas to equalise. Henry's action preserved Johnny Brown's record.

At home in Belfast, there was no fuss that George Walker can remember: 'I can't think it mattered to us, it was more that he was off to play international football. He left international jerseys in Lecumpher Street for us to wear, not that we did, that would have been showing off.'

In the close season Brown would return to Belfast to see his family. As George says: 'In the summer Johnny would come home from Wolves full of the jargon of the young professional player of the time. In my eyes he seemed quite a sophisticated character with his fancy sayings. He always had to have a boiled egg in the morning – hard, not soft. After that we'd go over to Ormeau Park and have a kickaround.'

These two FAI internationals were not covered in the Belfast press, which could explain the lack of fuss. In the Dublin-based *Irish Times*, a 'Special Telegram' said the France game 'was played in brilliant sunshine on perfect turf' and that Brown's volley 'gave the French goalkeeper no chance'.

The FAI archive resides at University College Dublin. Unfortunately, the records skip from 1936 to 1938, so official, internal feelings about this tour are not known.

What is known is that Brown played again for the IFA Ireland against Scotland six months later, then against Wales in March 1938. Coventry City were about to come fourth in the Second Division, one point off promotion, and Brown played in 40 of the 42 games.

It was May 1938. The FAI again called on him, for their forthcoming tour to Czechoslovakia and Poland. Belfast-born Harry Baird, then playing with Jackie Carey at Manchester United, was also called up.

But if there had not been public grumbling, privately relations between the IFA and FAI had been strained by Brown, Jordan and Breen's appearances in 1937 and by the FAI's ongoing insistence that they be called 'Ireland'. The IFA had used this name since 1882 and were not minded to lose it. They lobbied the International Football Association Board (IFAB), arguing the FAI should not be selecting players outside its jurisdiction.

The IFA lobbying won. After Coventry had given Brown permission to travel with the FAI, the English FA overruled them. Neither Brown nor Baird travelled to Czechoslovakia. After two caps, Brown's FAI career was over.

He continued to play for northern Ireland, winning his tenth and last cap in March 1939, the IFA's last international before the Second World War. He was 24 and listed as a Birmingham player for that game. Brown had excelled at Coventry but as season 1938/39 dawned he was out of the team. Something was afoot and on 10 September, 1938 the *Midland Daily Telegraph* reported: 'Brown Goes To Birmingham: Substantial Fee.' It said negotiations 'had been in progress for some time.'

It also said: 'For two seasons Brown was Coventry City's chief goalscorer. A player of craft, he will be remembered for a long time by Highfield Road supporters for the deadly quality of his shooting.'

Bar the fee, which was estimated at £3,000, no reason was offered as to why Brown was sold. It seemed abrupt. Then, many years later, the book *Coventry City 100 Greats* stated that Brown 'was involved in an unsavoury incident in a Coventry ballroom … Storer decided to cut his losses.' There were no further details.

The same month, September 1938, just prior to Brown's transfer to Birmingham, the *Midland Daily Telegraph* had been reporting on disturbances in Coventry city centre. There were headlines such as: '300 Irishmen in Street Fight'; 'Fierce Clash of Coventry Gangs.' It said trouble had occurred outside 'a dance hall' in Ford Street and it was not the first of its kind:

> *While Coventry City Police today denied that they experienced*
> *any difficulty in quelling the fight, they were prepared to admit*
> *that it was among the worst street brawls they have ever had to*
> *deal with. As on previous occasions in these fights, which unfor-*
> *tunately have become an all-too-regular feature of weekend night*
> *life in the city, the real trouble started when the police attempted*
> *to make an arrest.*

Set against this dramatic language was the fact that only one man was arrested, a Dennis Houlihan of Lower Ford Street, and there were letters to the paper about exaggerated reports. The editor replied that over 200 readers had written to him about Coventry's Irish question.

Irish immigration into England's Midlands was steady during the 1930s as people sought work. Coventry was viewed as a city of factories and men flocked there from both north and south of Ireland's border. There was the potential for old conflicts to be renewed, and some correspondence mentioned that. It is conjecture.

What is not is that the IRA were active in England, and in Coventry, in the late 1930s. In 1939 the IRA issued a statement instructing the British Government to remove its presence from Northern Ireland. It began a bombing campaign in Britain and there were explosions in Manchester, London and in August 1939 the campaign reached Coventry. On a Friday afternoon on Coventry's main shopping street, Broadgate, a 5lb bomb was placed in the basket of a bicycle and left leaning on a shopfront. The explosion killed five people. There were 70 wounded. This represented an upsurge in the IRA's capacity.

Understandably it caused outrage and Coventry police quickly named their chief suspect as Dominic Adams – uncle of Gerry Adams. In the end two other Irishmen were convicted and hanged, though the man thought to be responsible, Joby O'Sullivan – or Joe B. O'Sullivan – was never caught.

Nine days later Britain declared war on Germany. Soon it would be the Luftwaffe dropping bombs on the Midlands. Coventry's Irish question all but vanished from England's memory, though not the city's.

*

THE SECOND WORLD WAR WAS LOOMING. A YEAR EARLIER, THE *Birmingham Mail* had page after page of news on Nazi Germany's increasing militarization, the fleeing of Czechs from the Sudetenland and the efforts of British prime minister Neville Chamberlain to oppose, or to appease, Adolf Hitler.

In amid reports on gas-mask demonstrations and the addresses of bomb shelters, the transfer of a winger from Coventry City to Birmingham (they did not add 'City' until after the war) did not eat up many column inches. But on 10 September, 1938, at the top of page 9 of the morning edition, was the headline: 'Birmingham's Capture'. There was a small headshot of 'Jack Brown' and the short report said he would be making his debut that afternoon against Stoke City at St. Andrew's. With Birmingham second bottom of the First Division, they needed something fresh.

That night's 'Football Final' edition recorded: 'Brown, the Irish international, was a great success on the right wing,' yet Birmingham lost, 2-1, despite Stoke being 'outplayed, overrun and reduced to ineptitude.' Stoke's own star winger, Stanley Matthews, 'seldom got a kick'.

Things improved the following Saturday at Chelsea, where Brown scored the opener in a 2-2 draw. He then missed a home defeat by Bolton, but it was because Brown was playing for Ireland versus Scotland, who had Bill Shankly at right half.

Brown returned to his new team to face second-placed Derby County. Birmingham won 3-0 and the Mail referred to Brown's 'scintillating play'. He scored the second goal, having 'trapped the ball neatly, then proceeded to 'walk it' round two Derby defenders before driving it past [Frank] Boulton. It was a brilliant effort worthy of the best player on the field.'

A fortnight later there were 60,000 at St. Andrew's to see Birmingham beat Aston Villa in the city derby and in the FA Cup a record 67,000 for the visit of Everton. Brown was praised for 'an encouraging willingness to get into the fray', but while Everton went on to be the last English champions before the War, Birmingham were relegated.

England's 1939/40 season lasted three games. Birmingham were joint top of the Second Division when it ended and Brown had just scored again at White Hart Lane. He was two months short of his 25th birthday when the Second World War started, an Ireland international and Birmingham City employee.

The Football League was suspended, obviously affecting income. Regional leagues were introduced but the city of Birmingham was the most heavily-bombed after London and St. Andrew's was hit. The club played in a Midland regional league for the remainder of 1939/40, but they could only play 16 times the following season in the Southern regional league. With St. Andrew's unable to host games, players would often guest for other clubs and Brown played three times for Nottingham Forest early in the war. Later he turned out for Walsall, Northampton and Grimsby.

All the while he was retained by Birmingham but on 4 May, 1946 Birmingham City placed Brown on the transfer list at a fee of £1,000. The club's private comments to the Football League cited 'conduct not satisfactory' and 'shown no interest' as the reasons for the decision. The club had a new manager: Harry Storer, the man who had signed, and sold, Brown at Coventry.

Two months later, Barry AFC in south Wales met Birmingham's fee. Brown, 24 at the beginning of the war, was now 31 and heading for 32. He had gone from scoring at Tottenham and playing in front of 60,000 crowds, to making a Barry debut at Worcester City in front of 4,000.

Having applied to join the Football League, which perhaps had persuaded Brown to move to Wales, Barry were rejected and instead were in the Southern League and the Welsh League. How they afforded Brown's wages is unknown – of all things, the club had staged a swimming gala to raise the £1,000 transfer fee. But he stayed two seasons at Jenner Park and played 98 times. He scored in one of the most remarkable games ever, when Barry were 6-0 down to Gillingham at half-time yet drew 6-6.

A former Coventry City team-mate, Leslie Jenkin Jones, took over as player-manager of Barry but the club was running at a loss and in April 1948, it was wound up. Although it quickly resumed as Barry Town, money was required and Brown was sold for the £1,000 Barry had paid Birmingham. So in May 1948 Brown joined Ipswich Town in the Third Division South. It was a transfer upwards and for the 33 year-old it was the beginning of a late flourish.

Scott Duncan, the Manchester United manager who had tried to sign Brown from Wolves a long decade earlier was now managing Ipswich. Duncan had brought Harry Baird with him from Old Trafford and Brown and Baird knew each other well from Irish duties. Brown was to stay three seasons at Ipswich.

He was the cause of animated early reviews from the *Ipswich Evening Star*. In his first three games, Ipswich won 6-1, 5-1 and 5-1. There were 18,000 at Portman Road. 'A Wizard and Worker' the paper called him: 'A real ball artist, he has already shown he is a team man too.'

Brown played 42 games that season as Ipswich finished seventh and he passed his 34th birthday. The next season was harder for the club and for Brown, though in October of 1949 they beat Norwich City 3-0 in the East Anglia derby. Johnny Brown got a hat-trick.

The local paper turned that into one of those cartoons of the era. Johnny must have been presented with the original because it is one of the few pieces of memorabilia the family possesses. Not that the paper was without criticism. In its match report it said Brown had 'in previous games not touched the form of which he is capable.' Still, he was at Ipswich a third season – 1950/51. He was 37.

*

LENNY FLETCHER WAS 21 THAT SEASON. HE MADE HIS DEBUT IN March 1950. Born in 1929, Fletcher is Ipswich Town's oldest player. He remembers well a man he calls Jackie Brown.

'Jackie was a lovely bloke, the finest striker of a ball,' Fletcher says, 'the team relied on him. I got on well with him, he was a real character on the field and off it. He was one of my idols.

'When I made my debut, it was at Bristol City, I was right-half and Jackie was outside-right. We lost 4-2, Jackie made our two. When he scored those three goals against Norwich it was all about how he struck the ball. He made those goals himself. Jackie was marvellous that day, he turned the left-back inside out, he was so skilful. I was on the bench, there were no substitutes then, I remember it.

'We used to train on a side pitch at Portman Road then, Jackie would go all-in in training. He had one particular phrase he repeated: 'Get the ball on the ground.' If you did, he would mesmerise full-backs.

'He was well-known around the town – he was an international. He lived mainly in the Bramford Road area, it's about half a mile from Portman Road. He was a real good darts player, captain of a team in one of the pubs. And he'd one or two lady friends.

'Jackie and Harry Baird, he was another Irish international, they had us in hysterics in the dressing room. On the train to away games they played a game called 'Halfpenny' – it cost you a pound or something.

'The thing was, Jackie and Harry both took to the beer. That got Jackie into a bit of trouble with the directors, but not with Scott Duncan – he'd been a player himself, a Scottish international as well as manager of Manchester United, he knew what it was like.

'Harry Baird took over as third team coach. He used to have a pet pub called the Zulu, on Wolsey Street. They'd go after training. I should remember – I married the landlord's grand-daughter.'

Fletcher thinks that at the end of the 1950-51 season Brown left Ipswich. Brown had at one stage been in Baird's third team and the club may have preferred younger players.

'By the end I think Jackie decided to leave himself, I don't think he saw out his contract,' Fletcher says. 'As far as I know, when he left the club, he went back to Wolverhampton. He'd a lady friend there too.'

Yet in August 1951 the *Evening Star* reported that Brown was preparing for the next season: 'This was before Jackie Brown was taken ill and rushed off to hospital for an internal operation. Jackie is still there, a slice of bad luck, particularly as he was determined to come back in a big way.'

A week later the *Evening Star* reports Brown is 'convalescing in Felixstowe'; in September he is 'convalescing in Bideford'; in November he is 'back from Devon'; in December 'he is waiting to go back into hospital for another operation'.

By January 1952 that unspecified operation for an unspecified illness has taken place and on 12 April, Brown's photograph is back on the front page signaling his 'welcome return to football.' Presumably that meant Brown was back in training and a fortnight later he was due to play for Ipswich 'A' against Whitton United. 'Jackie Brown will turn out', the paper said.

But if he did, it went unreported and on 3 May the *Football Star* named the 21 players 'offered terms' by Ipswich Town for season 1952/53. Brown was not one of them and if he was still living in Ipswich, the edition of 23 August will have come with a thump. Here was a photograph of 30 Ipswich Town players and staff and Brown was not there.

A first-team player since his Belfast Celtic debut in 1931, this visible absence from the squad photograph will surely have hit Johnny Brown hard. It must be a moment that hits all professional footballers hardest: that first squad photograph you are not in. Your playing days are over.

*

GEORGE WALKER WAS IN HIS EARLY 30S IN BELFAST. WHERE JOHNNY Brown went immediately after Ipswich Town is guesswork but George says he remembers his mother, Johnny's sister Margaret, leaving to find him.

'By that time I was aware that my mother was going over to England on her own to 'bring Johnny back," George says. 'I'm not sure where she found him but I think it was in east London, near West Ham. He then appeared in our house in Roslyn Street. Johnny moved in with my mother and father and got a job as a crane driver at Harland & Wolff. It seemed like an important job in the shipyard. He was such a bright character, always singing.'

George has a vague memory of Brown trying to use contacts in Ireland and England to move players, an early form of agent, but he is not sure.

'I think he'd tried to represent players but working in Harlands then, there was a long walk, a full day's work and a long walk home. There can't have been much time for anything else.'

In the background, then and later, hovered Johnny Brown's personal debts.

'Johnny was very fond of the drink, though not over-fond like some,' George says. 'He was fond of the horses too. In those days, in those social conditions, there were so many people gambling not simply as fun but as a way to try to earn money. Anyway, he owed my mother money and didn't know how he was going to repay it.'

Johnny Brown sounds like a worried man and one day – 7 July 1963 – all those woes and disappointments got on top of him. It was a long time since he had been scoring for Wolves against Arsenal, playing with Peter Doherty and Jimmy Dunne for Ireland, 'dazzling' in front of 60,000. It may have felt longer. Was anyone asking him then about Stanley Matthews or Bill Shankly?

'He was in the house on his own and must have thought he'd had enough,' George says. 'He'd no children to worry about, he'd never married.'

Aged 48, on a joyless, oppressive Belfast Protestant Sunday, in his head Johnny Brown had made the irrational rational. He committed suicide, gassing himself in the kitchen in Roslyn Street.

He was discovered by his brother-in-law, Jimmy Walker, who was George's father, and by George himself: 'I'll never forget it and I will never forget my father saying: 'He did it himself, he did it himself,' over and over. Why hadn't my father noticed the signs? Johnny had put up 'beware gas' signs on the front door, on an inside door and above the mantelpiece. Maybe he was hoping someone would notice and come in before he did anything. A cry for help. He was lying on the kitchen floor. I'll never forget it.'

*

SUICIDE HAD BEEN DECRIMINALISED IN THE UNITED KINGDOM IN 1961, though not in Northern Ireland until 1966. In 1963 it remained a crime and it retained a stigma.

There were just two short death notices in the local press regarding Johnny Brown, beginning with the word 'suddenly' in brackets. 'At his brother-in-law's residence. Funeral from the Belfast Co-operative Society, 90 Shankill Road, tomorrow. No flowers please. House closed. Very deeply regretted by his sisters and brother and family circle.'

'It was kept quiet,' George recalls.

Johnny Brown was taken to Dundonald cemetery in the east of the city and was laid in the same grave as his parents. Thomas and Susan Brown had died within the space of four months in 1938, when Johnny was 23 and at Coventry City. With hindsight, Johnny lost his parents not long before he left Highfield Road. Now, as it says on the black headstone, 'Their son John', is buried with them. In the grave were also two of the Browns' grandchildren, who died young.

The headstone stands. It is a glum site and it is a grim sight. There is no indication of the life and times of Johnny Brown from his grave, no mention of Belfast Celtic or Wolves or Ireland caps or derby-day hat-tricks or interest from Manchester United.

There were no obituaries, it seems. Lenny Fletcher never knew what had happened and presumably other former colleagues, except those in Belfast, did not know. If they did, it was probably 'kept quiet'.

Two months later, another winger, from a mile up the Cregagh Road, made his debut for Manchester United. George Best put everyone in the shade and gradually Johnny Brown faded into the distance. When the Internet arrived a Jackie Brown Wikipedia page was created, maybe by a Wolves fan. It contained a broad statistical outline of Brown's career. It said he died in 1990.

*

JOHNNY BROWN WOULD HAVE BEEN 75 HAD THAT BEEN THE CASE. Sadly it was not true. By 1990 possibly the only people mentioning his footballing achievements were George and Tommy Walker. Tommy grew up in that house on Roslyn Street.

He had followed his uncle Johnny into the Irish League, first with Distillery, then with Crusaders and Ards. He won the 1952 Irish Cup for Ards against Glentoran at Windsor Park, 20,000 there. Tommy had agreed to join Second Division Luton Town a year earlier but changed his mind, even though Luton's manager Dally Duncan travelled to Belfast to conclude the deal.

From personal experience, and from his uncle's experience, Tommy knew the game could be fragile. He had been forced to retire temporarily from football in 1949 aged 23, due to pleurisy and a broken jaw sustained in an Irish League match. Distillery staged a testimonial and Blackpool, who had just finished seventh in the First Division, sent over their first team – minus Stan Mortensen and Matthews.

Not that this absence bothered the paying public at Grosvenor Park. Guesting for Distillery were players of the calibre of Davy Walsh and Jackie Vernon, both of West Brom (and both Irelands). And then there was the star guest: Charlie Tully of Celtic.

Back in Belfast at the end of his first season in Scotland, Tully was named in the team in the testimonial programme. Then his new manager in Glasgow, Jimmy McGrory, said Tully could not play. Tommy didn't mind because instead Tully walked onto the pitch and waved and where Charlie Tully was concerned, for many that was enough.

*

CHARLES PATRICK TULLY OCCUPIES A PARTICULAR PLACE IN THE history and imagination of Irish and Scottish football.

He was born on McDonnell Street, off the Falls Road, in Belfast in 1924. It was 11 July and as Tully came to joke: 'I always regretted I wasn't born on the 12th of July – just to be awkward like.'

He was the second of 13 children and perhaps felt an early need to stand out. Which he did. At 15 Elisha Scott saw enough to put Tully in Belfast Celtic's reserves. Tully was 'nervous as a bride' and recalled how Jimmy McAlinden, Martin O'Neill's future manager at Distillery, shoved shinguards down his socks. '(Before this I had used magazines and newspapers).'

The following morning one of those newspapers described Tully as an 'outstanding discovery'. He was signed by Belfast Celtic that day. Tully was off. An almost portly left-winger, he would defy perception and inspire fascination. From Belfast Celtic he joined Glasgow Celtic. At the former he became 'Cheeky Charlie' due to his stylistic and verbal impudence; at the latter, 'Tullymania' broke out.

There were Tully ties, Tully drinks, Tully ice creams, there was a newspaper column: 'Tullyvision'. He had an effect on people way beyond medals. His natural humour touched supporters: of his Celtic debut he said he hadn't 'set fire to everyone's tonsils'; when later asked his opinion of Celtic's full-backs, he replied: 'Passable.'

Scotland was dominated by Rangers and Hibernian when Tully arrived in 1948. Celtic would not win the title post-war until 1954, but Tully was like pain relief to Celtic fans. He stayed a decade at Parkhead and when he died, Jock Stein carried his coffin on the Falls Road as Joe Bambrick watched on and Tully's manager at Celtic, Jimmy McGrory, said: "I regarded him as one of the most, if not the most, valuable signings for Celtic."

Mourners smiled at the reminiscing but there was sadness at yet another footballer of that era who died far from wealthy despite being the main attraction to vast crowds. An example of that had come four months after Tully joined Celtic. They played Third Lanark in the Glasgow Cup final and there were 87,000 at Hampden Park on this Bank Holiday Monday.

As the *Glasgow Herald* reported: 'A queue eight-deep stretched from platform 10 to the bottom of Central Station ... many holiday-makers wanted to go because they had never seen Charlie Tully in action.'

Tully made his Ireland debut that year, though it is his appearance against England in 1952 at Windsor Park which added to the folklore. Tully was marked by Alf Ramsey and set about the future England manager.

'Surely you know what he did to Alf Ramsey!' says Harry Gregg roaring with laughter. 'Charlie was up against him and left the ball and walked away. Ramsey didn't know what to do. Charlie walked away, he walked away from the ball! Ireland v England! He walked away from the ball and he had the fella Ramsey so transfixed it was untrue. But it was true. Charlie Tully, he was the funniest man I ever met.'

To increase that day's legend, Tully scored twice in a 2-2 draw, one a left-foot volley from 20 yards, the other with his right direct from a corner.

Along with taking throw-ins off opponents' backs, scoring direct from corner kicks was a Tully trick. People could not believe it and nor, famously, could a referee at Falkirk who disallowed one Tully corner-goal and ordered it to be re-taken. Tully repeated the action and scored again. There was a pitch invasion.

Tully roused such wild reaction. Celtic had beaten Rangers just once since the war when Tully signed. In his sixth game for the club, Celtic won 3-1 and he set up all three. Rangers were torn apart by a player who would reduce the game to walking pace.

'Great players don't run and run and run,' says Gregg, 'they stop the ball, like Denis Law. Charlie was like Stanley Matthews – they stopped the game and they did it for a reason, because they were gone. Speed is in your head.'

Defenders took to lunging at Tully, most notably Rangers' Sammy Cox in 1949. Cox floored Tully with a kick that should have resulted in a penalty. Nothing was given, Celtic fans raged and Old Firm lore had another riotous chapter.

One good thing about that Glasgow afternoon was that the greatest sportswriter in Britain, Hugh McIlvanney, was there. McIlvanney saw Charlie Tully in the flesh and in context. He has kindly written this appreciation for Green Shoots:

> *His outstanding skill is by no means the only reason that Charlie Tully will always have a special niche in the history of Scottish football and especially, of course, in the history of Celtic. It was how he applied his talents that kept him vivid in the memories of all who saw him play and caused tales of his feats to be passed through generations of Celtic supporters.*
>
> *There was a taunting impertinence about everything he did on the field, a clear intention to disrupt the composure of challengers by not only beating them but embarrassing them with his close control of the ball and endless trickery.*
>
> *The effect was heightened by the fact that the stylish damage was being done by an unlikely physical specimen. With his prematurely thinning hair, hints of a pot belly and an arse that jutted out noticeably, he looked anything but an athlete in his prime. But to watch him in action, as I did a few times in my teens, was to realise how gifted he was at creating chaos in defences with his dribbling and the inventiveness and accuracy of his passing. He could show remarkable technique, and surviving admirers will tell you that scoring on several occasions directly from corner kicks*

wasn't as freakish as it seems.

His contributions were erratic but the best of them tended to come in big games and, unsurprisingly, he was always striving to shine against Rangers, which fed the pride of Celtic fans and deepened their devotion to him. They revelled in his ability to dismiss tacklers with an almost mocking air of superiority. Neutrals, too, enjoyed that. As was true much later of Jimmy Johnstone, sometimes Tully's bewildering of opponents was so audaciously brilliant that the natural reaction was to smile or even laugh out loud.

Tully had no pace to speak of and he wasn't nearly as dynamic as Wee Jimmy but in terms of entertainment there could be legitimate comparison. Whether Jock Stein, who attached huge importance to tempo, would have chosen to fit talents of Tully's kind into the greatest of Celtic teams must be open to question.

In that debate, another factor would be the Irishman's insistence on taking gamesmanship to the borderline of acceptability, and now and then beyond it. Stein wanted his players to be bold and challenging but nobody appreciated more than he did (to my mind, nobody appreciated anything about football management more than he did) the potential cost to a team when a player's behaviour becomes that of an outright provocateur.

Here it must be stressed, however, that Tully was often abused by opponents and that in the most notorious incident involving him he was entirely blameless. I was a 15-year-old spectator at Ibrox on the day in 1949 when serious crowd trouble erupted at a Rangers-Celtic match after Sammy Cox blatantly swung his foot over the ball to kick Tully and bring him down. Cox was one of the best Scottish footballers I've seen but his guilt then was as indisputable as his victim's innocence. When, instead of awarding a penalty, the referee waved play on, he was starting a trail of injustice shamefully extended by the SFA's ludicrous ruling that Tully was as culpable as Cox.

In the immediate aftermath of the foul, the fury at the Celtic end of the terracing went hideously out of control, and yet another of this fixture's unforgivable scenes of mayhem ensued. Bottles were hurled in a terrifying shower, people sought refuge on the running track and arrests were made.

I had been taken to the match from Kilmarnock by a middle-aged family friend who had a liking for Rangers and we had travelled in a supporters' club bus. It had been parked close enough to the Celtic end to put us at serious hazard when the game was over and violence spilled on to the streets. I am glad I can associate much happier memories than that one with the extraordinary Charlie Tully.

*

TULLY WAS ONE OF THE FINAL FLOWERINGS OF BELFAST CELTIC. Having won the last five Irish League titles before WWII under the management of Elisha Scott, the club resumed its primacy in 1947 by winning the Irish Cup at Windsor Park in front of what some claimed was a record attendance. It was against Glentoran and Charlie Tully scored the only goal.

And when the full Irish League season restarted in 1947-48, Belfast Celtic won it again, though the sale of Tully encouraged rivals to believe Belfast Celtic were vulnerable, which turned out to be an accurate description.

Boxing Day fell on a Sunday in 1948 so the traditional 'Boxing Day fixture' between Linfield and Belfast Celtic was played on the 27th. With the two rivals at the top of the Irish League, there were 30,000 at Windsor Park. The game finished 1-1 but the scoreline was an irrelevance.

On the final whistle of a game in which two players were sent off and another two were carried off with serious injuries, Linfield fans charged onto the pitch. Jimmy Jones, Belfast Celtic's centre forward, was upfield and furthest from the dressing rooms.

This was no benign invasion, this was menacing and the Celtic players knew it. Eight weeks earlier the two clubs had met at Celtic Park and Linfield striker Billy Simpson was thumped by Celtic goalkeeper Kevin McAlinden. The referee did not see the incident but supporters did and in the build-up to the Boxing Day game McAlinden was the target of anonymous threats sent to the club.

The visiting players could sense tension when they arrived at Windsor Park. As playwright Padraig Coyle has noted, the match programme referred to this an 'Old Firm' fixture; and when Celtic captain Harry Walker won the toss he chose to play in the direction of the Railway End, meaning his teammates would be closest to the changing rooms in the second half. The Celtic players thought they might need a quick escape and those fears were well-founded.

Jones, down near the Railway End, had furthest to get back. It was his tackle on Linfield's Bob Bryson that led to Bryson's departure and a half-time Tannoy announcement that Bryson had a broken leg only inflamed the crowd and increased their focus on Jones.

While the other Celtic players battled through the spectators to get to the dressing room beaten and bloodied but standing, Jones was not so lucky. He was thrown from the pitch onto the concrete terracing and was kicked and stamped on so badly his right leg was broken. It could have been worse.

*

OVER 40 YEARS LATER, SITTING IN THE FRONT ROOM OF JIMMY Jones's house in Lurgan and Harry Walker's in Belfast, the men went over those events.

'I knew the feeling before the match,' Walker said, 'so when I won the toss I chose to play in the direction that would leave Kevin McAlinden closest to the pavilion. 'I told our fellas: 'When the final whistle goes, all go for Kevin. He's the one they're gonna pick on.' I saw the crowd coming over but we pushed our way – no, we fought our way – through them. After a few minutes in the dressing room I noticed one player was missing. 'Where's Jimmy? Where's Jimmy Jones?' I said.'

Jones explained where he was: 'Chasing a long ball …

'But a whole crowd had come on from the Kop end and I was looking and wondering who they were after. In next to no time I was among them. Somebody hit me on the back of the head with his fist and I turned around and, goodness, there was that many of them there was no point in arguing. I tried to leg it to the players' entrance, but there was no way I was going to get there. I had seen police all around the ground during the match so I thought I'd get over to where police were. But they had all gone: they were up at the players' entrance.'

Jones was around 30 yards from safety.

'So I tried to run down the track, but someone came and pushed me off the pitch on to the terracing. I landed on my hands and knees – I remember that as I cut my right knee. That was the leg that got broke too. I got up to run but everybody was kicking at me. I fell, somebody kicked me or tripped me, and then some boyo … my leg was just lying like a piece of wood … and he jumped on it.

'It was sore, but I never thought about it. I just thought of getting myself out of the way. I got up to run but my leg was wobbling about. So I just had to lie down.'

Even a tough man like Jimmy Jones thought the worst. Then out of the crowd came a savior.

'These boys were kicking away at me and then this fella throws himself right over the top of me. He had a hat on and he was shouting: 'It's all right Jimmy, it's Sean McCann.'

'Now Sean played in goal for Ballymena, but he had an uncle who was a watchmaker in Lurgan, so I knew Sean. He'd been playing that morning against Cliftonville and was sitting in the stand. He saved my life, there's no doubt about it. They [the crowd] didn't know if he was a detective or what, but they sort of eased off and then a policeman appeared with a baton and started pushing them back.

'I was black and blue all over and whenever I looked at my leg, when I first looked at my leg … it was broken. The St. John Ambulance people came along and got me on a stretcher and tied my legs together. One fella just turned my foot up and I remember thinking, I hope he's turned it the right way.'

*

WINDSOR PARK WAS CLOSED FOR A MONTH AFTER WHAT BECAME known as 'the Jimmy Jones incident'. There were questions asked in the Northern Ireland parliament about policing, about the Royal Ulster Constabulary's passivity during the riot. Despite such spectacular violence, there had been no arrests.

At Belfast Celtic and other Irish League clubs the official response was regarded as tokenistic and an example of Northern Ireland's institutional sectarianism.

Besides, the directors at Celtic Park had already committed themselves to a drastic decision: their club was to fold and leave the Irish League. The men who ran it had had enough. They told Jimmy Jones of their decision that night in hospital, but they told no-one else.

Celtic fulfilled their fixtures until the end of the season before setting off for what was a farewell tour of North America. In New York they met Scotland, 1949 winners of the British Home Championships. Belfast Celtic won 2-0 in an ill-tempered match.

And then, after 58 often glorious, often violent years the club was gone. Belfast Celtic's directors walked away from the Irish League. The sectarianism in the bones of the city had damaged their players and the authorities had not provided due protection. Who could blame them?

There were always rumours of a return, as had happened in 1924 after Celtic's previous withdrawal from the League. But though Elisha Scott still turned up for work at Celtic Park, there was no comeback. Players were sold to England, Crusaders stepped into the Irish League and Celtic Park, the scene of Joe Bambrick's goals and so much history, became solely a greyhound track.

And then, in 1983, Paradise was demolished. Today it is a shopping centre and

Padraig Coyle and other volunteers man an impressive mini Belfast Celtic museum. Many have felt the Irish League has never been the same since 1949 and there was an echo 23 years later when another Irish League club of largely Catholic support, Derry City, felt compelled to withdraw from the Irish League, again due to security concerns. Irish politics had taken another bite out of Irish football.

*

AS FOR JIMMY JONES, HE LAY IN PLASTER IN HOSPITAL FOR NINE-and-a-half months while his mates were in New York and Toronto and his employers folded. On one particular day the surgeon prepared to amputate Jones's right leg but decided to re-consider.

Jones was glad he did. He was just 20 when this happened. He was a bullock of a centre forward who had the potential of a brilliant career. He took out a compensation claim for malicious injury against the city council and was awarded £4,000. The amount, Jones discovered in court, was based on the £16,000 Newcastle United had offered Belfast Celtic for him two months before the match at Linfield. The Celtic directors had not told Jones of this offer. He only found out during the court case.

Jones emerged from hospital with his right leg one inch shorter than his left. Yet he got himself fit and went to Fulham. But Manchester United wanted him – Matt Busby turned up at his house in Lurgan – and United disputed his Fulham registration. It dragged on, Fulham gave in and Jones, disillusioned by United's attitude, returned to the Irish League with Glenavon. They won it three times. He retired in 1961.

He still had a limp 30 years later and what trace of bitterness he contained related to Busby and United's blocking of the Fulham transfer. Of Boxing Day 1948, he was resigned. It happened, and he knew it could; because Jimmy Jones was a Protestant whose father refused to speak to him for three weeks when he signed for Belfast Celtic.

*

AS FOR JOE BAMBRICK, THREE YEARS AT CHELSEA WERE FOLLOWED by an unusual move to Walsall in the Third Division South. When the Second World War started, Bambrick returned to Belfast, to Linfield, where he joined the club's staff as a coach and scout.

The latter role would lead him, two years after the war, to a house on Windsor Avenue in Coleraine. Along with Linfield administrator, Jack Smith, Bambrick knocked on the door and asked if it was the home of a young goalkeeper who had just performed superbly against the Linfield Swifts youth team.

Harry Gregg was 15 at the time. He replied: "That was me.' And that's when Jack Smith said: 'This is Joe Bambrick."

Almost 70 years on, Harry Gregg is still impressed. Did he know of Bambrick?

"*Head, heel or toe, slip it to Joe*? By God, I knew who he was. I nearly fell down. It was a Sunday, he was tall, silver-haired, very well dressed in a navy coat. Silver, silver hair, he was a good-looking man. Incredible.'

Gregg signed amateur forms with Linfield and a goalkeeping career that helped define Irish and British football in the second half of the 20th century was under way. Bambrick had scored again.

Gregg did not break through at Linfield and returned to his local club Coleraine. There, in 1951, he made his senior debut in an Irish League match against Ards. After just eight minutes, the 18 year-old keeper conceded his first senior goal. It was described in one newspaper report as: 'A 20-yard drive that was in the net before young Gregg, making his debut for his hometown club, got a sight of it.'

The scorer was Tommy Walker.

*

AS FOR THE BALL WITH WHICH JOE BAMBRICK SCORED THOSE SIX against Wales, the ball laced by young Frankie Kerr, it was seized by the Welsh captain, Fred Keenor, on the final whistle.

There was no malicious intent. Keenor took it into the Wales dressing room at Celtic Park and had it signed by every player. That night at the two teams' sporting dinner at the Grand Central Hotel, Keenor called a halt to proceedings, produced the ball and presented it to Bambrick.

'I wish you the best of luck, Joe,' Keenor said, 'you deserve it. I only wish this may not go to your head, boy.'

Bambrick, 'who was more or less embarrassed,' according to the *Belfast Telegraph*, replied: 'If my head gets any bigger I will stick a pin into it and let it out, just as you would with the ball.'

We must assume that Bambrick left the hotel that night with the ball under his arm, a precious commodity. He died in 1983, aged 77, and at some point over time the ball made its way to a sporting auction. Today it resides in a glass case at the

National Football Museum in Manchester.

It is there beside a medal Joe Bambrick was presented with for his six Irish goals in February 1930.

> *Head, heel or toe,*
> *Slip it to Joe.*

*

AND AS FOR FRANKIE KERR, PRESUMABLY HE WENT HOME FROM CELTIC Park that evening in 1930 with his head racing about the deeds of Joe Bambrick.

But Kerr had other considerations. There was the worsening conflict in Belfast, the lack of employment, particularly for Catholics, and then there was his boxing career.

Kerr had been born in Belfast in 1914. His father, John Kerr, was a senior officer in the British Army and had been sent across the globe to protect the Empire – to India, Egypt and Baghdad among other places. When the First World War broke out, John Kerr was fighting at the Battle of Mons in Belgium on the Western Front. It coincided with Frankie's birth and for that the son was given the nickname 'Monsie'.

John Kerr survived the war and by 1927 was in barracks in the army town of Aldershot, 40 miles south-west of London. It was there that Frankie Kerr won what his family think was his first boxing title: Aldershot Boys Champion 1927.

Frank 'Monsie' Kerr's relatives know this because in the house where he eventually settled, 93 Cooley Road, Drimnagh in south Dublin, the Aldershot Boys Champion trophy was on the mantelpiece. This went unmentioned, perhaps because young Frankie won so many other titles.

After Aldershot, the Kerrs had moved to barracks in Armagh, then John Kerr left the Army and got a job in Belfast in a hotel. This is why the family were there the day Bambrick struck.

Young Frankie's prowess at boxing saw him reach the amateur Flyweight Ulster Senior Final at 15 – even though he was under-age and did not weigh enough. Moving to Bantamweight he won consecutive Irish titles in 1933, 1934, 1935 and 1936. He was to fight across the world – it was on the boat to a fight in New York in 1933 that Frankie heard about the death of his mother.

By 1937, now 23, Frankie went to the European Championships in Milan. In the quarter-final he outclassed his Italian opponent but lost. Kerr's descendants recall the opponent as being 'Benito Mussolini's son-in-law', but if that part of the story may be an exaggeration, the injustice is not. As compensation, the Italian organisers presented Kerr with a specially-made medal: 'The Most Scientific Boxer in Europe'.

It was another item for the Dublin mantelpiece. The Kerrs had moved south from Belfast around 1933. Frankie got a job in the Dunlop factory and carried on boxing out of the Arbour Hill club. He married, started a family and used those nimble fingers to become a tailor. On retirement from boxing Frankie became a four-nights-a-week boxing coach at a club in Drimnagh and at Trinity College. He was mixing with different classes.

In March 1953, son Brian was born. Like his father, Brian was soon sports mad, just like the boy from the same street, Eamonn Coghlan. Brian says that for all his father's sporting excellence, Frankie Kerr did not speak of his sporting career often. But there was one occasion – Brian thinks it was Christmas 1962 – when Frankie casually dropped in a remark about Joe Bambrick.

'It must have been a Saturday because my Da was at home,' Brian says. 'He'd have been back from work in O'Connell Street, he was a tailor. On Saturdays he'd leave work at 6pm and come back with a bag of prawns. The fish market was behind where he worked and there'd be a bit of barter, so we'd have prawns on a Saturday night. Me Ma would cook them up, me Da would sit with the papers. I remember that he'd sit reading and the paper would fall on his face as he fell asleep.

'I would have been nine and I got a book called A Compendium of Sport – I think that's what it was called. I got it from Santa. It was a collection of sports results – I can still see the green cover and I think Jesse Owens was going through the tape. It had lists from A to Z and I used to read these lists out, reading hockey results from India, all sorts of things.

'I must have been looking at British Home Championships results in my new Compendium and I see this result from Belfast. I must have said: 'Da, can you imagine that, some fella called J. Bambrick scored six in one match?'

'And he just said to me: 'Yeah, I made the ball for that match. I actually dropped it round for the game.'

'Now it was years later that it came to me what he had said. I knew he had this skill of lacing a ball – leather footballs were very scarce then but we'd play in the street with one, and it was precious. You'd be playing and it was falling to bits.

'When the lace got frayed, there'd be four or five holes on each side. But my Da had these little tools that would allow the ball to be re-laced and pumped up again. He'd sew it with this little stick he had, he'd lever it under the leather. Boys would knock on the door and ask. It wasn't frequent because the balls were so scarce, but I've seen him do it.

'He must have learned that as part of his trade in the Athletic Stores in Belfast, along with the racquet stringing. I can remember racquets being around the house along with footballs.'

Sadly, when Brian was 14, in January 1968, Frank 'Monsie' Kerr died. He had only seen his son play football a couple of times for local side Rialto. So Frankie did not see his son Brian start coaching in his late teens, join Shamrock Rovers and manage St. Patrick's Athletic to their first League of Ireland title in 34 years in 1990. He did not see Brian become the coach who led the Republic of Ireland to third place in the World Youth Cup in 1997, then to the European Championship titles at U-16 and U-18 the following year. He did not see Brian decorating his own mantelpiece.

Above all, in January 2003, Frankie Kerr did not see Brian Kerr become manager of the Republic of Ireland. The young man from Belfast who laced Joe Bambrick's ball in 1930 was the father of the Dublin-born son who became Ireland manager 73 years later. Frankie Kerr had threaded more than a ball at the Athletic Stores that morning.

'On the day I got the job, I thought about him,' Brian says of his father. 'Oh yeah, fucking hell: 'Imagine if me Da saw me now? What would he think?'

'I told myself to be smartly dressed that day. I do remember thinking about my family that day, and that all he ever saw of me was a 14 year-old kid running around playing ball – soccer, Gaelic. I loved sport, all sport. My image of my father was this brilliant boxing man, who I didn't know because he was always out. For years after, people would tell me he was a brilliant boxer. He never talked about it. Others said he was like a ghost when he boxed, about what a lovely man he was, a great dresser.

'People ask me why I got into coaching so young. I must have picked up ideas from watching my Da coaching boxing. He was great with people, there were always people in our house, sleeping on the floor. He had a great belief about the decency of people who had been through war and conflict. He had this genius, the links he had with people lasted forever. Joe Bambrick's ball, that was my old father's part in Irish football history.'

ALAN MCLOUGHLIN'S
POST

Wiltshire, England, 1990

THE MORNING MAIL WAS LYING ON THE DOORMAT OF THE HOUSE in Swindon's Chandos Close. Alan McLoughlin had just moved in. He was 22 and this was his first mortgage. The décor was, he says, 'fairly sparse. There was a second-hand sofa, a TV.'

McLoughlin had been training that morning with Swindon Town. It was February 1990 and Swindon were prospering near the top of the Second Division. Ossie Ardiles was their manager.

On returning home, McLoughlin stepped over the post, making for the kitchen to get the kettle on. Then he went back to the doormat and picked up what he thought was the usual clutch of bills and takeaway pizza flyers. Only there among the assortment, McLoughlin saw something different, a crisp white envelope. If this was strange, more so was the logo in the corner. It was the Three Lions of England's Football Association.

'I wasn't quite sure what it was,' McLoughlin says. 'I opened it and read. To my surprise – to my great surprise – it said I'd been called up for England 'B' to play against Ireland 'B' in Cork. Completely out of the blue.'

McLoughlin was flummoxed. He then thought of his uncle John, who lived in Co. Limerick, and whether John would be able to get to the game. Then he thought of his mother Nora in Manchester. She knew professional football had been harsh as well as kind to her son. Alan reached for the phone and dialled.

'I phoned home, Mum picked up and I blurted out the news. I remember I asked her about uncle John, that was as exciting for me as being recognised for doing something with a good Swindon team. My Mum was delighted for me, she knew that I'd moved from Manchester to Swindon to play and what moving had meant to me.'

McLoughlin grew up in south Manchester, the family lived at 126 Maine Road in the shadow of Manchester City's old ground. He had been recruited by Manchester United, though, and came through its youth system in the mid-1980s under Eric Harrison to play for the reserves without quite breaking through to the first team. He then suffered the rejection and dejection of being released. Lou Macari offered McLoughlin Swindon Town as a new start.

The McLoughlins of Maine Road were a tight family. Nora had come over from Limerick in the 1960s to find work and got it in the Dunlop factory. Pat McLoughlin had made the same journey, only from Mayo, at the same time to work in construction. Pat and Nora met. They settled in Fallowfield with many similar Irish families and stories around them.

Alan McLoughlin put down the phone and returned to the kitchen, his mind buzzing. 'The fact the game was against Ireland in Ireland, that made it even better,' he says. 'Now I was thinking: 'Do I respond? Who to? Should I ring Ossie?' I needed to calm down.

'So I go back to the kitchen and the other letters. If there's bills, I'm thinking, I better pay them. There's this brown envelope, hand-written, no logo on it. I didn't know what this was. I open it and it's from the FAI. They're saying I've been called up to play for the Republic of Ireland against England in Cork. It was surreal, not something I'm likely ever to forget.

'I was frantic. I ran back to the phone, called my Mum again and said: 'You're not gonna believe this.'

''What are you going to do? she said.'

''I'm going to play for Ireland,' I said. It wasn't a debate in my head. It just seemed the natural decision to me.

'It wasn't contrived. I've a Mancunian accent and I was born in England, but I love my parents and I love their backgrounds. We grew up in an Irish community in Manchester, my sister was Irish dancing from a young age. My Dad once took me to Old Trafford when I was very young just to see George Best. When I spoke to my Nan she'd tell me about the Black and Tans. As I said, it just felt natural.

'The thing is, I wasn't even thinking about international football, of any level. There'd been no Irish representative at games as far as I was aware. I'd been through a tough time, released by United. Playing international football did not cross my mind.'

But it crossed the minds of others. Tony Galvin, the Huddersfield-born winger who played 29 times for the Republic of Ireland, was at Swindon, the last stop of his playing career. He had asked McLoughlin about his roots – 'You must have some Irish in you with that surname?'

Although McLoughlin had replied that he did come from an Irish family; he did not know that Galvin had passed this snippet on to Jack Charlton.

McLoughlin now had to inform Ardiles and Swindon Town of his choice. In the days of faxes, two were sent from the club to the respective FAs. McLoughlin spoke again to Galvin, who 'gave me a flavour of what to expect, he cemented my decision.'

The next month, at Turner's Cross, Cork, Alan McLoughlin lined up for the Republic of Ireland against England in a 'B' international attended by his mother, father and uncle John. 'When the national anthems were played I looked at them.

'Then I had to focus on the game. We, I, wanted to put on a good show, and we did.'

Some around the England set-up will have known of their letter to McLoughlin but it was not something he had broadcast. He is realistic about his possibilities with England, the differences in the size of the talent pool available to the two countries. 'They had most of the Arsenal back four in that England squad, Tony Adams, Dixon, Winterburn, Seaman, they'd David Batty, David Hirst. The chances are, if I'd got on, I'd have won one England B cap. I played 42 times for Ireland.

'Our squad for that game was thinner, I noticed that on the two letters, England's list was longer. Sub-consciously I probably thought about that too. We'd Mike Milligan, who I knew from Oldham, I was familiar with Terry Phelan and I knew of Denis Irwin. I'd heard of David Kelly and Niall Quinn of course.'

He did not discuss the two letters on the doormat with anyone: 'I didn't feel it was appropriate to mention. Close family knew about them but I never really spoke publicly about it until years later.'

There was a packed crowd and an intense atmosphere on a wet afternoon in Cork. Dalian Atkinson gave England the lead. There then must have been some rueful English looks when the Irish equaliser arrived. It was scored by Alan McLoughlin. David Kelly and two goals from Niall Quinn made it 4-1.

'I can't remember much about the build-up but I hope Mum and Dad and uncle John had umbrellas. It was wet, noisy, the crowd were on top of you. The dressing rooms were so small. It felt significant that the game was in Cork, not Dublin. It gave me a feeling of what it is to play at a higher level. And to score, in front of Jack Charlton and Maurice Setters, I was euphoric when I saw my parents afterwards.'

McLoughlin could not know it then but less than three months later at Italia 90, he would face England again, in Sardinia, coming on as a substitute for John Aldridge in the World Cup finals. Ten minutes after McLoughlin's introduction, Kevin Sheedy equalised Gary Lineker's opener for England. The post in Swindon had delivered.

*

IN REPLACING ALDRIDGE, MCLOUGHLIN KEPT THE NON IRELAND-BORN quotient in the Irish team that afternoon at Cagliari at seven. This was making an impact as great as Swindon's postmen. Irish identity and authenticity became a question, debated at length inside and outside Ireland.

'We were called a bunch of mercenaries by the English press,' McLoughlin recalls, 'they never mentioned that John Barnes was born in Jamaica. Then we had people at home questioning Tony Cascarino, Andy Townsend.

'But you could be born in Ireland and move to England when you're two years old. You'd be Irish but growing up in England. For anyone to say they don't understand Irish culture or what it means to be Irish because you're not born in Ireland is bullshit. My parents moved to Manchester to make a life for themselves. But they always referred to Ireland as 'back home', they never forgot who they were. It wasn't rammed down my throat at home but I knew my identity. I lived in an Irish community in Fallowfield, lots of my friends were from the same background.'

One of McLoughlin's classmates was singer Noel Gallagher – whose mother Peggy came to England from Mayo.

And in terms of professional assimilation into the squad, McLoughlin never experienced any kind of antagonism or suspicion from the Ireland-born Irishmen. 'Packie [Bonner], Roy [Keane], Paul [McGrath], Kevin [Moran], they never made me feel anything but comfortable. No-one ever said: 'You don't sound Irish.' I never came across it.'

*

ONE OF THE SHOUTS HE REMEMBERS HEARING WAS: 'ENGLISH BASTARD.'

It was three years on from Cork and McLoughlin had become a Portsmouth player. He was still an Ireland international too, but to some in Belfast Alan McLoughlin remained irritatingly English. That, however, was a small detail in the turmoil of an occasion that he says was 'ugly'.

Ugly does not seem a large enough word to describe the maelstrom of sectarian hatred and sporting animosity that engulfed Windsor Park on 17 November 1993. Even those who knew their history, the geography of Belfast and what the ground meant in terms of Jimmy Jones and Linfield, were shocked.

It was a night that posed important questions about whether the two teams representing Ireland are a manifestation of the divided island – true in the literal sense; but also whether those two teams from two Association re-enforce that division officially, and culturally. In the middle of such questions was a young man born in Manchester.

'English bastard, Fenian bastard,' McLoughlin had his identity encapsulated through abuse.

'I didn't take it personally,' he says, 'I was expecting it. I knew that it would be different playing in Belfast and there'd just been those killings and bombs.'

Twenty-five days before the match, two young IRA members exploded a bomb in a fish shop on the Shankill Road, killing ten people including one of the bombers. The target was the leadership of the UDA, supposedly meeting in a room above the shop. Over the course of the next week the UDA responded by killing 14 people, eight of them in a bar in Greysteel. It was in this atmosphere of a society again turning upon itself, that Northern Ireland were to host the Republic of Ireland in the last qualifier in the group.

Had it been meaningless regarding qualification for USA '94, the evening might have less charged. But it was far from meaningless. The Republic began the game as one of three teams who could qualify. Spain and Denmark were the others and they met in Seville.

Denmark, European champions, were favourites to gain one of the two qualification places, but there was a combination of results that would see Spain and the Republic of Ireland go to America. The combination was a Spain victory and a draw in Belfast.

After 63 minutes Fernando Hierro scored the only goal in the Spain-Denmark game. That was good news for Jack Charlton and his players as the score in Belfast was 0-0 when news of Hierro's goal came through.

Eleven minutes later, however, Northern Ireland striker Jimmy Quinn changed all thinking with an extravagant 30-yard volley. There was delirium at Windsor Park: Northern Ireland could not qualify but they could stop the Republic doing so. The Irish could beat the Irish; or, to more accurately reflect the political sentiment of those present, the British in Northern Ireland could beat the Irish from the South, and their Englishmen.

At this stage Alan McLoughlin had been on the pitch four minutes having replaced Ray Houghton. McLoughlin was a roving midfielder tasked to get an equaliser. That had been his role since Jack Charlton saw him in Cork.

McLoughlin scored that day, and now he did so again. In the 76th minute he chested down a Gerry Taggart clearing header and, from the edge of the area, amid all the tension strangling Windsor Park, McLoughlin beat the Northern Ireland goalkeeper Tommy Wright with a calm left-foot volley that flew just inside the post. There was delirium once more, a different kind of delirium, quieter.

The game ended 1-1 and the Republic of Ireland were through to their second consecutive World Cup finals.

The security situation had been such that the team had had to fly to Belfast, not go by road. They flew back to Dublin airport where Taoiseach Albert Reynolds was waiting on the tarmac with a bottle of champagne. Given the angst across Ireland, this was a scene beyond the everyday considerations of politicians, Reynolds was there as a national leader. This transcended sport. Just as the match had done, it revealed the real status of football on the island: crucial, symbolic, divided.

*

MUCH OF THE AFTERMATH FOCUSED ON JACK CHARLTON'S SPAT with Northern Ireland manager Billy Bingham. It was Bingham's last game as manager and he, too, had led an Irish team to two World Cup finals.

Windsor Park meant something different to him: he had played there when Northern Ireland qualified for the 1958 World Cup by beating Italy in two games, the first of which involved a riot and a pitch invasion. Bingham had acquired a posh accent along the way, but he and Charlton were essentially the same working-class characters, who had chiselled out their own playing and managerial careers from backgrounds in shipyards and pits. The two men had a sporting rivalry that dated back to the 1950s, but they knew each other as friends. Nine months earlier Charlton had been a welcome guest on Northern Ireland's trip to play Albania in the same qualifying group. Charlton stayed in the Northern Ireland team hotel.

As managers, both men were pigeon-holed as pragmatists. It was a downplaying of their intelligence and experiences and, certainly in Bingham's case, a failure to fully understand resources. What he would have given for Paul McGrath; what Charlton would have given for Norman Whiteside.

Both knew their Irish history, too. Bingham knew it from the ground up as a Belfast boy who threw stones from his Protestant side of the Belfast streets at Catholic children in the Short Strand area opposite – as he told Eamon Dunphy in an interview the week before the game. Charlton knew it from the public revelation of 'Sean South from Garryowen' being played on the Irish team bus as it approached Lansdowne

Road for matches and the outcry it sparked in England and Northern Ireland.

Had the political situation been different, November 1993 would still have been tense because qualification was at stake; it was early 1990s politics and security which pushed it to the extremes.

There was a 'ring of steel' around Windsor Park, where no Republic of Ireland fans, officially, were allowed. Nor was Amhran na bhFiann, the Irish national anthem played. The whole occasion was seen as a giant suspect device, with McLoughlin saying players were joking nervously about who would be assassinated first. They settled on Charlton due to his long neck.

When Northern Ireland took the lead, Bingham's assistant Jimmy Nicholl said 'up yours' to Charlton's assistant Maurice Setters; when the game was done, McLoughlin having equalised, Charlton sought out Bingham to say: 'Up yours, Billy,' and immediately regretted doing so.

Regret: many felt it the next day. A country, or two, had been convulsed by a football match. Playwright Marie Jones immortalised it on stage in *A Night in November*, a title that has lasted.

In terms of sport, what mattered most was that the Republic of Ireland had reached the 1994 World Cup. Amid waves of emotional reflection and a Taoiseach on the tarmac, there was the reality of Irish qualification for a fourth consecutive World Cup. Relegated to footnote status was Jimmy Quinn's goal.

*

JIMMY QUINN PLAYED FOR READING, HIS SEVENTH DIFFERENT CLUB in England. One of those was Swindon Town, where Quinn had started his professional career in 1981, then returned in 1986. In Quinn's second spell at Swindon he came across a young lad just released by Manchester United who was living on his own: Alan McLoughlin.

Quinn was eight years older, established. 'I'll never forget what Jimmy did,' McLoughlin says. 'I was a young lad away from home, living in digs and he invited me over to his house to have meals, to have some company. Jimmy was already at Swindon, knew the club and the area, he wasn't aware of my background. We got on, I just thought he was really likeable.'

On the night in Belfast, the two had barely spoken, not because of rivalry, just the sheer tumult. And when the time did come to discuss it, they reverted, as friends do, to jokes.

'We shook hands on the pitch and he'd have called me a name,' McLoughlin says.

'Jimmy goes and scores a worldie and because of my goal it gets a bit lost. When he scored, the crowd thought they'd done it.

'Of course we spoke later, but it was football talk, just taking the piss. I'd spoiled his big night. It wasn't about nationality, it wasn't vicious.'

*

ALAN MCLOUGHLIN WROTE AN AUTOBIOGRAPHY: A DIFFERENT *Shade of Green*. It is a title that applies to Jimmy Quinn and to many others on the pitch, in the dugouts and in the stands that night in November.

The match was presented – and has been remembered – in block colours: black-and-white, orange-and-green. For some, those pouring sectarian and racist abuse on the visiting players, this was the case and there were those on both sides of the Irish border who read into Quinn's full-throttle jubilation at scoring something beside sport.

But that was incorrect. Quinn's celebration was not a reflection of where he came from, Jimmy Quinn was born a north Belfast Catholic. He was not playing 'for God and Ulster'. His enthusiasm at scoring stemmed from the thing he would like to be remembered for: goals.

Almost 25 years on he says: 'I scored 40 goals for Reading that season, you know? I think I might have the most club goals by a Northern Ireland international in England, more than Derek Dougan, more than George Best. I think so?'

Quinn is almost correct, he did score more than Best, but in terms of Football League goals, he was five short of short of Dougan.

Quinn grew up in Rathcoole, an estate long considered Protestant and Orange. But it was not always so clear. He was born in 1959 to William, an Ulsterbus driver, and Frances, who looked after the nine children. 'It was all mixed,' Quinn says, 'I'd friends who were Protestants. Our family was Catholic, but not religious at all.'

Non-religious Catholicism – it is a strand of Irishness which received little air-time and as the Troubles broke over the city in the late 1960s, religion began to physi-cally separate people. And not only were the Quinns a Catholic family in a largely Protestant area, three of Jimmy's brothers had joined the British Army. There were shades of green within the Quinn household and as with McLoughlin, this brought correspondence through the letterbox.

'Three of my brothers joined the Army,' Quinn says, 'and we started to get threaten-ing letters. I was about eleven or twelve, [1970-71]. We moved around Belfast, but it was affecting my mother's nerves and she just wanted us to go, leave. We came to England, felt like refugees. Through the Army we got a house in Wiltshire, and eventually we got a council house in Amesbury, near Salisbury.'

After school in Wiltshire, Quinn found work in north-west England and joined Oswestry in the Northern Premier League. 'I scored a few. There were two or three clubs after me, I signed for Swindon Town after a trial match.' It was there he later met McLoughlin. Quinn says all the senior players helped the younger ones, downplaying his kindness.

Of November 1993, he remembers: 'The match was massive for both. The Republic could get to the World Cup, but it was also Billy Bingham's last game in charge and we wanted to do well for him.'

Given his background he could hardly revel in the sectarianism of the occasion, but he does add another shade of green to the overall picture.

'There were bragging rights too. Our lads were all born in Northern Ireland [bar Kevin Wilson] and if you weren't, to play for us it had to be through your mother or father. For the Republic it was through grandparents and you had some playing for them who didn't even know where Ireland was. We moaned about that [in the squad]. Religion never came into it, our squad was always mixed and if you might have had the odd joke, it was never serious. But we moaned about that, about Cascarino and so on.'

Of his goal, he says: 'Everything I hit was going in that season. Kevin Wilson laid it back, I hit it and Packie Bonner was clutching at air. It was a fitting goal to win the game. Then they got it back. Alan scored.'

Jimmy Quinn got 41 goals that season.

*

ALAN MCLOUGHLIN'S STRIKE AT WINDSOR PARK MEANT THAT ON 18 June 1994, in the Giants Stadium, New York, the Republic of Ireland met Italy in the first game of World Cup Group E. After eleven minutes Ray Houghton scored a winner celebrated in homes and pubs across Ireland.

In one bar, the Heights in the Co. Down village of Loughinisland, they were watching the Irish performance when two UVF gunmen walked in and sprayed sixty bullets into the clientele. Six men were murdered. Irish football had again been used.

Eighteen years later the Ombudsman's investigation found 'collusion' between the RUC and the Loyalist paramilitaries who carried out the murders.

MR JOHN ROWLAND OF FINSBURY PARK, LONDON, HANDED OVER his shoes to the frail Irish teenager standing in front of him. Liam Brady had just arrived in London, it was the summer of 1971 and Arsenal were celebrating winning the League and FA Cup Double with a grand ball. They invited along the 15 year-old boy from Glenshesk Road in north Dublin, whom they had just signed.

'It was at Claridge's, black tie,' Brady remembers. 'I was an apprentice. I didn't know what day it was. And I had his shoes on, Mr Rowland's. He lent me his patent leather shoes to go to the reception.'

Given that at 15 some of Brady's opinions were as sure as his flowing talent, and that he had already displayed a willingness to take on injustice, Brady also had the wit to recognise decency and a generosity of spirit. Arsenal had placed their new recruit in the care of the Rowlands of Finsbury Park and Brady, while aware of his Irishness in 1970s London, was also aware of his hosts' Englishness.

'England made me so welcome,' Brady says. 'You're placed in digs when you come and I moved into an English family. Mr Rowland, he showed me the ropes, where to the get the bus, the tube. And I had his shoes on.'

What the Rowlands made of Brady is another matter. He was bringing an urban, soccer, southern Irishness, with him, an identity he had to fight for in Dublin. As part of that fight, Brady left school early.

Clearly a natural player, Brady was born in February 1956 into a working-class football family in Whitehall, north Dublin, to Eileen and Edward, a docker. Liam's older brothers Pat and Ray preceded him into the professional game with Millwall and Queen's Park Rangers and before them came Frank Brady, Liam's great uncle. Frank Brady played for the Irish Free State team, as it was known, in 1926 against Italy in the first ever FAI international. It was in Turin, the city Liam was to move to after Arsenal.

Liam Brady was steeped in Irish football but when he went to his local school, St. Aidan's Christian Brothers, his personal and family culture, his soccer culture, was more than frowned upon.

Brady's outstanding ability saw him selected for national honours and in April 1971 he was asked to captain the Republic of Ireland under-15s against Wales in Cardiff. Brady thought his school would be proud of him, or at least be pleased for him, but the school's response was to inform him that this was the same day St. Aidan's had a Gaelic football challenge match against a school from Galway. Brady was told that if he did not play for St. Aidan's, he faced expulsion.

'I was only a kid,' he recalls. 'My decision was that I wanted to play for my country and I wanted to play soccer. By this time I'd been going over to Arsenal and I was going to leave school in a few months to join Arsenal. I was proud and the Ireland match was such a big thing for me because the year before I got left out. I'd been playing a year above my age and we'd played up in Belfast against the North, not a schoolboy international but close to that, and we drew. I was taken off at half-time, I was a small kid and a lot of them were big. The team went on to play England and I was left out.

'So the next year I was doubly motivated. I'd helped the school win a couple of big trophies in Gaelic football and you'd have thought that the Brother would say 'well done' about the Ireland call-up. But no – and there were two or three other Brothers in the school who would have agreed with him – I was betraying my [Gaelic] culture.'

Brady's Irish culture was not something he took lightly. He played for his country and left St. Aidan's. The school disputed whether he had been expelled. They had to respond publicly because Liam's angry father contacted a reporter.

'It was my Dad. He went to the newspapers and the *Evening Herald* printed it on the front page – the front page. That must have been a big blow to the GAA and Christian Brothers schools, that they were exposed. A lad representing his country – captain of his country – any other school would be celebrating. That really embarrassed them.

'I came from a football tradition, my brothers were footballers, my great uncle was a footballer. There were great Irish players in England at the time that everyone followed. And yet the Brothers were trying to say: 'That doesn't exist.'

'They maybe came from a rural background, and if you look at soccer in Ireland, it's urban. That's where the British were in Ireland – Sligo, Cork, Athlone, Dublin. A lot of the Brothers came from Monaghan, Cavan, Tipperary, these places. They were from very Nationalist homes. They had a hatred of football, cricket – English games. You were almost betraying your country by playing them. Absolutely ridiculous. So in many ways you were taking on a tradition or a culture. It was a culture that needed to be taken on.

'The government knew it was going on, just like they knew there was child abuse going on, but they didn't take that on either. They just shut their eyes to it. It was wrong. It took a long time to change. I'm not saying I changed it, but I think my Dad being brave enough to do what he did was certainly a blow for the right cause. It has since altered, a little bit. There's less and less Christian Brothers for a start.'

It may have marked out the Bradys as Irish independents but it was a stressful, unnecessary episode. Just three years later he was in the senior Ireland team making his debut at Dalymount Park against the Soviet Union in a European Championship qualifier. 'I wonder what that Christian Brother was thinking.'

Brady settled into the Arsenal team and into a London-Irish culture. He carried with him his urban, soccer Irishness and had uncomfortable moments as the Troubles dominated the daily news bulletins. But he also placed one foot firmly in England's culture, lived with his English family, made English friends.

'When you're living in England and you're Irish, it was the News,' he says. 'London, England, wasn't an easy place to be. During the day at the club you'd forget about it, it was just when you came back and you're watching the News, the portrayal of what was going on at home, what the [British] government were saying. You'd be angry, you knew what was being said wasn't true. We'd been brought up knowing governments deny things that are true.

'Mr and Mrs Rowland didn't know it was wrong, but I knew, even though I was only 15. I would never argue with them. But in '72 we'd Bloody Sunday.'

Brady is no stage Irishman. He walked the line of an emigrant in England at a time of conflict and knows sometimes he crossed it. He laughs at himself as he recalls that when pushing to leave Arsenal for Juventus a decade after wearing John Rowland's shoes, the Arsenal secretary Ken Friar said to him: "You know you're going to a foreign country, Liam, if you leave.'

'My reply was: 'I'm in a foreign country now, Ken. I've done it once.'

'Ken has reminded me since – a few times – and he keeps reminding me, sometimes when other people are there.'

*

TWENTY YEARS AFTER ARRIVING IN NORTH LONDON, LIAM BRADY would have understood the unnecessary predicament facing another 15 year-old, this time north of the Irish border in Larne. The religion was different – Larne is a Protestant town – and the sporting culture was different. But Gareth McAuley experienced the same cultural pincer Brady had felt.

Like Brady, McAuley came from a football background; like Brady, McAuley attended a school which went out of its way not to appreciate this. Larne Grammar's preferred boys' sport was rugby, as was the case across the grammar school system in Northern Ireland.

'My granddad Archie Todd played for Bangor and won an amateur international cap – my granny had his cap,' McAuley says with no little pride.

'He did all right locally. His son Brian played for Larne and Ballymena United, so there was a bit of football on my mother's side. My granda's brother, he played for Ballyclare Comrades, in fact a few Todds played for Ballyclare. Football was never really pushed at me, though I can remember my granddad throwing a ball to me when I was really young. I got frustrated because I couldn't control it.'

By the time of grammar school, McAuley could control a ball. He joined Lisburn Youth, a club prolific in terms of future Northern Ireland internationals.

'We'd a good team,' he says, 'Dave Healy, Aaron Hughes, Grant McCann, a load of boys who went on to play international football.'

McAuley was an emerging centre-half, beginning to attract 'bits and pieces of interest from England. I was at the Man United school of excellence in Belfast for a bit, I went to a similar thing set up by Tottenham.'

But at Larne Grammar they saw McAuley differently. There he was a rugby player, an out-half or a centre.

'They didn't play football at all,' he says. 'I was captain of the rugby team on a Saturday morning, then I'd go and play football in the afternoon. It was difficult and when I got around fourth form, I told the school I didn't want to play rugby anymore. The headmaster called me in and told me I'd never have a career in football, that I'd never do this or that, but through rugby I could meet people who would help my career. It was pretty snobby really. What he was implying was that rugby has a better standard of person. When you think about it now . . .

'I stood my ground, told him I wanted to play football. Because of that I was, shall we say, overlooked when it came to things like being a prefect at school. After that meeting the last couple of years at school were difficult for me, things were made quite awkward. I just kept my head down. I did Art, Geography and Biology at A-Level and started a Civil Engineering degree. I did the first year, ended up being a draughtsman, doing computer design for a glazing company in Mallusk.'

At 16 McAuley joined Linfield, the first step on a long ladder that led him, 15 years later, to be a former Larne Grammar pupil in England's Premier League.

*

TERRY NEILL TELLS A SIMILAR STORY. BORN IN EAST BELFAST – 'HARPER Street, within the shadow of the Oval' – the Neill family moved out to Bangor.

'But a lot of relatives and my grandparents were still in east Belfast,' Neill says. 'My uncle Norman was in the same class at school as Dickie Best, George's father. Billy Bingham came from the area, Danny Blanchflower. And we all supported the Glens – I went home and away with my Dad and uncles to watch Glentoran. I can remember us stopping the car on the way back from Coleraine and lifting peat off the roadside and whipping it into the boot. Have a look round, make sure no-one was coming. But the Glens didn't fancy me.

'I'd passed my 11-plus, went to Bangor Grammar School. I left because they didn't play football. They said I'd to play rugby. I went to the Technical College and started playing for Bangor, became a schoolboy international.

'Suddenly the Arsenal came in when I was just reaching 17. I'd no idea. I was sitting in the Tonic cinema in Bangor one Saturday night having played for Bangor. I was sitting there getting cramp and the *Ireland's Saturday Night* came round. In the middle it read: 'Neill for Arsenal'. It was the first I knew.

'Arsenal thought I'd snap their hand off. But I said: 'I don't know.' They were gobsmacked and Bangor had no money. We were el gypos. Anyway, I went after a few weeks. Cried myself to sleep.'

*

'WHEN I WENT TO SCHOOL – ST. MICHAEL'S – THE CARETAKER WAS a man called Mr Coote and he would come out and confiscate the ball if he saw us playing soccer. When we saw him coming we'd pick up the ball and pretend we were playing Gaelic football.'

Brian Kerr is recalling schooldays in Inchicore, Dublin in the 1960s. This was an era when what became satirised as 'Official Ireland' continued to glare at a game it insisted be called soccer. Football, that was a Gaelic sport, an Irish sport. Soccer was foreign, English, the 'Garrison Game'.

'Coote was representative of an old Ireland, or an older Ireland,' Kerr says, 'the Ireland where GAA players had their heads bowed in soccer photographs in the paper so you couldn't see their faces. They'd get banned if they were recognised.'

The GAA did indeed ban players it discovered participating in soccer. This did not extend simply to those who played soccer, but those 'caught' turning up at a soccer match were also penalised. Nor was this just directed at families such as 'the Cooneys near us who played for the Dublin hurling team,' as Kerr says. In November 1938 Douglas Hyde, no less than President of Ireland, was removed from his honorary position at the top of the GAA for attending the Ireland-Poland soccer international at Dalymount Park in Dublin.

Under 'The Ban' – or the GAA's Rule 27 – players were not allowed to participate in, attend or promote soccer, rugby, hockey or cricket. It was a ruling that may have had contemporary rationale when it was introduced in 1902 and Irish Nationalism was embroiled in a political and cultural battle that would see the Irish independence arrive within 20 years. But it looked increasingly anachronistic, spiteful and unrealistic as the decades passed.

Yet it was 1971 before 'The Ban' was lifted. And while Rule 27 was lifted, Rule 21 remained in place. It forbade members of the British security forces from membership of the GAA. Introduced in 1897, it was removed after the Good Friday Agreement of 1998 and the replacing of the RUC with the Police Service of Northern Ireland (PSNI).

'You'd get suspended,' Kerr says of Rule 27. 'It wasn't always implemented in Dublin, but it could be. Maybe down the country, if someone made a complaint, it was more frequent. We didn't live in that atmosphere, there was a difference between rural and urban.'

*

'I WAS REARED IN TUAM, CO. GALWAY, WHERE MY LATE MUM WAS from. I'm a big Galway supporter, hurling and football. My first game was at Tuam stadium in 1950 when Galway played Tipp in an all-Ireland hurling semi-final. I fell in love with the maroon-and-white there and then. Galway got beat 4-7 to 2-6 but, sure, that was it. To a five year-old that doesn't matter. St. Jarlath's, the stadium, it only opened that year. I was at the opening.'

Paddy Mulligan was to win 50 caps for the Republic of Ireland and play six years for Chelsea and Crystal Palace as the swinging sixties turned into the 1970s. He was part of the Chelsea team that won the European Cup Winners' Cup in 1971, beating Real Madrid in the final.

Mulligan can talk about the Bernabeu stadium, King's Road glamour and all that; he can also recall 'doing the beet with the Conways next door' in the fields of Tuam and 'just sitting on the wall', a memory that will resonate with many of that generation. 'I was so fortunate to grow up in that era,' he says.

If Mulligan experienced two different cultures as child and adult, he also saw two in Irish sport. 'My aunts and uncles in Tuam, and my aunt in Sligo, they were very sports orientated,' he says. 'There was no soccer in the family, it was all GAA. Soccer, it was alien, oh yeah. Very much. It was foreign, no question.

'Then we came to Dublin, to Chapelizod. St. Patrick's Athletic were playing in Chapelizod in the old greyhound stadium – Alex Stevenson was their manager, *the* Alex Stevenson. There was a speedway track around the pitch. We were spoilt for choice. Nobody had any money, but we'd everything else.'

It was 1956. Mulligan played Gaelic games at school and loved it. He then started playing soccer in Dublin's street leagues and while he wanted to be Stanley Matthews or Paddy Coad, soccer was 'very much frowned upon'.

Contradicting that attitude, domestic Irish soccer was enjoying a boom and some of those enjoying it, as Mulligan points out, were Gaelic footballers. Dublin's Kevin Heffernan, one of the all-time greats, was one who would go to Miiltown to watch Shamrock Rovers, for whom Mulligan played from 1963 until he joined Chelsea.

'I think people had the good of sport in their minds,' Mulligan says. 'I played Gaelic football as well and I know lots of Gaelic lads who played soccer – Kevin Heffernan loved soccer. The official view was forced upon them and they rebelled to a degree. In our own quiet way, it was our small, quiet cultural rebellion. People voted with their feet. The attitude was: 'Nobody's going to stop me going to a soccer match if I want to go to a soccer match.'

'I mean, the Gaelic lads weren't allowed to go to a soccer match, but they'd put on a cap, pull their coat up around their face. They'd go. The great Galway goalkeeper Johnny Geraghty came up to Milltown to see how we trained and he trained with us – in the middle of Galway's three-in-a-row in the All-Ireland. Mick O'Connell came across to see me in England, 1973-ish, to see how we trained at Crystal Palace. Stayed for a week.

'It was the hierarchy who were opposed to soccer. It was like Archbishop Mc-Quaid in 1955. He said: 'Don't go to the game.' Something like 28,000 went. On a Wednesday afternoon. We had minds of our own. Just because he said it was the wrong thing to do … No. It wasn't.'

Mulligan is still visibly annoyed by the condescension and outright antipathy soccer attracted from official Ireland.

At its summit was Archbishop John Charles McQuaid. McQuaid was a strident figure in southern Irish society for decades, as Archbishop of Dublin from 1940-72. His influence preceded that appointment as one of those who advised on the 1937 Ireland constitution and with religion woven into the state officially and culturally, McQuaid's narrow opinions held sway over decision-making to a degree which sounds, at best, unusual to modern ears. McQuaid had a Paisleyite level of cultural influence.

In 1950, when the FAI were trying to organise a friendly with Yugoslavia for the following year, McQuaid reminded them of the oppression of Catholics in the semi-Soviet state. There was no friendly against Yugoslavia. In 1952 the FAI and Yugoslavia were again in communication but the FAI felt obliged to ask McQuaid his opinion on the proposed friendly. McQuaid again said No. The Association was obedient to his command, the way the church and McQuaid liked Irish citizens to be.

But the FAI was also frustrated. In September 1949 the FAI's Ireland had gone to Goodison Park and defeated England 2-0. This was four years before Hungary beat England at Wembley, one of the milestones of 20th century European football.

Ireland thus became the first 'foreign' team to beat England in England. Con Martin and Peter Farrell scored the goals and as Tom Finney, who played that day, was to say:

> *If you ever go to Southern Ireland, don't try and claim that England have never been beaten at home by any team other than the home countries. Eire may not be Continental, but they definitely regard themselves as 'outsiders' ... worth remembering if you should cross the sea to Ireland for an off-the-ration steak or two.*

This was an historic breakthrough, an indication of the football talent in Ireland. Also in 1949, Jackie Carey was voted Footballer of the Year in England. And yet there was a struggle. Soccer was still seen as foreign by many within the hierarchy of southern Irish society and by sections of the population.

The FAI began coaching programmes around the time of the England victory and in 1951 appointed Scot Dougie Livingstone as the country's first recognised National Coach. Here was a measure of ambition and organization not always associated with the FAI, then or later.

There were individuals thinking differently, too, as Mulligan shows: 'Joe Fitzpatrick, my manager at Home Farm, had me playing as a protector in front of the back four in 1959 – that's because he'd go to Germany to see what was going on. Home Farm, 1959, that was innovation.

'In 1956 Ireland beat West Germany in Dalymount with six or seven League of Ireland players in the team. The Germans had won the World Cup in '54. In this country there's always been players. That same year Ireland went to Rotterdam and beat Holland 4-1. Holland learned. After that game they turned professional and look what happened. It's taken us a long time to learn.'

Only after that Irish defeat in May 1956 did Dutch football embrace professionalism, a compliment of sorts.

Livingstone had got to work. His impact was far from revolutionary but he had done enough in two years for the GAA President, Vincent O'Donoghue, to refer to him as 'the chief of the new Saxon recruiting campaign ... busy enticing young Irish boys by various inducements to become happy little English children.'

Irish soccer men such as Mulligan and later, Brady, felt the full weight of this kind of sneer, and though they understood it was not one shared unanimously by the players of Gaelic games, it made their sporting life difficult. But it did not put them off.

And in 1955, at the third attempt, Yugoslavia were at last due to play in Dublin.

Arrangements had been finalised when, one week before kick-off, McQuaid suddenly thumped his fist again. It seemed there was a familiar submissive role for soccer to play as official Ireland walked away from the FAI. Radio Eireann had planned to broadcast the match but withdrew coverage. The Irish Army band, primed to play the national anthems, cancelled.

The Irish players, meanwhile, turned up at Dalymount Park and as Mulligan says, so did over 20,000 on a Wednesday afternoon. Yugoslavia won 4-1, but that was not the overriding issue in Ireland.

'It didn't matter to us, we were going to see sport, to enjoy ourselves,' Mulligan says. 'It was an education. Think of Dynamo Moscow, Honved, the great Hungary team of the 50s, you want to see them. I went to the cinema with all my pals to see Pathe News to get a snippet of the England-Hungary match at Wembley. McQuaid said Yugoslavia were Communists – ten of them were Catholic.'

*

IN FEBRUARY 2007, CROKE PARK STAGED THE IRELAND-ENGLAND SIX Nations rugby international. The GAA had allowed their Dublin home to be used as Lansdowne Road was being re-developed. That was the logistical background. Rather more prominent was the symbolism. This was a sport deemed 'foreign' taking its place at the home of the GAA, scene of the British Army killing 14 spectators in November 1920.

The GAA has attracted criticism for the mythologising of its role in trying to create an 'Irish Ireland' and in *Sport & Ireland: A History* Paul Rouse gives the origins of Croke Park's Hill 16 as an example. Before it was Hill 16 with its Easter Rising connotations, it was Hill 60 – named from the battle of Gallipoli in 1915, where Irish soldiers in the British Army served. It was not until 1931 that it became known as Hill 16.

That the same British Army fired on Croke Park in 1920 is not in dispute, nor is the GAA's sense of defiance, pride and self-determination in the face of such events anything other than understandable. For the GAA allowing England to play at Croke Park was the crossing of a hostile border with an outstretched hand and this magnanimous gesture was extended to soccer a month later. The Republic of Ireland played Wales in a Euro 2008 qualifier.

Brian Kerr was at both matches. 'The England rugby game, it was sensational,' he says. 'If anything was going to have an impact in the post-Troubles time, that was it. The feeling in the ground was that all this is finished. There were some old hardcore

UDA men there that day, I was in the same box as them.

'When I was manager of Ireland, I would have loved to have taken the team to play in Croke Park. A lot of Gaelic fellas wouldn't know that. I still get cracks about watching the 'wrong' game when I'm seen at a Gaelic match.

'But that's where I started. My school in Inchicore is now a museum for the 1916 Rising, because it was used as the overflow for Kilmainham gaol. We'd play all sports, I didn't have an anti-GAA thing. A few of us were good at soccer and even if it was known as the Garrison Game, the Brothers recognised we were good. We'd a couple of Brothers in the school who were very broad-minded.

'In my head, I would have loved to be the manager that day at Croke Park. Not for any nasty reason, but for the enlightened people who didn't look down on soccer as the Garrison Game.'

ARGUABLY THE MOST SIGNIFICANT FOOTBALL MATCH IN THE HIS-tory of Ireland was not a football match. It was a ruse.

What does it say about the status of football in Irish and English eyes that on Easter Monday 1916 Garry Holohan and Paddy Daly led a small company of young volunteers towards the Magazine Fort held by the British Army in Dublin's Phoenix Park pretending to be a soccer team having a kickabout?

It says soccer was regarded by both parties as an English game and, therefore, that these young Dubliners could not raise suspicious thoughts among the soldiers guarding the Fort. Holohan and Daly and those about to launch the Easter Rising knew this would be the soldiers' perception.

The term 'Garrison Game' stemmed from the British Army camps located around Ireland when it was part of the United Kingdom and garrisons were stationed there to maintain the Empire. As Association football – soccer – grew in popularity through the late 1800s, British soldiers took their game outside the garrison and into towns such as Sligo, Dundalk, Athlone, Limerick. There were other avenues of origin for the game in Ireland but 'Garrison Game' stuck, although today, as Dave Hannigan wrote in *The Garrison Game,* it is a phrase that 'belongs in a history book.'

Hannigan quotes Michael Collins saying in 1908: 'There'll be no garrison games for Ireland … there should be no soccer for Gaels,' and that was the atmosphere of the times. It was an attitude that enabled the Phoenix Park kickabout to occur.

'Paddy Daly and I went on bicycles and called at Whelan's on Ormond Quay, where we bought a football,' Holohan said in his statement to the Bureau of Military History. 'After a few minutes' chat together, as if we were a football team with followers, we moved around to the front of the Fort in a casual way, some of the lads kicking the ball from one to the other. When we got near the gate they rushed the sentry.'

Paddy Daly explained his part in this pose: 'I was to ask the sentry where the soccer ground was while Paddy Boland would then jump on him and disarm him. We did this.'

The Easter Rising was under way. The Magazine Fort produced its own kind of match report and teamsheet and whether the week of the Rising is considered an all-out success or not, five years later there were two Irelands: an Irish Republic and Northern Ireland.

*

WHILST FOOTBALL-SOCCER WAS NOT THE ISLAND'S MOST PRESSING item in the seven years from Easter 1916 to the end of the Irish Civil War, like the rest of Irish society it was changed radically – utterly – by those years.

When the Irish League resumed after WWI in 1919/20 two Dublin clubs, Shelbourne and Bohemians, were willing participants in a division based around five Belfast clubs and Glenavon in Lurgan. A year later those two Dublin clubs were two of eight in the first League of Ireland. This was the moment of fracture in Irish football, 'The Split', as it came to be known.

It was led by the Leinster FA, the administrators of the early game in Dublin. In June 1921 they informed the Belfast-based IFA, to whom they were affiliated, that Leinster would be running its own affairs. The secession had been coming. For years there had been grumbling, often well-founded, that the northern governing body held an anti-southern bias as revealed in fixture venues, committee make-ups and the selection of the international team – among other things. There was a civic, geographic tension between Dublin and Belfast, too, plus cultural differences such as playing games on Sundays. In Dublin this was common practice, in Belfast this was a religious taboo. There was also a lot of small 'p' backroom, committee-men politics.

But it would be naïve to separate the split in football from the overall politics of the time. The fact is that when the first post-war Irish League season began, there was one, unified Ireland. By the start of the first League of Ireland season, the creation of two entities, the Irish Free State and Northern Ireland, was under way.

In September 1921 the Football Association of Ireland, an enlarged version of the Leinster FA's administration, was established. The island of Ireland now had two football governing bodies and two Leagues.

Plenty of people thought, indeed some in each organization, that this was temporary – a fracture, not a break – and that in time it would heal or be healed. The first evidence of that belief was not far away.

The League of Ireland was a success in its first season, supporter interest and turnstile income were healthy. The Irish League suffered. By December 1922 there was sufficient concern in the north about the split for Linfield to request a charity match in Dublin by way of beginning reconciliation. When the FAI and IFA then met for a first meeting to discuss differences, in the Shelbourne hotel in Dublin, it ended with Linfield withdrawing the charity match offer. The meeting had not gone well.

That was February 1923. Yet just three months later, at the IFA's annual meeting, the mood was optimistic. Chairman James Wilton referred to a north-south 'old-time friendship' and as Cormac Moore writes in *The Irish Soccer Split*: 'To loud applause, he [Wilton] concluded with the wish 'that before their next annual meeting they would have a 'United Ireland'.''

Indeed, that summer of 1923, there was a groundswell of opinion in Dublin that returning to the IFA and Irish League under amended circumstances was appealing for sporting and commercial reasons. Simultaneously, though, the FAI was lobbying for formal international recognition and when a French club side, Gallia, travelled to Dublin for two matches, the new state, and the new Association, had its first taste of continental validation. It liked it, and that mattered as the FAI wanted to establish its own Ireland team and play its own internationals.

The problem was that IFAB – the International Football Association Board – was a UK organization. It consisted of the Associations of England, Scotland, Wales and the IFA. Stymied by IFAB, the FAI went to FIFA, a newer organization formed in 1904 in Paris. In August 1923 FIFA granted the FAI provisional membership. The FAI's sense of self-determination was altered. It felt it had a chance.

Two months on, IFAB called a meeting in Liverpool and both FAI and IFA attended. There was no agreement reached but the Liverpool conference led to another, in Belfast in March 1924.

This was significant in that the IFA offered, in modern parlance, parity of esteem. Domestic bureaucracy and international team selection would be shared. The FAI delegation was surprised by the cordial offer and when they left the Belfast meeting it seemed there would be a reconciliation. Some newspapers even reported the fact of it; the FAI received some congratulatory telegrams.

But there was one stipulation that disconcerted the FAI when it got back to Dublin: it was that the chairman of the international selection committee would be from the IFA, permanently. Therefore, for example, if there was a six-man committee with three selectors from the north and three from the south, the chairman would always give the north a majority. This bothered the FAI as it considered the Ireland team more often than not to be the IFA's version of Ireland. The FAI wanted a real and recognizable 32-county Ireland team. They wanted internationals staged alternately in Belfast and Dublin. They wanted their flag to fly.

Just eight weeks after the Belfast conference, the FAI got their wish. A football team representing the Irish Free State, organized by the FAI, appeared at the Paris Olympics. The team was amateur, fitting the Olympian ideal, but of greater significance the team was called 'Ireland' and played under an Irish Tricolour. Their anthem was Let Erin Remember, not The Soldier's Song. The team wore blue, possibly the St. Patrick's blue of the professional IFA team. Ireland beat Bulgaria at the Stade de Colombes, then were beaten by the Netherlands, but here was a start, visible progress northerners could not ignore.

Negotiations with the IFA were ongoing and after the English FA suggested alternate chairmanship of the international selection committee, as well as alternate venues, this was accepted by the IFA. A solution was imminent. Then, as it tends to, money talked.

The IFA, while willing to accept Ireland internationals in Dublin, wanted to retain the receipts, not give them to the FAI despite the matches being played in their jurisdiction. The FAI, needing income to exist, refused. The split remained.

In March 1926, the FAI found the resources to send a team to Turin for their first, professional international. This is the game Liam Brady's great uncle Frank played in – the FAI said that only those born in the 26 counties of the new Irish Free State were eligible for selection. This was another moment in the development of the FAI's Ireland, and in strengthening the split. Then, a year later, FIFA stated that the IFA's international team should be called 'Northern Ireland' from thereon.

There was a ball rolling but England and Scotland maintained it was the IFA team which would be called 'Ireland', as did the IFA. In 1932 came another attempt at finding a solution, a two-day meeting, the first day in Dublin, the second day in Belfast.

On the first day the IFA agreed that the FAI could keep its receipts from internationals staged in Dublin. This was the breakthrough, or so it appeared. On the second day, the FAI asked for one of the two IFA seats on IFAB. Taken aback by the timing as much as the request, perhaps feeling ambushed, the IFA refused and in a manner that left no room for further negotiation, not then or in the years that followed.

It meant the split had time to grow and settle and it was 1946 before a meaningful international gesture was again made – each Association allowing players from the other's jurisdiction to be selected for forthcoming matches.

But there was always the broader political landscape: in 1948 the Republic of Ireland Act was passed in Dublin which led, formally, to Irish withdrawal from the Commonwealth. A separate identity, as a fully independent Irish Republic was growing and in football two Irish teams entered the 1950 World Cup. FIFA wanted clarity: which players represented which Ireland? The days of players being able to appear for both were coming to an end.

Neither Ireland qualified for the finals, and in March 1950, when the IFA Ireland fielded FAI players in their qualifier against Wales in Wrexham, it was to be for the last time.

*

CON MARTIN PLAYED THAT DAY FOR THE IFA'S IRELAND IN WALES. He had, five months earlier, scored for the FAI's Ireland. That, too, was in a World Cup qualifier, in Dublin against Sweden.

Martin was a versatile footballer. He had made his full FAI Ireland debut as a goalkeeper in a 1-0 win in Spain in June 1946; he made his IFA Ireland debut as a wing-half against Scotland five months later. But Martin's flexible availability went too far for FIFA and, as he explained in his house in Drumcondra in 1999, Con Martin's dual soccer Irishness went too far for others.

Martin's sporting brilliance had revealed itself first in another code: Gaelic football. 'I won a Leinster Senior Championship medal way back in 1942,' Martin said, 'but the medal was never given to me until 1972. I was disappointed because I would have won an All-Ireland medal with Dublin, I was on the team. But I was suspended completely from Gaelic because I preferred the soccer. I had to make a choice.'

Martin described that choice as 'another political thing'. He had moved from the League of Ireland club Drumcondra to Glentoran for £500 in the summer of 1946 – 'Elisha Scott tried to sign me for Belfast Celtic but the Glentoran people offered twice the sum.'

Martin was unable to say why he chose to live in Ballysillan in north Belfast but said 'it wasn't a big deal' to be a Dublin Catholic living near the top of the Shankill Road or playing for Glentoran: 'I never sensed anything at all, I stayed with the Protestant people up there. There were times when I went up the Falls Road and was heckled for playing for Glentoran. It never dawned on me that the situation would become violent.'

At Glentoran Martin played alongside Danny Blanchflower. It was not for long – 22 matches – as Leeds United offered £8,000 for Martin and he was sold. Previously he had turned down Manchester United. 'Matt Busby came to Belfast to sign me as a goalkeeper, because Jackie Carey had recommended me,' Martin said, 'but Leeds wanted me as a centre-half.'

By the time of the northern Ireland game at Wrexham in 1950, Martin had moved from Leeds to Aston Villa, where he again linked up with Blanchflower. Both men played in Wrexham. The IFA's northern Ireland team contained seven northerners and four from south of the border – Bud Aherne, Reg Ryan, Davy Walsh and Con Martin. All four had played against Sweden in the FAI's last World Cup qualifier months earlier. There was an international reaction to this, clarification was demanded.

As Martin explained, there was also a domestic reaction and it was just as decisive. Jackie Carey had not been given permission to play for the IFA against Wales because Manchester United had a match – against Villa, Martin's club. United won 7-0.

'The next day the Villa chairman called me into his office,' Martin said, 'and showed me a lot of letters from people in the south calling me Judas for playing for the north. Villa were getting threatening letters saying they wouldn't be welcome in the south if I kept playing for the north. That was when the director of Aston Villa asked me to refuse to play for northern Ireland ever again. That was the turning point.'

Villa had a relationship with Shamrock Rovers and Rovers' chairman Joe Cunningham pressurised Villa. Martin said that he and the other three players involved, and other southern Irish players, received a letter from Cunningham urging them not to play for 'the small part of Ireland'. Nine days after Wrexham the *Belfast Telegraph* reported: 'Martin To Play Only For Eire'.

Martin had written to the IFA to say he would no longer be available. Similar letters were sent from other players. This prompted another headline: 'Four Footballers Who Weren't Asked Refused To Play'.

'I enjoyed playing for northern Ireland and I enjoyed the people,' Martin said. 'I was sorry and if I'd had my choice, I wouldn't have done that [written a letter]. It was Aston Villa – and they were good to me.'

Martin felt his loyalties lay 'half and half really' and that one Ireland team, or two Ireland teams, was 'always an issue'. He said the 'players got on great' and recalled Billy McMillan from Carrickfergus being handed a vial of Holy Water before the FAI game in Spain and 'taking a swig of it.'

But after Wrexham, hardening attitudes and FIFA's new criteria meant there would be no more dual Irish internationals like Cornelius Joseph Martin. The Split had again been re-enforced.

GREEN SHOOTS

*

'I WAS EXCITED ... AND WHY WOULDN'T I BE? ... THE EXCITEMENT IN my voice and body language was palpable ... my hands were wet with the sweat of the nervous tension. Here, I thought, we were talking about history in the making.'

It was 1973 in a London hotel room before the term 'All-Ireland' was again used with capital letters and serious intent.

This is Derek Dougan speaking, of how he sat down with the IFA's leading administrators, Harry Cavan and Billy Drennan, and told them of two phone calls he had recently received. One was from John Giles in Leeds, the other from Louis Kilcoyne, FAI president. What the two men had to say stimulated Dougan: Brazil, world champions in 1970, were going to Dublin and would play an Irish XI.

'Then came the moment I shall remember for the rest of my life ... I was confronted with a cold and stony silence ... For me, the idea of the All-Ireland team created the possibility of contributing to the healing of divisions ... a temporary sporting unity would be a major achievement.'

Cavan told Dougan he would put the idea to the IFA. But in Dougan's recollection, Cavan did so 'tersely'.

The Northern Ireland team had gathered in London en route to Cyprus for a World Cup qualifier. Dougan was captain again. This was his 43rd cap, he had played at the 1958 World Cup, spanned the Peter Doherty-George Best generations. But Northern Ireland lost 1-0 in Cyprus and as Dougan said: 'I was never selected again to play for my country.'

He was still good enough to finish that season with Wolves in the First Division, and to play the next season there too. He was also good enough to be asked by Giles and Liam Tuohy to be part of the All-Ireland XI that met world champions Brazil in Dublin in 1973.

Giles was still a Leeds United player while about to take over as manager of the country now known by FIFA as the Republic of Ireland. Kilcoyne was Giles' brother-in-law and had lobbied Joao Havelange, Brazil's FA president and a man ambitious to unseat England's Stanley Rous as head of FIFA in its 1974 election. If Kilcoyne could deliver an FAI vote for Havelange, Havelange could deliver Brazil in Dublin for a friendly.

Brazil were on a 1973 European tour to acclimatize for the 1974 World Cup in West Germany. They agreed to an Irish visit, bringing the lustre of Jairzinho and Rivelino to Lansdowne Road, but it had to be for a charity match and the opposition had to be 32-county in make-up. For that reason, Giles called Dougan.

Dougan came from Avon Street in the shadow of the shipyard in east Belfast. He could only have been more Protestant if he had tried. But he had been in England for 16 years by then, beginning with Portsmouth, and looked at the daily, bloody news from Belfast with an emigrant's eyes. He was a changing man. The words above come from his book: *The Sash He Never Wore*.

Dougan had something of the Brian Clough about him. He had strong opinions and was keen to voice them. As the Troubles descended into increasing violence in 1971 and '72, Dougan was part of the Northern Ireland squad unable to play at home. He was determined to try to do something and was proposing his own cross-border friendlies when the Brazil game arose. He jumped at the opportunity to play Brazil and in July 1973 he was there, along with Allan Hunter, Bryan Hamilton, David Craig, Pat Jennings, Liam O'Kane and Martin O'Neill – all Northern Ireland players.

The team could not be called Ireland or All-Ireland. Dougan said that Rous later told him that Cavan had been busy behind the scenes ensuring the team's name had no Ireland title. Whatever Cavan did, it had an effect. The team was called a Shamrock Rovers XI despite no-one from Shamrock Rovers being on it.

Brazil won 4-3 in front of 35,000 – One headline was: 'Brazilians Rocked by United Irishmen'. A gesture had been made and one man there who would have understood both the day's possibilities and its limitations was Con Martin. His son, Mick, recently transferred from Bohemians to Manchester United, was playing.

'I was delighted to be part of it, to be selected against the best team in the world,' Mick Martin says. He and Dougan both scored for the Irish.

'I don't know if all the players felt as strongly as Derek but we knew what it was about, the cross-border element to it. I don't know if you'd call it an agenda, but Derek had the idea of an All-Ireland team, similar to the rugby. How could the rugby lot do it and football not? I spoke to Derek a few times about it: 'How good a team could we be?' he'd say. That bit was about sport.

'We all knew there were going to be difficulties if you tried to make it happen, you could end up with some enemies. You'd have both sets of committee members for a start, then there would be the staunch people in the north. Where would you play? Who would be manager? Those things. But I felt the bigger obstacle was the bureaucracy, with their jobs and their perks. *Me Feiners.*'

After the game Martin remembers a group, including Hunter and Craig – northern Protestants – going out for a drink in Dublin together with himself, Don Givens, Terry Conroy – southern Catholics. 'There'd have been singing, traditional, the lads had no problem.'

Dougan and many others saw the game as a success and as an example. He wrote afterwards: 'They didn't say it couldn't be done, they said it shouldn't be done. It was done and afterwards they couldn't find any fault with it, so they said nothing.'

But it caused more than a ripple and there was, three months later, a meeting in Belfast between the two Associations described as 'lengthy and amicable'. There was another in early 1974. There was a gap until 1978 but then the two Irish FAs met in Dundalk and issued a joint statement on discussions that included 'the possibility of an All-Ireland Football Federation which would be responsible for international matches'.

Had Harry Cavan and the IFA thought again? Cormac Moore quotes a newspaper report from 1979 where Cavan says 'that two teams in a small island like this was nonsensical', although Northern Ireland players of the era raise their eyebrows at the notion of Cavan as a force for change.

Plus, as Mick Martin says, the two teams were direct opponents by 1979, drawn in the same European Championships qualifying group as England. This meant that on September 20 1978, for the first time, the two Irelands lined up against each other. The game was at Lansdowne Road.

'That was the first one,' says Liam Brady. 'Among the players it was kind-of, 'let's get this over with'. It was at the height of the Troubles. It was 0-0.'

Just over a year later came the return in Belfast. Mick Martin missed the first match in Dublin through injury but was now captain. His opposite number with Northern Ireland was Allan Hunter, one of his colleagues from the 1973 'Shamrock Rovers' team.

'Tense, that's how I remember it, a bit fiery,' Martin says. 'We stayed in a hotel up north, went straight to Windsor Park on the bus. It was a tight ground in a Loyalist area, flags, you knew what you were going to get: 'Fenian bastard'. And you did. You just assume there's going to be enough protection if there's a pitch invasion, whatever. It went OK.'

Northern Ireland won 1-0, a Gerry Armstrong header from a Sammy Nelson cross. Nelson was one of six Arsenal players who played in the two matches. Nelson, Pat Jennings and Pat Rice were from the north, Brady, David O'Leary and Frank Stapleton were from the south.

Brady was incensed. In a book in 1980 – *So Far, So Good* – Brady devoted a chapter to the international situation, writing: 'The day the European Championships groups were named, six Irishmen at Highbury sat down and faced up to a sickening and depressing reality … I remember vividly how stupid and senseless the whole thing seemed.'

Brady was 'bitterly disappointed' not to be able play on the same Irish team as George Best and almost 40 years on, Brady says: 'It was heartfelt, I would have loved to have seen an all-Ireland team. When you see the rugby team, they can get on together. I never had any doubt the players could get on together, as long as the way we were portrayed wasn't as 'The Republic' with a Tricolour. There had to be a softening of that, as there has been in the rugby.

'But, looking at the history of Irish football, and any other sport, once you split, it's difficult to get it back together. Boxing didn't split, cricket didn't split. I have met cricket people, and there's friction between north and south, but they manage to keep it together. 'I was always saying that there should be one team. Maybe that was naïve. It was so entrenched, particularly up north, they weren't going to give that status up and they probably never will. And let's face it, I don't think there was much appetite from the Football Association of Ireland. It's like turkeys voting for Christmas, 50% of the blazers would have to be hung up.

'Would I like to see a united Ireland team today? Absolutely. But I think it can only happen when things get better between the two peoples. Back then it needed leadership. Dougan almost broke the mould.'

Brady was injured for the 1979 match in Belfast but, not wanting to look 'like some kind of chicken', he went to Windsor Park with his teammates and, at least once, laughed.

'I sat on the bench. Gerry Daly got hit with something thrown from the crowd. It nicked his head and Sammy [Nelson] tells the story of how he went over to Gerry and says: 'Fucking hell, Gerry, you've been shot!'

'Gerry looked at him – with shock. He nearly did die, but it wasn't because he was mortally wounded. Sammy was a great joker.'

*

IN BETWEEN THOSE TWO 'TWO-IRELANDS' MATCHES IN THE EURO 1980 qualifiers, there was another cross-border game that demonstrated how problematic a reconciliation would be. In the 1979/80 European Cup, the winners of the League of Ireland, Dundalk, were drawn against the winners of the Irish League, Linfield.

On this news, a fog of apprehension fell at once across Ireland. Dundalk, as a town, and Linfield as a club, had reputations.

The first leg was scheduled for 29 August, 1979. Two days before the match, off the coast of Co. Sligo, the IRA blew up the boat of Lord Louis Mountbatten, killing him and three others. Later the same day, around 20 miles from Dundalk, the IRA exploded another bomb at Warrenpoint, killing six British soldiers. Half an hour later, another explosion killed a further 12 British soldiers who had rushed to the scene. Firing shots across the border, the British Army killed a civilian. In Belfast the UVF murdered a man. There were 24 people killed in less than 24 hours.

That the Dundalk-Linfield game went ahead is as incredible now as it seemed then. Not only did it happen, Linfield were able to bring a large travelling support and as every man, woman and child in Ireland expected, there was serious trouble. 'I remember the Guards running across the pitch as the game went on,' says Roy Coyle.

Coyle was the Linfield manager. He grew up close to where Derek Dougan was born, went to Orangefield Secondary with Van Morrison, joined Sheffield Wednesday in 1972 and was capped five times by Northern Ireland in 1973. In 1975, aged just 29 he was appointed Linfield player-manager. In Belfast, a city not short of them, Coyle was regarded as a hard man, but even he calls Dundalk that day 'scary'.

Dundalk's ground, Oriel Park, was a basic facility where fans were free to roam if they chose to. Linfield's fans wished to do this, to get to a flagpole in particular. It was flying a Tricolour.

'We went down the day before, stayed overnight, I forget where,' Coyle says. 'It wasn't in Dundalk, I know that. There was a lot of security on the way down and we were shepherded by the Guards once we got over the border. They were waiting for us and escorted us to our hotel. There were quite a lot of people outside the hotel.'

Once Linfield got to Oriel Park, Coyle says: 'You had to try to blank it out in the dressing room, you'd a job to do.'

But as the game kicked off a riot began, there were policemen running across the pitch as play went on. 'The referee and players just stood and watched them. There were fans climbing up onto the roof of the stand, firing bottles and everything. Madness.'

Remarkably the 90 minutes were completed and a 1-1 scoreline recorded. But the trouble continued after the final whistle in the streets around Oriel Park and UEFA's response was severe. Linfield would not be allowed to play the second leg at their home, Windsor Park. Nor would they be allowed to play it elsewhere in Belfast, nor in Northern Ireland, nor anywhere in the UK. UEFA produced a radius within which Linfield were not to organise the second leg and so seven days later, the two Irish champions found themselves across the Irish Sea and across the North Sea on the outskirts of Amsterdam, at the home of HFC Haarlem.

'We were banned for three games and there was a specific radius and within that we couldn't play,' Coyle says. 'We'd to go beyond England. We went to Haarlem because we'd a youth team that played in a tournament there for a few years, so we'd a connection. We knew Barry Hughes, a Welshman who managed Haarlem – Ruud

Gullit played for them then.'

On a calm, sunny day, in front of a few intrigued Dutch locals, Linfield lost 2-0. 'It wasn't like Dundalk,' Coyle says. 'We got hammered, well, Warren Feeney missed a penalty at 1-0. But the most important thing was there was no trouble. Neither set of supporters travelled. The big thing was to get it played and done.'

A year later Linfield were back in Haarlem, 'hosting' France's champions Nantes in the European Cup. But they were also, as Coyle recalls, back across the Irish border. In the late 1960s in an effort to provide some all-Ireland football, the two Leagues had agreed to the Blaxnit Cup, which became the Texaco Cup and then the Tyler Cup. There was Association co-operation involved; but only so much could be done.

'We'd played Athlone in the Tyler's All-Ireland Cup final [August 1980] and this car kept coming past us,' Coyle says of the journey home. 'Our bus driver stopped, made a phone call. Turns out there was a massive crowd waiting for us at Dundalk. The Guards went ahead to sort that out, the police went into Dundalk and dispersed them. We got over the border, into the North and away.'

*

THAT WAS THE LAST OF THE CROSS-BORDER COMPETITIONS – UNTIL 2005. In 1983 the FAI accepted that 'there will be no settlement of the split in Irish soccer' until Irish politics changed.

Ten years later Alan McLoughlin turned up at Windsor Park and nine years after that Neil Lennon was warned in an anonymous phone call that if he played for Northern Ireland against Cyprus he would be 'seriously hurt'. Lennon, a Northern Ireland captain playing at home, retired from international football after that.

Lennon played his club football at Celtic, whose manager was Martin O'Neill. Former captain of Northern Ireland, now manager of the Republic of Ireland, O'Neill crossed the border in Irish football. It will soon be 100 years old.

The men of the IFA and FAI back then thought their split was a fracture, but like a temporary Belfast peace wall it morphed into a permanent divide and both parties learned to live on either side of it. The divide became the culture, the border became a culture of separation, not just in football.

'I don't think it'll change now,' says Alan McLoughlin, 'and I don't think it needs to change. It works for both countries at the moment.'

West Bromwich Albion ended the 2016/17 season with five players born in Northern Ireland. Three – Gareth McAuley, Chris Brunt and Jonny Evans – play for Northern Ireland; two – James McClean and Marc Wilson – play for the Republic of Ireland. To be born on the island gives you dual nationality, a choice.

'Your heart has to be in it, that's the biggest thing,' McAuley says. 'International football is a privilege, and it's a choice. You don't have to play it if you don't want to and for me, if you don't want to be involved and give everything you can, then there's no point in being here. For both the lads born in the north who play for the south, I think that's the way it is. You can't force people, your heart has to be in it.'

Today any cross-border discussion usually entails a complaint from the IFA about a northern boy choosing to play for the FAI. It is why Northern Ireland manager Michael O'Neill and youth director Jim Magilton knock on doors such as that of Belfast teenager Shayne Lavery. Thriving at Everton, Lavery has played for the IFA but has attracted the attention of the FAI. He is one in a long line.

In retrospect, one of the most striking aspects of the past century was the success of the 1980s and 1990s. In 1982 and 1986 Northern Ireland qualified for the World Cup. In 1990 and 1994 the Republic of Ireland qualified for the World Cup.

Those successes were an indication of the quality of Irish footballers and brought pride and praise. But those qualifications and appearances at the highest level of the sport also enhanced separate Irish identities and sustained a divide. In 1994 very rare was the Irishman who declared that Irish footballers had just played in four consecutive World Cup finals. But they had.

PART II

EARLY NORTHERN THINKERS

WILLIAM, BILL AND PETER THE GREAT

WILLIAM MCCRUM

SWING SOUTH-WEST OUT OF ARMAGH CITY, ABOUT A MILE OR SO down the Monaghan Road and on the left lies the village of Milford. It is trim, red-brick, a model village built for cotton and linen in the 19th century, some low-rise industry among the orchards of rural Co. Armagh. It is quaint.

Here in the quiet, leafy lanes of the tractor, the hotbed cities of global football feel a long way away, yet Milford is part of every one of them. This pastoral scene is plugged into not just Irish football, but into every stadium and pitch across the world. Turn left into the village and the welcome sign reads: 'Milford: Home Of The Penalty Kick'.

Think back to all the penalties there have ever been – from Panenka's to Baggio's to O'Leary's – all the scored and all the missed and every single one of them originates here on a playing field off William Street in Milford, Co. Armagh.

It's still here, the patch of grass on which William McCrum first came up with the idea. As player, administrator and observer, McCrum assessed the unsporting and sometimes outright violent behavior plaguing the new, growing game of Association Football in the 1880s and thought it must be countered. There must be a fitting punishment found to halt it. There must be a penalty.

McCrum was a thinker, a maverick from Big House Ireland, where the richest family in a village or small town dominated the landscape literally and figuratively. His father, Robert, was a wealthy linen-mill industrialist who constructed Milford to supply his mill with workers. Robert McCrum was also a thinker, and an inventor and teetotaler. Notably for Ireland, he built Milford without a chapel, church or public bar.

Son William, known locally as 'Master Willie', would join the family business and village life. He was an amateur dramatist, who formed 'The Milford Players' troupe, and he was a sportsman. Cricket was the first game William came to, but this new sport of association football also took him.

*

BORN IN 1865, WILLIAM MCCRUM ATTENDED THE ROYAL SCHOOL, Armagh and Trinity College, Dublin, where he graduated in 1886. Back in Armagh he was instrumental in forming Milford Cricket Club and then the Football Club.

Milford FC may sound a marginal, parochial team, but not at the time. This was immediately a significant, aspirational club and Milford were included in the inaugural Irish League season – 1890/91. The Irish League is the second oldest national league in the world after England's and Milford FC were the only club in it from outside Belfast.

It did not go well, however. Milford played 14 matches and lost 14. Unsurprisingly they finished bottom, conceding 62 goals. Those statistics will have been felt acutely by William McCrum because he was Milford's last line of defence. The man who invented the penalty-kick was a goalkeeper.

It was from that goal-line perspective that McCrum had begun to ponder how to improve the new sport. Even before that first Irish League season, as a 'keeper McCrum will have experienced the unchecked – though legal – physicality of forwards. He will have been aware of stories travelling over from England of incidents of grievous bodily harm and worse on pitches around the country. From one local league game near Leicester came news of a player's death from a deliberate violent challenge. The perpetrator was charged with manslaughter.

These were days when the referee was more a timekeeper than an interventionist adjudicator, when there was no 18-yard box as we know it and, of course, no penalty-spot, because the penalty-kick had not been invented.

Crime and punishment were on McCrum's mind. His solution was in motion when he forwarded a proposal to a receptive colleague at the Irish Football Association, its general secretary Jack Reid. Reid, like McCrum – like many involved – was a player as well as an administrator and an evangelist for the new game. Reid's position at the IFA also gave him a place on the International Football Association Board (IFAB), the lawmakers of the game.

Reid saw the value in McCrum's idea and took it to IFAB. It was 1890, McCrum was 25. Reid and McCrum were hopeful of a good hearing, but they were disappointed. Apparently IFAB had a full agenda.

Although the Board agreed to return to the issue, it may have sensed the revolutionary nature of McCrum's proposal. Certainly when the penalty-kick idea was publicized the reaction was hostile. Football in this era was still under the ownership – emotional and physical – of England's public schoolboys. It is revealing of the era that McCrum's idea was scorned as 'the Irishman's Motion'. It was something to be mocked. The 'death penalty' some called it.

One of the complaints McCrum's penalty idea attracted was functional: a penalty-kick would interrupt the flow of the game. 'Gridiron' was one concern. Another was spiritual: to accept such a punishment for deliberate fouling was to imply England's public schoolboys were capable of deliberate fouling.

C.B. Fry, a towering figure of the age, a future England test cricket captain and Corinthians FC captain was a vocal critic. Fry said that that it was 'a standing insult to sportsmen to have to play under a rule which assumes that players intend to trip, hack and push opponents and to behave like cads of the most unscrupulous kidney. I say that the lines marking the penalty area are a disgrace to the playing field of a public school.'

The so-called Irishman's Motion was, in modern Northern Ireland phrasing, parked. But it was not scrapped and for all the outcry, it was not parked for long.

While it waited on a hard shoulder, Notts County played Stoke City in an FA Cup quarter-final at the Trent Bridge cricket ground in Nottingham. Towards the end of the match, with County winning 1-0, Stoke had a shot cleared off the line by a defender's hand. Stoke were awarded a free-kick almost on the goal-line but it was indirect – as the rules stated – and County massed their players along the line. Stoke failed to score, the whistle blew and Notts Co. had won.

All knew it was an unfair result. England's administrators had already been made aware of McCrum's proposal the previous year. There was a possible solution to Stoke City's unwarranted defeat.

In June 1891, IFAB met again, in the Alexandra Hotel on Bath Street, Glasgow. On this occasion the Irishman's motion was not only heard, it was admired, it was accepted and it was implemented. With minor tweaking, William McCrum's idea became Law 14 of the Game. It still is.

The 12-yard penalty spot was initially a 12-yard line. It was 1902 before the spot was introduced to the playing fields of the world and, in the beginning, goalkeepers were allowed to advance six yards to try to save the kicked penalty. That was later amended, keepers being required to stay on their line. Gradually new pitch markings were brought in.

There is a debate as to when the first ever penalty-kick awarded. In his history on the subject, *He Always Puts It To The Right,* Clark Miller says that two months later in Belfast, Linfield were playing a Canadian touring team. There was a handball, disputed as ever, but the referee gave a penalty-kick. A centre-half called J. Dalton stepped up and scored. Dalton had been born in Ireland and emigrated. Here he was back to score the historic first penalty.

McCrum's motion took root and changed the sport. Milford FC, however, left the Irish League after just one season and McCrum himself disappeared from public consciousness. He was still seen in the village, 'Master Willie', and played some part in the family business, but according to one descendent, it was a damaging, gambling role leading to the eventual closure of the mill.

This descendent is Robert McCrum, Literary Editor of The *Observer*. He wrote about his great-grandfather in July 2004, shortly after England had been knocked out of Euro 2004 6-5 on penalties by Portugal.

Where some saw sporting injustice as the origin of William McCrum's invention, Robert McCrum saw stagecraft too:

> *The penalty kick, of course, is the kind of penalty that only a goalkeeper could have invented, a supreme moment of drama and self-sacrifice that places the goalkeeper, generally a bystander, at the centre of the stage. Yes, it stacks the odds against the goalie, but it does make him, heroically, even tragically, the star of the show. Master Willie was not just a sporting show-off. He also devoted hours of recreation to amateur theatricals in the Milford village hall, the McCrum Institute.*

Not that Robert McCrum knew much about his ancestor. For decades William McCrum lay in St. Mark's cemetery, Armagh, his contribution to the history of football as quiet as the grave.

McCrum was said to have died 'alcoholic, penniless and alone' in a boarding house in Armagh in 1932; actually it was after a seizure in Armagh County Infirmary and the local paper reported 'the death of a brilliant scholar, raconteur and renowned sportsman'.

His grave has recently been restored by appreciative Northern Ireland fans. There is a black-and-white football on the grey gravel – take a sharp right at the cemetery gates.

The citizens of Milford also began a push for recognition in 1997 when the patch of grass off William Street was threatened by a housing plan. The citizens won, 'Linen Green' was developed and today there is a bust of McCrum on top of a marble block. It was from standing here, on the green in the middle of Milford, that William McCrum set in motion a sporting revolution, a change to the geometry, rules and fairness of football. It was some invention.

BILL MCCRACKEN

STAND ON NANSEN STREET OFF THE FALLS ROAD IN BELFAST AND there is nothing to suggest that one of the most influential thinkers in the history of football came from here. Then again, maybe Bill McCracken had enough recognition during his lifetime.

Described as infamous more often than famous during his contrary, effervescent 24-year playing career, as with William McCrum, McCracken attracted scorn before his thoughtfulness changed the laws of football forever.

Scorn is possibly too gentle. As one of the greatest pieces of sports writing you could come across asks of the widespread animosity McCracken inspired: 'Who but a snake charmer would fall in love with a serpent?'

McCracken would doubtless have appreciated such colour. Having had access to some of his personal papers, this was a character who would quote Walter Scott in a scouting report and who would sign off those reports with 'Your old cigar' or 'Your old Irish Stew'.

These papers relate to the second, perhaps third or fourth act of Bill McCracken's canny career. The reports date from the 1950s and 1960s; he was a Newcastle United scout until 1958, then joined Watford in the same role, where he suggested they sign Newry Town's young goalkeeper, a lad called Pat Jennings.

In June 1955 McCracken had recommended Newcastle sign Millwall's Charlie Hurley. They didn't and Hurley joined Sunderland, becoming their 'player of the century' and winning 40 Irish caps.

That was ten months after McCracken sent the Newcastle manager, Stan Seymour, a report from Ireland which began: 'Here is the latest bulletin from the land of spuds and buttermilk'. In this he outlined the ability of a 17 year-old playing for Ards in the Irish League, George Eastham.

'All one would gamble on is his physical make-up. He has got everything else', McCracken wrote. Two years later Eastham joined Newcastle and three years after that started the legal procedure which would overthrow the retain-and-transfer system in English football leading to the abolition of the maximum wage. It was one of the landmark rulings in the history of professional football.

McCracken would have understood, because he knew a lop-sided situation when one presented itself. It was this visual perception which caused his fame, or infamy.

'It was exciting to have been discovered by an authentic football pioneer,' Eastham was to say of McCracken. 'Bill was the brilliant Newcastle and Ireland full-back who, almost single-handed, had brought about the change in the offside law in 1925.'

Here lies Bill McCracken's claim on the history of football: that he changed it forever.

*

THE CHANGE MCCRACKEN WAS TO BE NAMED RESPONSIBLE FOR came in 1925 but a decade earlier he was sufficiently well-known in Britain for *Thomson's Weekly News* to serialise his life story. McCracken's opening line in this series was: 'I have been heart and soul in the game.'

He was born in Belfast in 1883, although biographical facts such as this had to be found elsewhere. In his weekly column, McCracken was straight into football, no mention of parents or family or his early life. What he did say was that he joined the Boys Brigade and 'paid two pence every week' to play for them.

He was soon asked, he says, to play for the 'Irish Brigades against the chosen of Dublin' and at 16 was signed by Distillery. He played 'about four matches' for Distillery's seconds and in one in Lisburn 'some temper was shown'.

McCracken had fouled one of two brothers. The second brother reacted aggressively to this. McCracken threw a punch and hit the first brother. 'The fat was now properly in the fire,' he writes. Quickly, enraged fans were on the pitch.

'I managed to reach what was called a pavilion, but not before I left the rowdies souvenirs in the shape of fragments of my jersey. The game had to be abandoned. Not the fight, however. All the way to the station they bade us an Irishman's farewell with stones.'

It was, McCracken reflects, his 'first offence'. It was to be the first of many provocations.

He was 17, an apprentice joiner in the shipyard and about to make his first-team debut: Distillery v Cliftonville, Christmas Day 1900. The next day he played for Distillery against Glentoran and says Linfield tried to sign him after the match. Distillery's response was to get his signature on a professional form, though McCracken insisted he finish his apprenticeship.

Distillery won the Irish League in 1901 and 1903 but the stories he tells are of scuffles and trouble. Playing in the Irish Cup final in 1903 in Dublin against Bohemians, which Distillery won, McCracken says 'some of the Bohs supporters attacked me'; against Linfield in the Co. Antrim Shield, he rescues the referee from a mob when 'just as we entered the door a 'representative from Guinness' crashed against the woodwork and broke into a thousand pieces.'

The apparent mayhem accompanying McCracken did not put off suitors. Arsenal, Rangers, Aston Villa and Liverpool were persistent and he almost joined Liverpool as John McKenna, so important in the early years at Anfield, 'was Irish'. McKenna came from Monaghan.

But McCracken was in no hurry. So when he did move, it was major news and prompted an FA inquiry. It was May 1904 when George Morrell of Rangers knocked on the door on Nansen Street. McCracken was at this time suspended by Distillery over a 'knee injury'. Morrell was told McCracken was not in but that he was not leaving Distillery, only to discover that Newcastle United director James Telford had already been up the same street that morning and McCracken was on his way to Tyneside.

Underhand payments were alleged, and McCracken, in another life-story serialization in the 1930s, said the FA wrote to him requesting to see his bank manager. 'I was only 21, I didn't mind anyone looking at my bank balance. I was not yet in the 'Rolls-Royce' class.'

Nothing irregular was found, 'but it was a big sensation while it lasted'. After staying over at the chairman's house, McCracken joined his new teammates on tour in Denmark. It was to be the start of a Newcastle United career that lasted 19 years, 444 matches and which brought McCracken three league championship winner's medals and an FA Cup winner's medal to add to his honours with Distillery. All this beside the national notoriety.

There were also 15 full Ireland caps (IFA). McCracken had just passed his nineteenth birthday when the first of these was awarded. It was in Cardiff against Wales, a 3-0 Irish win. Andy Gara from Roscommon scored a hat-trick on his debut.

There were nine more by the time Ireland hosted England in Belfast in 1908 and an eleventh cap was due when McCracken was called up again. But having discussed money with two Newcastle colleagues who played for England, Colin Veitch and

Albert Gosnell, McCracken discovered that while the IFA paid its players two guineas, the English FA paid theirs £10.

'I wrote to the Irish FA accepting their invitation to play if paid the same as my clubmates in the English side,' he said. 'No reply ever reached me.'

McCracken turned up for the game, at Solitude: 'But I declined to play. It was represented that this was a last-minute decision of mine but actually I had stated it clearly in a letter some 10 days previously. I went to the match, mainly because I wanted to show my conscience was easy. However, there was some unpleasantness when I was recognized and I was obliged to manoeuvre my wife into a doorway.'

The IFA banned McCracken. He was their star player, one of the biggest names in Irish and British football, and they banned him for asking for the going rate. The ban lasted until 1919, by which time he was 36. 'I was made to feel very uncomfortable about it.'

The Irish selectors missed out on a once-in-a-generation talent, a point of reference for every other footballer in England. By 1919 McCracken had long perfected the art of offside and with that helped Newcastle United to their Edwardian supremacy.

When he came to explain how this had come about, he returned to his first match with Distillery. Asked to play full-back alongside Jimmy Welford – 'not as young as formerly' – McCracken found himself doing the running of two men and frequently in the opposition half. The offside rule then stated that three opponents – usually the goalkeeper and two defenders – had to be between a player and the opposition goal.

'Of course, a player could be offside in his own half in those days,' McCracken wrote.

That part of the law was changed in 1907 but what he noticed from that first senior game was that with some forethought, opponents could be caught offside on a counter-attack if a full-back was sufficiently advanced and willing to step up.

No-one had done this before, either because they had not thought of it or because they deemed it unsporting, which many did. It was a powerful argument, the spirit of the game.

McCracken thought being clever was also part of its spirit, as did his Newcastle teammates. They spent hours in midweek team-talks discussing moves and systems. This approach was new, too, and McCracken praised these 'serious-minded men'.

He admitted not all the talking was 'one hundred per cent successful' and that some players did not like this innovation. But, he concluded:

> One and all tried to make United into a team, in the best sense
> of the word. As everyone knows, we did become the finest in the
> country. Five Cup finals and three League Championships in

seven years speak for themselves … and when the other side broke away, the moment they came past me the whistle went. At times it was almost laughable to see opponents fall into the simplest of simple traps.

McCracken became madly popular on Tyneside but his antics, as they were labelled, made him distrusted by the authorities and detested in a pantomime fashion by opposition fans and players. At Stamford Bridge he was spat on, at Villa Park a fan threw a pipe that hit him on the head, at Roker Park he was assailed by apples and oranges – 'the pitch looked like the fruit market'. At Manchester City he sparked a pitch invasion and when he once questioned a refereeing decision, by writing to the FA, they banned him for a month.

His response to supporter criticism was: 'If they knew more about football than we do, there would be 50,000 players and 22 spectators.'

Yet the most telling comment on McCracken's offside was that others imitated him. And it was this which led to a rule from 1866 being changed in 1925. From now on, two players – the goalkeeper and one defender – were required to be between the attacker and goal, rather than three players. It was intended to assist forwards, and goalscoring rates increased, but over time the extra attacking risk would bring extra caution to defensive lines. The McCracken-inspired ruling altered the very way teams lined up and approached football.

The man himself considered his original tactic to be 'an attacking move – I realised that by going up field I could practically dictate to opposing forwards how far they should come. If they came past me they were offside. I was an overlapping wing-back before the term was invented.' And if his ploy failed, McCracken argued, the damage would be done a distance from his team's goal.

Bill McCracken was 42 by the time the 1925 rule change occurred. He was manager of Hull City, having departed Newcastle in 1923 after 19 years at St. James' Park.

The ruling had an effect: First Division goals went up from 2.6 per match in 1924/25 to 3.7 in 1925/26. In 1927/28 it was over 3.8 and Everton's Dixie Dean got 60 of them on his own.

Funnily enough, there was one club were there was no immediate avalanche of goals in that first season after the rule change: Hull City. In their first seven games of the Second Division season, they conceded one goal. Bill McCracken may just have understood the change more than his contemporaries.

In 1930 Hull were relegated but only after reaching the FA Cup semi-final. Leading Arsenal 2-0 at Elland Road with 20 minutes to go, Hull drew 2-2 then lost the replay

1-0. McCracken was shattered. He moved on to Gateshead, Millwall and Aldershot before re-joining Newcastle United on a £300 per annum salary as the scout sending those idiosyncratic reports.

In one of them from October 1954 McCracken mentioned Liam Tuohy's potential at Shamrock Rovers and a month later sent this to St. James' Park: 'Mr Cunningham, the man who with his wife runs Shamrock Rovers ... confirmed promise that Newcastle will have first option on any of their players.'

Having then moved to London, McCracken was 75 when he started scouting for Watford. Amazingly, his last report is from 24 April 1971, a reserves match between Crystal Palace and Leicester City. It was three months after his 88th birthday.

Bill McCracken was nine days short of his 96th birthday when he died in 1979. He had been heart and soul in the game.

He had once joked in a questionnaire several decades earlier that his ambition was to be 'King of Ireland' and yet McCracken is largely forgotten, unheralded, even in his native Belfast.

It is all the better therefore that a brilliant contemporary wrote an appreciation of McCracken. Don Davies worked for the *Manchester Guardian*, having previously played amateur football for England and cricket for Lancashire. He was one of eight reporters killed in the Munich air crash in 1958.

In 1962 a collection of some of Davies' writing was published and it includes a sublime profile of Bill McCracken. It is a worthy tribute to two brilliant men:

> *William McCracken was an Irish international right-back and a storm centre of his generation. He was a specialist in off-side tactics and as such was the cause of more demonstrations of hostility and resentment than any other player before or since.*
>
> *Being an Irishman, he naturally took a deep delight in that most of his playing time was spent in twisting the tails of British players. Being an artist he played sixteen times for Ireland and nigh on twenty seasons in one of the most illustrious club sides of all time, Newcastle United of the early 1900s.*
>
> *As a zealous student of Association football as well as one of its foremost practitioners, he applied all the resources of a keen mind to the problems of defensive strategy with such success in off-side moves that in his day he could reduce the cleverest forward line to a rabble of hesitant and bewildered units.*
>
> *That McCracken, though widely respected as an individual*

*and always feared as a player, was not exactly a universal favou-
rite is understandable. Who but a snake charmer would fall in
love with a serpent?*

*It was his province as a setter of off-side traps of unwonted
slickness and cunning to jolt his contemporaries out of their
conventional ruts and make them substitute adaptability and
resource to rule of thumb; to force them to realize that the only
antidote to subtlety and deceit was even greater subtlety and
deceit. In short, he made them think, and that has never been a
popular mission.*

*Crowds flocked to watch him, composed mainly of angry
and prejudiced men, and few there were who had the patience to
acknowledge the beauty of McCracken's technique in the abstract.*

*Tempers frayed and angry scenes developed. On one occasion
at Hyde Road, McCracken teased and tormented the Manchester
City forward line to such purpose that the crowd felt obliged to
intervene.*

*… Thus the old law which had stood untouched since 1866
was scrapped, mainly, as men thought, through the perverse genius of an Irishman who loved to meddle in British affairs. Not
for the first time in our island story was a decision made which
seemed to penalize those who used their brains in order to make
things easier for those who could not or would not use theirs.*

Davies then notes drily of the effects of the offside rule change in that first season,
1925/26.

*A certain Yorkshire club, Hull City, was seen to be oddly stubborn
in its refusal to conform to the prevailing fashion of giving away
goals like largesse; on the contrary, it was making scoring so difficult that in the first five matches of the season not a single goal
had been scored against it.*

*'Chilly doubts again assailed observers. Not McCracken
again, surely! But facts were facts and soon the alarming rumour
spread, later confirmed by eye-witnesses, that the enterprising
coach, critic and tactical adviser to the Hull City Football Club
was none other than our old friend the Irish Mephistopheles,*

William McCracken, as ever a peerless defender in his own day, still adding cubits to his stature as the game's arch-obstructionist. Thoughtful men peered into the future with alarm and misgiving. The ghost was still walking.

PETER DOHERTY

ON 14 FEBRUARY 2016 LIONEL MESSI SHAPED TO TAKE A PENALTY-KICK for Barcelona against Celta Vigo at the Camp Nou stadium. Instead of striking the ball at goal with his left foot, Messi tapped it sideways to his right. There, suddenly, was Luis Suarez, who stroked the ball past the baffled goalkeeper and into the net.

Across the world fans swooned. Charmed by the impudence of the goal, while questioning its validity, some were quick to say that it was legal and that Thierry Henry and Robert Pires had tried to perform the same penalty-kick trick for Arsenal in 2005. They failed to accomplish it. Others produced footage from 1982 of Johan Cruyff and Jesper Olsen scoring the same style of penalty for Ajax.

In general there was a sense of pleasure at this creativity, Messi and Suarez brought a smile to faces. In the north-west of Ireland there was a similar reaction, only there it came with knowing nods and the comment: 'Aye, The Doherty Penalty.'

Twenty-five years before Cruyff – nearly 60 years before Messi – Northern Ireland had faced Portugal at Windsor Park in a World Cup qualifier for the finals in Sweden in 1958. This was a maturing Irish team and 2-0 up, they were awarded a penalty.

Danny Blanchflower stepped forward to take it but instead of shooting, Blanchflower nudged the ball sideways. Running in from behind him was Jimmy McIlroy. With the Portuguese goalkeeper flummoxed by something he had never seen, McIlroy calmly side-footed the ball in. The referee, Hugh Phillips of Scotland, had never seen this either and in a panic, or because he thought McIlroy had encroached, ordered a re-take. This time McIlroy converted conventionally.

The rest of the Northern Ireland players had not been expecting this experimental penalty, especially on such an occasion, but a few of them suspected instantly where the idea came from.

Peter Doherty had been appointed Northern Ireland manager in 1951 while he was player-manager of Doncaster Rovers in the Second Division. It was his last playing role in a career that saw him compared favourably with anyone who had ever kicked a ball.

To the generation who saw Doherty play, he made a profound impression, one that deepens and spreads with every page of research. One former player turned commentator, Maurice Edelston, described Doherty as: 'Unorthodox, incalculable and inspiring. He was a discontented footballer. Not in the sense of sulkiness … the kind of discontent that makes for experiment and restlessness.'

It was this restless inventive spirit which saw Doherty, as far back as 1945 according to Stanley Matthews, perform the penalty-kick Lionel Messi took in 2016.

'Peter Doherty guested twice for Port Vale in 1945 and caused a stir in one of the games,' Matthews wrote in his autobiography. 'He elected to take a penalty but instead of shooting for goal, he laid the ball back for a team-mate to run on to and duly score. I know of only one other incident of it happening – Johan Cruyff did exactly the same.'

Harry Gregg was playing for Northern Ireland that day in Belfast in 1957 when Blanchflower and McIlroy produced their audacious effort.

'I can't remember whether he [Doherty] told them to do it or whether they knew about it and just did it,' Gregg says. 'Peter would have known about it, I'm sure. He'd done it himself, long before then. It was known as 'The Doherty Penalty', that's how I knew it. He did it at Doncaster Rovers and he did it before Doncaster Rovers.'

Another Irish international, Johnny Crossan, offers further, personal evidence. 'I was at the match at the Brandywell when Peter Doherty did it. He was player-manager of Doncaster Rovers. I remember the match as if it were yesterday because we were dumbfounded. The whole of the Brandywell was silent for about ten seconds.

'It wasn't Derry City, it was a north-west select, with Kevin Doherty picking the local team – the two brothers. The referee was Gorman Young, OK? The goal was scored at the Show Grounds end. I was on the greyhound track.

'I remember when the penalty was given. The crowd began to chant 'Peter, Peter'. He looked at his boots. I think it was Harry McShane he passed it to. He came in and nearly tore the net off. The reaction was silence. The referee gave a goal, which was the right decision. Phenomenal. We talked about that in Derry for an eternity.

'That's what shows how Doherty thought. He thought about things in a different way. There's that old saying about being one step ahead of the posse, Peter Doherty was miles ahead. Genius.'

Crossan was far from the first person who saw Peter Doherty in the flesh to use the term genius. Read any old book from an opponent or teammate and genius is the word they choose time after time.

'Without going overboard, you *had* to see the man play,' says Harry Gregg, who was bought from Coleraine by Doherty at Doncaster.

'Peter Doherty was better than George Best, he was. I'm very proud to have known George, I'm lucky enough to have met some wonderful players. I got a letter from Germany recently asking me to name the best I'd played against. I named five Germans – Bert Trautmann, Fritz Walter, Franz Beckenbauer, Uwe Seeler and Gerd Muller. See Muller? I'd be lying on the ground asking: 'Can you at least try to make it look hard?' The only one who could compare with him was Jimmy Greaves. But Peter Doherty, he was a man apart.'

Len Shackleton, the great English individualist, was just as forthright: 'Peter Doherty was surely the genius among geniuses. Possessor of the most baffling body swerve in football, able to perform all tricks with the ball, owning a shot like the kick of a mule, and, with all this, having such tremendous enthusiasm for the game that he would work like a horse for ninety minutes. That was pipe-smoking Peter Doherty, the Irish redhead who I am convinced, had enough football skill to stroll through a game smoking that pipe – and still make the other twenty-one players appear second-raters.'

Matthews had some reservations about Doherty off the pitch, but on it, he says: 'Peter Doherty was a genius of an inside-forward. Prior to the emergence of George Best in the sixties, Doherty was to my mind the greatest footballer to come out of Northern Ireland.'

Trevor Ford recalled a post-war Swansea-Derby friendly when the Vetch Field fencing gave way 'so excited' was the capacity crowd with 'the wizardry of Peter Doherty'. Stan Mortensen selected his all-time team from these islands and said: 'I would have to concentrate on Englishmen. I would have [Jackie] Carey from Ireland, and Doherty from Ireland. No Scots, no Welsh.'

When Manchester City won the first League title in their history in 1937, it was after signing Doherty a year earlier for a club record £10,000. The team jumped to the title from ninth place in 1936.

Arthur Walmsley was sports editor of the *Manchester Evening Chronicle* and when on the thirtieth anniversary of that title Walmsley looked back, he wrote:

The most glittering jewel in City's 1937 League championship crown was peerless Peter Doherty. Peter was in his middle twenties when he joined Manchester City and such was the tremendous effort he put into every game that my ecstasy – yes, that is not too strong a word – was tinged with a melancholy apprehension that he would burn himself out before he was 30. How little I needed to have feared. Peter was still playing League soccer when he was 41, broke a leg and still came back again. If ever a player had everything, then that player was Peter Doherty. In his Maine Road days they used to sum him up by saying: 'Doherty is worth 90 goals a season to City – he scores 30, makes 30 and saves 30 at his own end.'

Joe Mercer was City's manager by 1967. 'Of all the opponents I faced,' he said, 'I particularly remember Doherty.' It was, apparently, England captain Billy Wright who christened Doherty 'Peter the Great'.

Doherty was not City's centre forward in 1937 but he was their top scorer, 32 goals in all in that season. He entered the club just as Matt Busby was making for the exit. The two men played only once on the same team, Doherty's debut against Preston North End. It was February 1936 against Preston and Doherty found himself marked by Bill Shankly, of whom Doherty recalled: 'He dogged my footsteps all afternoon, muttering: 'Great wee team, North End, great wee team."

Shankly was impressed. 'Peter had wonderful skills,' he said. 'Peter never gave in because in his mind he was always winning. You could lace into him and harry him and flurry him, but you couldn't knock him off the ball. [Denis] Law had a similar nature to Doherty's.'

*

PETER DOHERTY WAS BORN IN 1913 IN THE SMALL TOWN OF MAGHerafelt, close to Lough Neagh. One of ten children, Peter's family moved north to Coleraine with their pet greyhound called Larry. Doherty went to school at St Malachi's, which he was to say was 'just an ordinary little elementary school with dingy classrooms and a cramped, asphalted playground [and] no school team.'

He was not to play organised eleven-a-side football until his teens but once Doherty did, he was quickly taken by Glentoran. At 19, Doherty scored in the Irish Cup final against Distillery.

'That Irish medal is still my proudest possession,' he said in 1949, by which time he had won the FA Cup with Derby County as well as that League title with Man City. 'It's of poorer metal than the English FA one, but has a much nicer design, in the shape of a cross with a shamrock engraved on it. My name is on the back of it. I've never bothered to have it inscribed on my English medal.'

Shortly after the Irish Cup final, Blackpool bought him, a £2,000 transfer concluded in Belfast's Abercorn hotel. England was hardly on the other side of the world yet arriving at Heysham on the boat from Belfast, Doherty felt: 'I was a stranger in a strange land.'

Blackpool were in the Second Division and Doherty could not get them out of it, but he was an asset the club could sell for ten times what they paid for him, even though he did not want to leave. He was sold to City regardless and expressed his annoyance, something a 22 year-old did at his peril in those maximum wage, retain-and-transfer days.

'In modern-day parlance you'd say he had an attitude,' Matthews said of Doherty.

'Acerbity' was the word Matthews chose, adding: 'For all his genius no-one really warmed to Peter.'

It was an opinion that would have surprised those eulogising Doherty because they did so, not just for Doherty's innate ability, but for his application, his willingness to challenge the status quo – his attitude.

The Doherty penalty became the most well-known and graphic illustration of his innovative thinking but there were others. He eschewed the clog-heavy football boot preferring a lighter, basketball style shoe, close to a modern trainer. He would take three pairs to matches and assess the pitch. He wanted players paid better and was vocal about it. When he became a manager he would sometimes switch numbers around on jerseys – unheard-of – and he once played two wingers on the same wing in an international. 'The opposition didn't know what to do,' laughs Gregg. 'He just wanted to confuse them.'

There were other penalty-kicks. 'People didn't practise penalties then, we did,' says Crossan. 'I remember practising for half an hour – corners and penalties – before playing England at Wembley. We trained at Hendon police ground.

'Peter was an out-and-out thinker. His family were all clever men, kind men. Such charisma, genteel with such amazing authority.'

A brilliant disruptor, most of all Doherty urged ball practice and coaching. Despite a row at the end at Blackpool, he had been impressed by manager Sandy MacFarlane and not because the two men gelled. It was because MacFarlane was 'systematic' in his approach to training, held a tactical discussion every Friday and would often make Blackpool stay in a hotel before home games.

MacFarlane had the Blackpool-Margate FA Cup tie in 1936 filmed to show to his players afterwards. 'Sandy pointed out our weaknesses in his most trenchant style … singling me out for a special rebuke,' Doherty said.

But this was professionalism, whereas in Ireland, with the IFA, everything Doherty found was 'slapdash'.

It infuriated him. After winning the title, City went on tour to Germany. In Berlin, Doherty said, 'we were expected to give the Nazi salute at the line-up but we had decided merely to stand to attention … [Germany] was rapidly becoming an armed camp.'

But he also saw there and elsewhere in Europe: 'The supreme value of coaching. Everywhere on the continent one can observe its results.'

And he knew that if he was given the opportunity, he could coach.

*

LIKE SO MANY, DOHERTY'S PLAYING CAREER WAS CUT IN HALF BY the Second World War. He had just had his 26th birthday when war broke out and he was 33 at the beginning of the 1946/47 season.

He was to play a mere 16 times for Ireland over a period of 15 years and looking back at his first couple of appearances in a green shirt, he noted 'a complete lack of cohesion'.

Shankly said Doherty was, in his mind, 'always winning'; not with Ireland. A committee in Belfast selected the team from players employed in England. There was minimal preparation, no coach and limited expectation.

'I have a deep-seated conviction that we are included in the International tournament to make up the numbers,' Doherty said. No Irish team played at Wembley until 1955 and this particularly annoyed him. 'Is it because we are not good enough?'

Having moved from Man City to Derby after the war, then to Huddersfield Town and on to manage Doncaster in the Second Division, Doherty was still playing at the age of 38 when the IFA had the nous to appoint him. The first proper Irish manager still had the committee to deal with.

The IFA players Doherty took over in 1951 had won two matches since the war. It was another three years before they won under him – in fact there were two Irish victories in his first 21 matches. Given resources – organizational and numbers, low morale and with no FAI players to call on, managing Northern Ireland was arduous and at times might even have seemed futile.

Yet with diligence, care and charisma, by 1958 many of the same players Doherty inherited were in the World Cup quarter-final in Sweden while England and Scotland had flown home. Wales also reached the last eight, but one difference was that Wales had a 22-man squad; Northern Ireland had 17 players, two of whom were uncapped, and were in the same group as the world champions West Germany, Argentina and Czechoslovakia.

To become the first Irishmen at the World Cup, Doherty's team had already eliminated Italy and Portugal. Against Italy in Rome, Doherty had a 5ft 5in forward, Wilbur Cush, at centre-half. Northern Ireland had also won at Wembley, beating an England side including Duncan Edwards 3-2. Doherty was showing what he could do.

But two other hurdles surfaced before Sweden: the playing of games on Sunday, which some within the IFA refused to countenance, meaning only two officials stayed with the squad; and the Munich air crash in February of '58. The crash left Jackie Blanchflower, Danny's brother, unable to play and it left Gregg scarred physically and emotionally.

The IFA thought Gregg, who had not flown since Munich, should get the train from Belfast to Sweden, which he did. 'Three days, third class by the way,' he says.

He was accompanied by an IFA official who flew back to Belfast as soon as the pair reached Sweden. That was over the issue of 'playing on the Sabbath'. Northern Ireland did not play a home game on a Sunday until 2015.

In the first training session Doherty then lost his striker Billy Simpson of Rangers to injury. Three games in Gregg was so injured he was using a walking stick. 'Against West Germany, I did my ankle,' he says.

Fortunately, or not, the Irish physio Gerry Morgan treated Gregg. 'I told Gerry not to take my boot off because I knew my foot would swell up and I'd not be able to get the boot back on. Gerry strapped up my ankle around the boot, then poured whiskey over it. That's true, you know. *Gerry Morgan.*'

Morgan's humour was an essential ingredient in the Irish formula. One piece of advice he gave to players was: 'Put iodine on your studs, so when you kick the bastards they don't get indigestion.'

Against rank-outsider odds, Doherty pushed the smallest country through the group at the expense of Argentina and Czechoslovakia.

'Respect is a very strong word,' says Gregg. 'Worshipped is a different word altogether, a different planet. Peter was worshipped by the players. 1958 was a triumph by Peter the Great, there's no ifs or buts in my mind. He made us what we were. He was far ahead of his time.

'His teamtalks were hellfire and damnation, but no bad language, he never swore. 'The will to win, you have to have the will to win!'; 'nobody can beat us!' It never changed. It was short and positive, really positive. Then he'd ask Danny [Blanchflower] if he wanted a word and he'd speak for two days.'

In the quarter final, Northern Ireland met France – Just Fontaine and Raymond Kopa up against Jackie Scott from Grimsby Town winning his second cap. France won 4-0. This was a fifth game in 12 days. Size had told.

'We thought we'd a chance, but we'd a lot of injuries by then,' Gregg says. 'Jackie Milburn was with us as a journalist. He said that if Peter had played himself Ireland would've gone further. He was 44, 45, but he'd run people in training.'

Terry Neill, future Irish captain and manager, makes a similar comment and links Doherty to Blanchflower and on to Best:

> *Historically, the Northern Ireland team, the founders of it were Peter and Danny, a Catholic and a Protestant. The two of them were like Siamese twins. Peter used to tell a story about Danny from '58 when they'd been to see the Argentinians, who they were about to play. Peter thought: 'Mmm, some players, Argentina.' They got back to the hotel and before Peter could say anything, the other players asked about Argentina and Danny said: 'We'll stuff them.' Peter was there gasping . . .*
>
> *Danny would always tell me if we won the toss to change ends. 'Make them walk,' he'd say. 'Yeah, but we've to walk too, Danny.' 'It doesn't matter, you're being decisive, you're ordering them about.'*
>
> *Then in the second half, even if you've kicked off in the first, try it again. The referee might not notice. We're little Northern Ireland we need everything we can get. And I got away with it two or three times. 'Do it with authority'. What an education.*
>
> *And the penalty [in 1957] I know where Danny and Jimmy got it from – Doherty. Peter was so inventive, such a thinker. Danny followed on in that tradition, put a few questions in the minds of the opposition. Can you imagine what that right back was thinking when he saw Peter had put on two left wingers? It's legitimate. And it's humorous. Bestie follows in that line too.*

A feeling of triumph accompanied the Northern Ireland squad home. Doherty stayed on for four more years, taking the job as Bristol City manager, then working for Aston Villa, Preston and latterly as a scout for Liverpool. He rang Bill Shankly about a young forward at Scunthorpe called Kevin Keegan.

Doherty died in 1990, aged 76. A blue plaque was unveiled in Magherafelt.

He had done what the greats do, he moved people, made them think, made them feel part of something special simply by being there. To those who saw him and knew him, Peter Doherty brought an aura to a room or to a stadium and left a vacuum when he was gone. A plaque seems insufficient recognition.

'I don't talk romantically,' says Gregg. 'I talk in black and white and it doesn't make me popular. But I don't have to be romantic when it comes to Peter Doherty, the man was incredible.'

*

POSTSCRIPT

MID-MARCH 2016, CLOSE TO 50 YEARS ON FROM THE BLANCHFLOWER-McIlroy penalty at Windsor Park against Portugal. In the hills above Burnley, Jimmy McIlroy reviews the footage. And again, and again.

Sadly, even though he is determined to smile, McIlroy has been trapped by the beginnings of dementia. He can barely recognise himself scoring, never mind remember the events surrounding the Doherty penalty.

McIlroy, like Doherty, won a League title. McIlroy did it with Burnley in 1960, where they said he was the brain of the team. Today there is a stand at Turf Moor named after Jimmy McIlroy.

'It looks so easy, simple,' he says of the penalty-kick against Portugal. 'I took penalties for Burnley, I never wanted to.'

Prompted, McIlroy speaks of Charlie Tully and George Best, two of those he played with in an Irish jersey. And Peter Doherty: 'Nobody wanted to upset him, he was a tough man. He was demanding, he really was.'

PART III

FOREIGN PIONEERS

PATRICK O'CONNELL – SPAIN

APRIL 2015, ST. MARY'S CEMETERY, KENSAL RISE, NORTH LONDON.
Over there in the corner by the railway, he lies, unmarked. Beyond the green metal fence is the rattle of the Bakerloo Line and the hum of the No. 18 bus scurrying up and down the Harrow Road. In the silent sky planes are in that slow Heathrow holding pattern.

Below on the gravel paths, there is another silence, a graveyard silence. Daisies and dandelions creep across graves dishevelled by the decades, unkept by families of Heffernans, O'Rourkes, Spillanes and Carrolls, who buried their relatives here, then moved on to concentrate on the living, the next generation Irish.

The first here, in 1858, was a Mulcahy, the first of 170,000 mainly Irish and Italians brought to St. Mary's on their final journey. There is some grandeur: the Emmet Mausoleum, made in Portland stone, salutes the life of one Robert Emmet, great-great nephew of the Robert Emmet; T.P. O'Connor lies here too.

But it is the flattened, unrecognisable graves of ordinary migrant lives that strike, and Plot 216 is one example. If there was a headstone, it no longer stands. If there were flowers, they are long gone. What remains is a three-sided outline of a grave where the masonry is dislodged, the weeds grow and only on bended knee can the faded inscription be read: 'In loving memory of Emily O'Connell who died 2nd Feb 1931.'

That surname is the clue, the sole clue, that this unregarded patch of London contains the bones of a man who lived a life of flesh, personality, politics, travel and football: Patrick O'Connell.

Patrick O'Connell, born in Dublin in 1887, should be familiar to all interested in football. His life and times possessed the drama of a thunderous novel, yet in the office at St Mary's, when cemetery director Michael O'Shea pulls the yellowing death register from March 1959, the handwritten black ink offers only the bare details of his funeral: O'Connell's body was brought from St. Pancras Hospital, NW1, on the 4th of the month; the burial cost eleven guineas; he was 71; he joined his sisters Emily and Christina in Plot 216.

These were the sparse finalities of a life that teemed with action. There was no mention here of O'Connell being captain of Ireland when, for the first time, they won the British Home Championships in 1914; no mention of him being captain of Manchester United; no mention of him managing Barcelona during the Spanish Civil War. And what about the bigamy? What about the United-Liverpool match-fixing scandal?

And what about when O'Connell was manager of Real Betis and they won La Liga for the one and only time in their history? That was 80 years ago that same week. He was tall, convincing, wore a hat. In Spain, he became 'Don Patricio'.

In north London, there is none of that, just the sad smack of an unmarked grave that did not even bear Patrick O'Connell's name. And a puzzle: how did a man who enjoyed six decades of vivid colour, accomplishment and intrigue end his seventh in poverty and obscurity, then disappear from our consciousness altogether under the weeds spreading themselves across this corner of St. Mary's cemetery?

*

PATRICK O'CONNELL WAS BORN IN DUBLIN ON THE NOW-DEPARTED Jones's Terrace, a street adjacent to Croke Park. In the 1890s, when O'Connell was a boy who had moved around the corner to Fitzroy Avenue with his ten brothers and sisters, it was not the Croke Park of today. It was a pitch where O'Connell played football.

He got a job in Boland's Mill and joined Liffey Wanderers. In 1908, as O'Connell was approaching his 21st birthday, Belfast Celtic offered him a professional contract and he moved north. He and newly-married wife Ellen were given accommodation on Albert Street off the Falls Road.

O'Connell stayed less than a year in Belfast, though he and Ellen had enough time to have their first child, Patrick junior. Although he became a defender, Belfast Celtic played him up front initially and O'Connell scored three goals against Linfield at Windsor Park in one City Cup match.

Such progression attracted The Wednesday of Sheffield, then fifth in England's First Division. But O'Connell's limited impact at Hillsborough saw him transferred to Hull in 1912. Hull were in the Second Division, but in 1914 Manchester United took O'Connell back to the First. The £1,000 fee made him an expensive signing. United made him their captain.

On the opening day of the 1914/15 season O'Connell scored for United at Old Trafford, quite a debut. Except United lost 3-1 to Oldham Athletic and by April had won just six league games. They were in danger of relegation when Liverpool visited.

Fortunately for United, they won 2-0 to ease concerns, but those reporting on the game, and spectators, saw nothing fortunate about the result. They saw a fix and O'Connell was seen to be at the centre of it due to his missed penalty-kick which the Manchester Echo said 'made a mockery of this great sport. A dark cloud indeed hangs over that penalty.'

When it became known subsequently that an unusually large number of bets had been placed on the 2-0 scoreline, there was an investigation by the Football Association and seven players, from both teams, were found guilty and banned. O'Connell was not one of them, but he had taken the theatrically bad penalty-kick.

There were still seven games of the season remaining, so this was not the result that ensured United stayed up by two points, but the bookmakers' price for 2-0 was 7/1 and those involved probably looked at the 18,000 attendance, the state of the First World War and thought they could do with some income to protect themselves from the future.

When the War was over, O'Connell, now 32, was no longer in Manchester, though his wife and four children were. He was in Scotland playing for Dumbarton, which was a curious destination. Those two words were to become an O'Connell characteristic.

Another surfaced when after one season, he moved back to England. O'Connell did not return to the north-west, he arrived in the north-east as player-manager of Ashington. It was 1920 Ashington were about to join the new Third Division North.

His family must have been disconcerted by this but it was nothing compared to what he did after two years in the coal town. He moved from Ashington to Santander. Without them.

*

O'CONNELL WROTE NO MEMOIR, LEFT NO STASH OF PERSONAL papers that would reveal his thinking at the different stages of his irregular career, but at some point, we must assume, he met Fred Pentland.

Pentland was a winger for Middlesbrough and England, who in 1920 had joined Racing Santander as their coach. He was now off to manage Athletic Bilbao.

The two men's playing days had overlapped, though even if they had not, Pentland would have heard of O'Connell. He had become well-known, and not just for United-Liverpool.

A year before, February 1914, O'Connell had captained Ireland when they won 3-0 against England at Ayresome Park. A month earlier the Irish had beaten Wales in Wrexham, which meant that in March Ireland had the chance to win the Home Championships for the first time if they could avoid defeat to Scotland in Belfast. They drew 1-1.

The game was due to be played at Cliftonville but the level of interest meant it was switched to Windsor Park. Over 30,000 attended. O'Connell 'had to leave the field for repairs', as one report put it – he had a broken arm – but he came back and played on. At the end there was a happy Belfast pitch invasion. Patrick O'Connell was an all-Ireland hero.

*

IN 1922 WHEN O'CONNELL LANDED IN SPAIN, ORGANISED SPANISH football was just 20 years old. The Copa Del Rey was a national competition but La Liga did not begin until 1929. Under O'Connell, Racing Santander won five regional titles and became founder members of La Liga.

He went west along Spain's north coast to Real Oviedo that year and then moved south to Andalusia, to Real Betis. He was a travelling 'Mister', a pioneer coach brought from English football to teach the game. Betis were in the second division but they won it in 1932 under O'Connell and then, three years later, won their one and only La Liga title.

He had met, and married, another woman by then. She was Irish and her name was Ellen – just like his first wife, whom he had not divorced and to whom he would send occasional letters with Spanish pesetas inside to help feed the four children he had walked out on. The second Ellen did not know about the first Ellen or O'Connell's children, yet.

After Betis, the second Ellen accompanied O'Connell to Catalonia in 1935. There is a letter in the Santander archive showing O'Connell had applied for the Barcelona manager's job in 1931 but the club declined; now, having won La Liga, O'Connell was appointed manager of FC Barcelona, but just as the Spanish Civil War was about to split Spain.

FC Barcelona's president Josep Sunyol appointed O'Connell, the club played as Les Corts, pre Camp Nou, and in June 1936 O'Connell's new team reached the Copa del Rey final. Barcelona met Real Madrid in the Mestalla stadium, Valencia, and lost.

The defeat was probably hurtful at the time but it was of no consequence when, six weeks later, Sunyol was murdered by General Franco's soldiers near Madrid.

La Liga could not continue and with Franco's troops closing in on Catalonia, neither could FC Barcelona. They had to flee and were offered a tour of Mexico by a sympathetic businessman. First they had to get to France and by stealth and train they crossed the border and arrived in Paris in May 1937. It was just as the Ireland team – with Johnny Brown – were beating France. O'Connell turned up at the Irish team hotel.

Mexico was followed by a detour to New York and the series of matches earned Barcelona not just enough money to clear their debts, O'Connell was able to return to Paris, where he had opened a bank account that Spanish authorities could not access, and place the tour profits of $12,900 there. This is why he has of late been known as The Man Who Saved Barcelona.

There is more to it than that – there is so much to Patrick O'Connell that even a lengthy review of his life would seem condensed. But without question, he played his part in keeping FC Barcelona going and he returned to the desperate city, whereas more than half the players on the tour had chosen to stay in Mexico or France.

La Liga resumed in 1939/40 and O'Connell was back in Andalusia, returning to Real Betis then moving to their city rivals, FC Sevilla. After that came a return to Santander and in 1949 he had been in Spain 27 years. He was 62.

He and the second Ellen would stay in Spain until the mid-fifties before moving to London, where Patrick's brother Larry ran a small, modest hotel near Euston station. It was here that the second Ellen discovered Patrick's first life. She left him; he applied for National Assistance. In February 1959, aged 71, he died, unheralded, in the St. Pancras hospital. No-one knew him then as the man who saved FC Barcelona.

*

MORE THAN HALF A CENTURY AFTER PATRICK O'CONNELL'S QUIET death, Jeremiah Dowd went to a talk in Dublin about the Spanish Civil War. When he came home, Jeremiah said to his son Fergus that he had just heard about an Irishman who had been manager of Barcelona. Fergus was a football fan and wondered why, if that was the case, he had not heard such a thing. Surely everyone would have known?

Fergus started digging. With others such as the descendants of O'Connell's first, Manchester family, when they had finished – about four years later – they had staged a resurrection.

By June 2017 Patrick O'Connell was back in Manchester. He was in the National

Football Museum with an exhibition of his life and career. There was a documentary in production; two plaques, one in Dublin and one in Belfast had been unveiled where O'Connell had lived; there was a bronze bust commissioned by Real Betis to sit beside their La Liga trophy; the boardroom at the Nou Camp has an O'Connell painting on the wall; the Football Association of Ireland has an alcove dedicated to O'Connell at their new headquarters; Sue O'Connell, wife of Patrick's grandson Michael, has written an evocative book.

Michael was brought up by Patrick's first wife, Ellen, and says he thought of his grandfather as 'a bit of a swine'. He knew the pain Patrick O'Connell had caused; he also knew some of the glory he had experienced.

But he knew little else. There was just not the coverage, either in Ireland, England or Spain, and if Ireland has a difficult relationship with the past, it is not alone. Spain has, from 2007, Ley de Memoria Historica – a National Memory Law. It relates to the Spanish Civil War, who is remembered, how they are remembered.

Such a sentiment applies to O'Connell – Don Patricio. For over 50 years his legend lay buried, his life like a great song we had never heard. No more. Above all, at Plot 216 in St. Mary's cemetery, Kensal Rise, there is now a clean headstone standing. Patrick O'Connell no longer lies over there by the railway line, unmarked.

JOHNNY CROSSAN –
HOLLAND & BELGIUM

THE WAY JOHNNY CROSSAN TELLS IT, ALFREDO DI STEFANO WAS descending the broad stairway at London's Café Royal in the manner of a 1930s Hollywood film star. Crossan was at its foot, looking up. Stargazing. 'You know,' Crossan says, 'I'm a wee man from Hamilton Street, Derry.'

He remembers Bobby Charlton being beside him, as was Scottish international George Mulhall. They had just shared a table with Billy Bremner at a Football Writers' Association dinner.

'I was looking up the stairway and I said to George Mulhall: 'Look, there's Di Stefano." Crossan says.

'George says to me: 'Are you sure?'

'I says: 'Yes, I'm telling you.'

'So we went up to him; and what does Di Stefano do? He holds out his hand to me and says: 'Standard Liege?"

Crossan rocks back in his seat and declares: 'Well'. It is one long, satisfied 'well'. Then he adds: 'Oh, aye – one of the greatest players ever. Mulhall couldn't believe it. 'Jammy bastard', he says.'

Delighted, Crossan concludes: 'Beat. That.' Except he uses the Derry vernacular: '*Bate. That.*'

In the course of a truly exceptional career, Johnny 'Jobby' Crossan could have selected any number of moments or individuals to show that he, too, like Alfredo Di Stefano, was once a player. Crossan's passage through football was incomparable to the point where unique seems too slight a description. Unique-unique might be more appropriate.

In conversation Crossan adds Peter Doherty to Di Stefano, and Faas Wilkes, Ferenc Puskas, Brian Clough, George Best among many others. That's on the pitch. Off it, Crossan touches on Fred Trueman, Pope John XXIII, Patrice Lumumba, Clement Freud, John Hume and the Beatles.

If, as Crossan says, there was a time in the late 1950s and early 1960s when Di Stefano could legitimately be called the best footballer on the planet, then there was a day around that time when Crossan could be labelled its most famous, or infamous.

In January 1959, six weeks after his twentieth birthday, Johnny Crossan – the wee man from Hamilton Street, Derry – picked up the *Daily Express* and saw himself, not on the back page, but on the front.

"BANNED FOR LIFE', it said,' he recalls – 'on the front page. And down the side there some piece about the new Pope.'

Crossan had been banned *sine die* – that is, indefinitely, forever – by the Football Association in London. His sentence applied to all football everywhere in the world. Crossan, who had joined Bristol City from Coleraine three months earlier, was told his career was over. He would never play professional football again. He was shaken. He was 20.

Elsewhere there was outrage. Crossan's 'crime' was that when he was a Derry City player at the Brandywell stadium – before moving to Coleraine and on to Bristol – he had received payments from Derry despite being an amateur. Also while a Derry City player, Crossan had discussed an £8,000 transfer to Sunderland and how the two parties – Derry City and Crossan – could divide the fee. These were illegal practices, although as common in professional football as rain in Ireland.

The source of the revelations was the board at Derry City. They were so enraged by Crossan that they were prepared to incriminate themselves in order to punish him. Derry informed on themselves to Alan Hardaker, secretary of the Football League in England.

Derry's frustration stemmed from Crossan's amateur status which meant that at the end of a season he was free to move from the club. He had been at the Brandywell since he was 15, before that as a ballboy. Crossan had declined a transfer before despite many offers.

Yet now he chose Coleraine. Derry City's grievance was that if Crossan was transferred, Coleraine would be receiving a fee, not Derry City. Coleraine could divide it with Crossan (albeit illegally) as they wished.

Coleraine were managed by Kevin Doherty; Bristol City were managed by Peter Doherty. The two brothers oversaw Crossan's transfer in October 1958 to Bristol for £7,000. This is when Derry City exploded. They complained, in private, to Hardaker.

The pre-Partition all-Ireland team that won the British Home Championships for the first time, in 1914. Including Patrick O'Connell.
Back (left to right): Referee (Unknown), Val Harris, Fred McKee, Davy Rollo, Patrick O'Connell. *Front:* E. H. Seymour (Trainer), Sam Young, Billy Gillespie, Alex Craig, Bill Lacey, Louis Bookman, Bill McConnell. *(Colorsport)*

The first post-Partition team to represent the Irish Free State as 'Ireland' abroad. Ireland at the Olympic games in Paris, 1924. *(Getty)*

Above: Joe Bambrick: The man who scored six in a day. 'Head, heel or toe, slip it to Joe.' *(Getty)*

Notorious Bill McCracken: The man from the Falls Road who changed the shape of world football. *(Colorsport)*

73 years after his father laced Bambrick's ball, Brian Kerr is appointed manager of the Republic of Ireland. *(Getty)*

The prolific Jimmy Dunne. The man Jamie Vardy never caught. Dunne played for both Irelands. *(Getty)*

Dave 'Boy' Martin: transferred with Johnny Brown from Belfast Celtic to Wolves for an Irish record £7,500. *(Getty)*

The boy from east Belfast plays for Eire: Johnny Brown, far left front row, kneels two places down from the remarkable Jimmy Dunne. The first game of the FAI's end of season tour to Switzerland and France, 1937.

Taoiseach Eamon de Valera (left) at Ireland v Poland 1938 with President Douglas Hyde (centre, moustache). *(Getty)*

Foreigners? Four years before Hungary win at Wembley, the FAI Ireland team defeated England 2-0 at Goodison Park. They became the first 'foreign' team to win on English soil. *Back-row (left to right):* Con Martin, Thomas Aherne, T. Godwin, T. Moroney, W. Walsh. *Front:* P. Corr, O'Connor, Johnny Carey, P. Desmond, P. Farrell, D. Walsh. *(Colorsport)*

Wrexham 1950: the last Ireland team to have players selected from both sides of the border. *Back (left to right):* Norman Lockhart (Coventry), Danny Blanchflower (Barnsley), Hugh Kelly (Fulham goalkeeper), Gerard Bowler (Hull City), Sammy Smyth (Wolves), Reg Ryan (West Brom).
Front: John McKenna (Huddersfield), Robert Brennan (Birmingham), Con Martin (Aston Villa; captain), Tom Aherne (Luton Town), Davy Walsh (West Brom). *(Colorsport)*

Master and apprentice: Peter Doherty (right) shows the banned Johnny Crossan what it's all about. *(Getty)*

The great Harry Gregg during Northern Ireland's 2-2 draw with West Germany at the 1958 World Cup in Sweden. Four months after the Munich air disaster Gregg was voted goalkeeper of the tournament. *(Getty)*

Fans everywhere: Ireland v Spain at Dalymount Park, Dublin 1966 shows the popularity of soccer in a contested sporting landscape. *(Getty)*

Windsor Park, packed and framed by the Belfast landscape for Northern Ireland v Holland in 1977. George Best's last Irish cap. *(Getty)*

An all-Ireland XI dressed up as Shamrock Rovers prepare to take on Brazil at Lansdowne Road, June 1973. *(Getty)*

Above: Expert export: Liam Brady in Juve stripes at the San Siro. *(Getty)*

Into the Bundesliga: Noel Campbell at Fortuna Cologne. *(Getty)*

One Arsenal, two Irelands: Frank Stapleton and Pat Jennings pose in the respective Irish kits. *(Getty)*

Wembley 1985: Jimmy Quinn, centre, celebrates Northern Ireland reaching a second consecutive World Cup. *(Getty)*

Alan McLoughlin, November 1993: An Irish Mancunian in Belfast after scoring the goal that took one Ireland to USA 94. *(Getty)*

Northern Ireland fans in Spain, 1982 *(Getty)*

That Stuttgart moment: travelling fans and Irish players go wild after Ray Houghton's goal against England at Euro 88. *(Getty)*

Ireland's favourite Englishman: Jack Charlton pleases his new public. *(Colorsport)*

Being there: Irish and English travelling fans have a kick about in Cagliari before the countries meet at Italia 90. *(Getty)*

Across a cultural border: Croke Park hosts soccer, a game it once banned. Republic of Ireland v Wales, March 2007. *(Getty)*

The Oval: home to Glentoran since 1892. Peter Doherty, Con Martin and Danny Blanchflower all played here in the shadow of shipyard cranes. *(Getty)*

Not Oriel Park: Dundalk's players on a stage fit for their talents. AZ Alkmaar 2016, a 1-1 draw in the Europa League. *(Getty)*

Cool captain: Martin O'Neill spins away from Miguel Alonso (father of Xabi) as Northern Ireland beat hosts Spain at 1982 World Cup. *(Getty)*

Jumping for joy: Michael O'Neill celebrates Northern Ireland's second goal against Ukraine at Euro 2016. *(Getty)*

The chance: Wes Hoolahan has his late shot stopped by the Italy goalkeeper Salvatore Sirigu. Wes came back for more. *(Getty)*

Always taking a step up: Gareth McAuley climbs highest to score Northern Ireland's historic first goal at Euro 2016 against Ukraine. *(Getty)*

Louise Quinn, No. 4: 'In no way will we accept a step backwards.' Irish women ready to fight for their sport. *(Getty)*

George Best back on the street where he grew up: Belfast's Cregagh estate. *(Getty)*

The matter quickly became public and official and Crossan was summoned to Belfast as the Irish FA mounted an investigation. Derry City co-operated and Hardaker was kept informed. Hardaker was a disciplinarian who liked to be seen as a disciplinarian.

Nevertheless, in January 1959, when the verdict of the investigation was announced, no-one was expecting a punishment so severe it put an unknown 20 year-old on the front pages. But it did, Crossan became a cause celebre. It was as if a boy caught nicking sweets had been jailed for fraud.

The lad nicknamed Jobby was denied his job, a footballer was denied football. His registration withheld so that no other club could sign him – ever – Crossan returned to Hamilton Street, Derry, where he lodged an appeal.

*

'I THOUGHT THE WORLD HAD ENDED. I WASN'T JUST SUSPENDED FOR three weeks, it was: 'You're banned from football for ever – *sine die*.'

'It was Peter Doherty who had said to me in the car going home from training in Bristol: 'I don't think you're going to be able to play for us.' Peter was broken-hearted and he was broken-hearted for me.'

Back in Derry, Crossan waited, and looked around him.

'I think Derry is really deprived. Tell me anything good in Derry that hasn't been in Belfast for centuries. It's very much a poor city. Lots of people went to England to work, at times it was depressing. You know, Derry City don't own their own ground. I could name you fishing villages in Donegal with more, their own pitch, floodlights. We had nothing. Maybe that made me a wee bit harder.

'You come from Northern Ireland, you're politically-minded, you're born with that as well. It wasn't the polarized city it became, certainly not, but it was fragmented, same as Belfast.

'I'd played most of my junior football for Foyle Harps. I never got a trial for Northern Ireland as a schoolboy but I was playing for Derry City when I was 17. I got an Under-18 cap in 1955. It was against Scotland at Greenock Morton. Then we played England at Leyton Orient. Jimmy Greaves got a hat-trick.

'I was inundated by scouts by then. It started with my brother Eddie being a player and him telling people this boy can play as well. I'd a choice, I was an amateur of course. I went to Everton – Eddie was at Tranmere by then – and Nottingham Forest. Sunderland made the biggest effort. Their manager Alan Brown came over to Derry a couple of times, offered Derry money.'

The sport then – mid-1950s – was, in the word of the Professional Footballers' Association, 'feudal'. Clubs owned and controlled players. Directors could dictate lives and some enjoyed the power. A parallel system evolved beside the official line and players, managers, clubs knew the system and worked it. Sunderland knew what they were doing and Crossan knew this was a moment, a rare one, when money could be made. Derry City knew too.

As he says: 'Derry were involved in everything. The fee was about £8,000. Sunderland upped it to £10,000 and I wanted £2,000. Derry didn't tell me it had been upped and they offered me a lot less than £2,000.

'But it wasn't a dispute, it was bargaining. My ultimate card was that I was an amateur and had the right to walk away at the end of a season. Every amateur could.

'Derry were clever enough. They knew what I came from – my Da, Johnny, was just a general labourer, my Granda had been a fisherman. We didn't have too much. Eddie, my eldest brother, he played for Derry City and was then transferred to Blackburn Rovers. I played for Derry City. My younger brother, Jim, played for Derry City. Liam played for Derry City reserves and Harry, before he drowned, had signed for Derry City. Five of us on Derry City's books. Hamilton Street was about 20 yards from Brandywell Avenue, so you were born into it.

'The directors thought I'd jump at whatever was offered. But I had been around Derry City all my life and I'd never had a penny. I thought I was entitled to this. We were a poor family. Let's be honest about it, I thought it was a chance to make a few bob.'

Coleraine, 30 miles away and with Kevin Doherty as manager, were monitoring the situation. 'The money I got from Coleraine for signing as an amateur was more than what Derry City were going to give me for being transferred for £10,000. That might throw a wee bit of light on how I was being treated.'

Crossan also knew that from Coleraine he would be sold on to Bristol City. This was a scheme, Coleraine were a holding bay – 'That's exactly what it was.'

It was the kind of open subterfuge football's system forced upon itself. The difference here was the scale of the sanction imposed on a 20 year-old and the reaction the punishment provoked.

Part of Crossan can comprehend Derry City's initial reaction to his transfer from Coleraine, but not how it developed: 'I can understand them being annoyed. But they'd every chance to put it right.

'What they did then was unbelievable – they reported me for taking money for playing for them. It was £3 a match. I said I took that money because I worked on an assembly line at BSR – Birmingham Sound Reproducers – on a Saturday morning and that was recompense for me missing hours. They were evil at that stage, they wanted to do me. And they did.'

Clement Freud, grandson of Sigmund Freud and a future MP, was working as a sports reporter at The *Guardian* then. He travelled to Derry to document Crossan's plight. 'Fair-minded people reading of the ban are incredulous that this has been imposed for his failure to get his share of the money,' Freud wrote.

Freud and Crossan stayed in touch after that. When Crossan got married to his girlfriend Barbara, the undertaker's daughter, Freud laughed.

The appeal took time. Crossan was, as he says, 'back in the family. There was no great reaction from them – this was Derry. I remember a couple of times being on my own thinking about what I was going to do and I got anxious then.'

There had been some re-assurance, though, from calls from clubs also waiting on the appeal verdict. When it came, Crossan was still banned, much to his dismay. The fines for Derry City and Coleraine stood; Bristol City had no new player.

The one consolation was that the ban now extended no further than the UK. It meant that Crossan could move abroad – he had no choice. It sounds straightforward, even appealing to modern ears, but Crossan was a 20 year-old who had lived in Derry all his life bar a few weeks in Bristol and who had never been abroad. 'I'd been to Donegal,' he says. He did not have a passport.

*

FOR FOREIGN CLUBS TO SHOW INTEREST IN JOHNNY CROSSAN THEY would need to have seen him play. Two had. The oldest club in Austria, First Vienna, had a scout at the England-Northern Ireland U-18 game and were first to get in touch. And then, as Crossan says: 'Denis Neville rang me.'

Denis Neville was one of those English coaches who became better known abroad than at home. In the 1950s Neville managed in Denmark, Italy and Belgium before, in 1955, taking over Sparta Rotterdam in the Netherlands. He too had been at that U-18 match.

Neville talked Crossan into a visit – 'I went out to Rotterdam to see digs and things, met a woman called Mrs. Rudolph. I could stay with her family.

'Had I been abroad? Not at all. When I went to Scotland to play, that was a foreign country. I didn't have a passport. I went to Dublin and got an Irish passport – I'm a Derryman. I was able to get a passport quick. Eddie was married into John Hume's clique and I think there were a few strings pulled.'

So in August 1959, instead of being Bristol City's new signing from the Irish League, Johnny Crossan ran out for Sparta Rotterdam against Fortuna 54 in the

Dutch Eredivisie. Sparta had won the League the previous season, so he was joining the champions. He would be playing in the European Cup.

"Be careful, son,' they said at home. But I wanted to be a footballer and this was a chance. The European Cup didn't mean anything to me then, but the glory game did.

'Most of the people at the club spoke English, not as fluent as they are now, and I did numerous newspaper interviews. You were only allowed two foreigners then. Sparta had some Hungarians who'd come out of Hungary after the Revolution of '56. I walked onto their team. I was a decent wee player.

'My first day? It was desperate. I knew I was alone then. I was in a hotel for a couple of days and I toyed with the idea of going home. But come the Sunday, we were playing and it all changed. I felt fantastic running out. We'd gone out for a warm-up beforehand – that was foreign to me, we didn't do that at the Brandywell. We did sprints, drills, came in and we had a cold shower before kick-off. I thought to myself: 'This is big time, all right.'

'The atmosphere was phenomenal – League champions, first day of the season and Rotterdam's a football city. Life started flying.'

Sparta received a bye in the preliminary round of the European Cup, then drew Gothenburg. They had beaten the Irish League champions Linfield 7-3 on aggregate, though only after Linfield had beaten the Swedes 2-1 at Windsor Park with Jackie Milburn scoring both. Milburn had three years at Linfield at the end of his career.

Sparta Rotterdam and Gothenburg drew 3-3 on aggregate in the last 16 and in those days that meant a third game at a neutral venue. It was in Bremen and Sparta won 3-1, Crossan scoring the second goal.

In the quarter-finals Sparta drew Rangers. This meant Crossan was back in the UK, playing football. But he was still banned.

The original ruling from the Football League, however, stipulated that Crossan's ban applied only to League football. That had already led to Crossan being selected by Northern Ireland for their British Home Championships game at Wembley against England in November 1959.

'The same men, essentially, at the IFA who got me banned domestically, then picked me for the international team,' Crossan says. 'Work that out.'

They did not pick Crossan again for three years, though. 'I got booked in the match for a tackle on Ron Flowers and Harry Gregg always says it was so bad the Queen crossed herself.

'Then Sparta drew Rangers, I was delighted. Living in Northern Ireland, we knew all about Rangers and Celtic. In Belfast you had Linfield and Belfast Celtic and then Belfast Celtic disappeared. Strangely enough, I'd no qualms about going to Ibrox.

They beat us 3-2 at our home in the first leg. We beat them 1-0 at Ibrox, I played well in that game.

'In those days there was no goal difference, you had a third match. So we played them again, at Highbury. They beat us 3-2, the decisive goal was an own goal. For me – for a man who was banned – I'd played at Ibrox, Highbury, Wembley.'

Crossan stayed two seasons in Rotterdam. He played against one of the city's greatest players – Faas Wilkes, Johan Cruyff's inspiration – and got married along the way. Unintentionally it would bring about his departure from Sparta.

'Dutch football was improving, it was largely amateur til the 50s, then they started investing and bringing some foreigners in. I played against Faas Wilkes, he was the man then. The reason I left was very simple – I got married and I told Denis Neville I needed an apartment and he let me down.'

Still banned from the UK, Crossan had attracted attention from next door to the Netherlands. Standard Liege won the league in Belgium in 1961 and fancied Crossan.

'I wanted to go to play in England but Standard offered money, I don't know how much. So I went.

'Barbara came to live with me in Liege. She was dead on but she would become homesick and she'd go home for a couple of days. Don't forget, I was only 20 and she was 17 when we got married. It was a 10 o'clock mass, wedding breakfast, and I was on the train to Dublin at 12. My brother Liam was in the station. He says: 'Have ye any money on you?' That's the type of family we were. Life was great.'

The two-foreigner rule applied in Belgium and Liege already had two. Paul Bonga Bonga, from the Congo, was one of them.

'We knocked about together, me and Paul, we roomed together. Paul was an extremely intelligent man. His children were educated in Paris. And he was a good player. The first president of the Congo was a man called Patrice Lumumba and his secretary was Janine, she was Paul's wife. There was an incident in the Congo, the Irish Army were out there. Paul had great difficulty talking to me about it.'

The Irish Army, under the United Nations, were involved in the Siege of Jadotville in September 1961; ten months earlier nine Irish soldiers had been killed in the Niemba ambush. Lumumba, leading Congolese independence from Belgium, was murdered because of his political activity, the CIA eventually admitting involvement.

*

'I HAD TO PLAY RESERVE MATCHES BECAUSE YOU HAD TO PLAY SO many games. But I played in the European Cup every time. Our manager was Geza

Kalocsay, he'd been a coach with the great Hungary team that won at Wembley in '53. Knew his stuff.'

In February 1962 Standard Liege reached the last eight of the European Cup, where they drew Glasgow Rangers.

'We got Rangers, again. It was the quarter-finals and we beat them 4-1 in Liege. I got two. Brilliant.

'Davie Wilson scored for Rangers. Davie was a pigeon man, he rang me a few times in Liege because Belgium was a big place for racing pigeons. 'Johnny, could you get me a couple of eggs?"

Rangers won the second leg 2-0 – 'Jim Baxter was outstanding' – but Liege were through to the semi-final. There they met Real Madrid, who had won the first five European Cups.

The first leg was in Madrid and Crossan remembers the team-talk well.

'I'd the job of marking Di Stefano. I was an inside left or inside right but we were going to the Bernabeu and Real Madrid were massacring teams there. Jean Prouff was our manager by then and he was determined to play defensively. There were 100,000 there or whatever. At the team-talk he said: 'Johnny, I want you to do this, do that. This Di Stefano's a clever player.' Bit of an understatement, that.

'We all knew how good he was. I ran about like a young foal. I tried to nail him once or twice, as you do. It was 2-0 at half-time. But look at that forward line – Tejada played outside right, Del Sol inside right, Di Stefano centre-forward, Puskas inside left and Gento outside left. I mean, come on?'

Di Stefano scored the first, Madrid won 4-0, then 2-0 in Liege. But Johnny Crossan from Hamilton Street, Derry, had played in the European Cup semi-final and, as Di Stefano was to show years later at the Café Royal, he made an impression.

*

HE WAS MAKING IT ELSEWHERE. EVEN THE BLINKERED IN BLAZERS AT the IFA had to notice that two of their players, Danny Blanchflower and Johnny Crossan, were playing in the European Cup semi-final. Blanchflower had captained Tottenham against Benfica.

Standard Liege finished second to Anderlecht in 1962, meaning no European Cup in 1962/63, but it was an end-of-season trip by England that would shape Crossan's next step. On the way to the 1962 World Cup finals in Chile, England played a friendly in Peru. The IFA's Harry Cavan was there and met an England selector, Syd Collings, who was also a director of Sunderland.

Alan Brown was still the Sunderland manager and the club were still interested in Crossan. The IFA needed as many good players as it could get. Here was the start of an expedient u-turn. It took another five months but Crossan's ban was lifted on October 1962, co-incidentally, on the day he left Standard Liege for Sunderland for £30,000 – £3,000 of which went to Crossan.

'It was all solved in Lima, Peru, in a side street,' Crossan says. There is no hint of admiration for the men involved.

'We loved it in Liege, an apartment in the centre of town, broad boulevard, fourth floor. I could speak the language quick-time. I got some coverage at home, Malcolm Brodie would come out and write an article for the *Belfast Telegraph*. I could have stayed but when you score two against Rangers in the European Cup, people take notice. Brodie was aware and there were times when we thought Brodie was picking the Ireland team.

'When I heard it was lifted, I still felt it was an injustice. I still feel that and I'm 78. Len Shackleton was partly responsible for bringing me to Sunderland and we know what he thought about directors.

'Sunderland were in the Second Division. I went there in October 1962, Clough got injured on Boxing Day against Bury. Brian had the operation, he was skint. I gave him £20. That's what he got a week. I was on £45 because I signed after the George Eastham ruling. There were no bonuses for him, you see, and Sunderland were good at the bonuses.

'Brian and I became friends, we went to the cricket all the time. We'd be in the Yorkshire dressing room – Freddie Trueman, Ray Illingworth. That was a great team. We'd go to Bramall Lane, when they had the cricket ground there, to watch Yorkshire. The first Test match we went to was at Old Trafford [1964]. We saw Bobby Simpson, captain of Australia, score 311.'

Sunderland were promoted at the end of Crossan's first season at Roker Park. They stayed up but in January 1965, he left for Manchester City, then in the Second Division. He was made captain and City were promoted in 1966.

He was also back in the Northern Ireland team – one month after the ban was removed. Two years later, winning his eighth cap in Wales, Crossan played with George Best on his Irish debut. When Crossan moved to City, the two knew each other well in Manchester.

'George was outside right, myself inside right, Sammy Wilson centre forward. The best in the world at one stage was Di Stefano. Then Pele came along. But for me, on his day, George Best was better than any of them. George was a sensation. We played nearly every game together for Northern Ireland for a few years, we'd travel together. I saw him go from footballer to Beatle, in fact we'd be out with the Beatles – they got a bit handy with a couple of players' wives one night. We'd two Miss Worlds in our house another night. Barbara thought the world of George. Manchester was phenomenal.'

From City, Crossan returned to the Second Division with Middlesbrough and then in in 1970, aged 32, the man who had been desperate to play in England moved back to Belgium. Crossan joined a third division club, KSK Tongeren, near Liege.

'There was contact through Standard Liege. Jean-Paul Colonval rang me, he was a centre forward, went on to work for Canal Plus. I went back to Liege, lived near enough next door to where I'd been. We'd children by then. We won promotion in the first season, got to a cup final [1974], played it at Heysel. Lost. I stayed five years. I must have been doing all right.'

NOEL CAMPBELL – WEST GERMANY

THERE ARE THREE MEN IN THE PHOTOGRAPH IN NOEL CAMPBELL'S hand. On the left is Gerd Muller, to the right is Franz Beckenbauer. In the middle is Noel Campbell.

'It was in the Cup, the 'Deutscher Pokal',' Campbell says. 'We beat them 2-1 in Cologne.' By 'them' Campbell means Bayern Munich.

'Then we travelled up to Munich the following Saturday for the return leg. We had about 400 team-talks and the main thing was to hold Bayern for the first 20 minutes. I scored an own goal after about a minute.

'They'd a player, Franz 'The Bull' Roth, and he'd a shot that was going 50 yards wide until I got a touch. They scored five or something. But beating them in the first leg, that was an achievement. We were a second division team then. We'd 28,000 there.'

With that Campbell lets out a chuckle. He is recalling an adventure, his adventure, into the old West Germany of the 1970s, when the lad from Kimmage in south Dublin, playing part-time for St. Patrick's Athletic in the League of Ireland while working for the Smithfield Motor Co. found himself rubbing shoulders with the two of the greats of post-war European football. The 'we' he refers to are Fortuna Koln.

'Franz Beckenbauer?' Campbell says, 'he is what he is. But Gerd Muller – he still doesn't get the credit he deserves. He was the most amazing player. He was the most amazing goalscorer, better than any of them, even Jimmy Greaves. Muller was an astonishing footballer.'

Sitting across the road from Connolly Station in 2016, we are back in Cologne in December 1971. Campbell had arrived in Germany in the summer of that year, aged 21, not a word of German to his name. He was alone at first, did not know Cologne or the league he was joining, the Regionalliga West. Signed by Fortuna, Cologne's second, smaller club behind FC Koln, Campbell was a novelty, a pioneer. After two seasons he became the first Irishman to appear in the Bundesliga and no-one has made the same journey since.

'It was a massive leap,' Campbell says, 'but it was too good to turn down. I could've gone to Shamrock Rovers.'

*

NOEL CAMPBELL WAS BORN IN TERENURE IN DUBLIN IN DECEMBER 1949. He was one of twelve children – seven sisters, five brothers – born to Anne and John. John worked as a bus driver for CIE. Anne had enough on her hands keeping home. After a while, the family moved.

'It was a small Corporation house on a Corporation estate in Kimmage, a nice estate,' Campbell says. 'Everyone had kids then, all big families. Two bedrooms and we'd be sleeping all together. You know, the usual. You think you're talking to Brendan Behan, don't you? But all me pals were the same. Those were good times.'

Sport – soccer – gripped the Campbell boys: 'My brother Johnny was a player, so was my brother Hubert, and Jim. They all played League of Ireland football. Johnny played for the great Drums team – Drumcondra. Hubert played for Sligo [Rovers] and Jim played with me at St. Patrick's Athletic.

'I played from being a baby. I joined one of the junior teams, Stella Maris. I was a forward, sometimes winger, inside forward. I used to go every Tuesday on the 16A bus, travel for an hour back and forward to train. I played Under-13 for them when I was 10.'

That last line – 'I played Under-13 for them when I was 10' – was delivered, like all Campbell's comments, with a matter-of-fact modesty belying its significance. In a sports-mad city such as Dublin in the late 1950s, playing teenage football aged 10 was not going to go unnoticed.

'Yeah,' Campbell concedes, 'I suppose I'd some ability. I hate even saying it, but I was a skilful player. I wasn't maybe as strong as some of the older boys. I'd great potential. As they say.'

When Campbell was 10 – December 1959 – Burnley were half way to winning the First Division title in England. Managed by Harry Potts, Burnley were a bit more than the Leicester City of their day – finishing first, fourth, runners up and third between 1960 and 1963.

Burnley were renowned for their youth system and scouting and they had noticed a precocious boy in Dublin: Noel Campbell. After Burnley's title-winning season, Campbell was brought to Turf Moor.

'There were a few clubs,' he says. 'I'd a week over at Burnley. Harry Potts was the manager, they'd Jimmy Adamson and Jimmy McIlroy. Alex Elder played. I was to go back when I was 15.'

It was agreed, 10 year-old Campbell would join Burnley. Then, he adds, as if it is an afterthought: 'Arsenal came in.'

Campbell had left his junior club, Stella Maris, to join his nearest local one, Larkview. Arsenal had a scout called Mick Heron who knocked on the door in Kimmage.

'I was 13 when Arsenal came in. Apparently there were a few clubs interested, but Arsenal said they'd bring me over, live with a family, go to school in north London. I went over for a week with my mother and my uncle to see what it was like, where I'd live.'

Arsenal, managed by Billy Wright, had outmanoeuvred Burnley. And so, aged thirteen-and-a-half, Campbell left his family and moved to London. On his own.

It seems hard to believe now that a young boy would be unaccompanied. Did his family not think he was too young?

'In those days there no great schooling for us here,' is Campbell's phlegmatic reply. 'There was no way I'd be going to university or college or anything. Not in a million years. So I went to secondary school in a place called Arnos Grove.'

He makes it sound seamless, even though Arnos Grove is in north London.

'I'd train Tuesday and Thursday evening, but I wasn't even old enough to play for the Arsenal youth team. I was the youngest at the club. They trained at London Colney. The first house I lived in was in a place called Bounds Green. Then I lived in Palmers Green. The families were nice, but it is unimaginable now. If I was truthful, it was probably the unhappiest time in my life. I was lonely, I was 14 and I was living in London.'

There was at least one early trip back to Ireland: 'Do you remember the name, Billy Wright? I'd been over in London a few months when they brought me home. Arsenal – Ian Ure, George Eastham – played against a Dublin selection and they took a photo of me with Billy Wright on the doorstep at the Gresham hotel. I was 14 by then I think.'

Campbell stayed until he was 16, earned his apprenticeship, made the youth team and had been joined by some other Irish boys. Then, after Wright's contrived resignation in June 1966, Bertie Mee became Arsenal manager.

'I was only 16, still at school,' Campbell says. 'I was playing for the youth team with Charlie George, Pat Rice, Eddie Kelly – Sammy Nelson came a bit later. There was another lad from the North, Derek Humphreys. He was a good friend of mine, later killed in a car crash.

'Bertie Mee took over. Anyway, he came in, and there were so many kids. And I wanted to go home. 'We don't mind,' he said. So they let me go.'

Campbell does not come across as a man tormented by regret. Even so, in another era he would not have been allowed to travel alone from Dublin to London aged 13 to join a football club.

'The saddest part of my life were the three years in London,' he says. 'It's only afterwards, when I look back now, that I understand that. I was there because I had to go. It was tough, when I look back. I was 13 in the big London, astonishing isn't it?'

He says it was 'a relief' to be back in Dublin, where he remained a valuable football commodity.

'I suppose I could have gone to any League of Ireland team but my Da was friendly with Gerry Doyle, who was manager of St. Pat's at the time. It was a terrible team, I was kind-of their big player. I did that for a couple of years.'

Campbell's description of St. Pat's as 'terrible' is by comparison to other experiences. While he was there, St. Pat's played in Europe.

'It was in the Inter-cities Fair's Cup. We played Bordeaux, lost in Dublin. In the second game in Bordeaux, I scored two, we were beaten 6-3. I was only 17. My son was going through his Guinness Book of Records and I was actually in it for that [youngest scorer] in '67. Probably not now. At that time I wasn't bad. I didn't worry about football then, I'd no inhibitions. I'd more when I was 25.'

*

BY THE TIME HE WAS 25, NOEL CAMPBELL WAS PLAYING IN THE Bundesliga. He stayed with St. Pat's, playing semi-professionally, looking for work and earned his first of eleven Irish caps while with the club. At the end of the 1970-71 League of Ireland season, when St. Pat's came third-bottom, Campbell was contacted by Ben Hannigan, a Dubliner who had just had a few months with Sligo. Hannigan, a rover, thought he would try his luck abroad.

'He was going around Europe trying to get trials,' Campbell says. 'He had one with Fortuna Koln. And he recommended me. A man called Oscar Schidler came over to see me. I went over there, trained with them, discussed things and then I signed. I don't know how much St. Pat's got.

'At St. Pat's I was earning buttons. I worked in a few different jobs while I was there, my last was at the Smithfield Motor Company. They were Ford Dealers. I was some sort of clerk, used to ship the broken parts back to Cork.

'In Germany I was earning very good money, I can't remember exactly how much, but very good. I felt this was my second chance, my second big chance. It took me a while to settle but I got there eventually. I was 21. The family were happy for me.'

At a time when few Irish people got further than Britain, Campbell arrived in West Germany in July 1971.

'I had my own apartment, then I got married, my wife Anne came over. I was there until 1979. I never got any German lessons, I just learned it as I went along and a lot of them could speak English. Everything was positive towards me, I was well-accepted. I was quite popular with the fans. I liked a drink and I was out and about.

'It was a good team. The standard was really good. I was being coached in a totally different way, fairly intensive. We were promoted to the Bundesliga in my second season and promotion was fantastic. Now they have Bundesliga 2 and 3, then it was the Bundesliga and Regional Leagues.'

There were five Regional Leagues. Each would send two clubs forward into two mini-leagues of five. They played the other four clubs home and away and the two winners of each group were promoted. As Campbell says: 'It took some doing.'

For Fortuna Koln, this was historic. Formed in 1948 via a merger of other local clubs, Fortuna had never been in the Bundesliga. They were very much Cologne's second club.

'FC Koln were massive, Fortuna couldn't get near,' Campbell says, 'but it was an excellent club in the southern part of the city. The owner was Mr Loring. He changed managers like an Italian.

'I lived in the same building as him for a while. It was murder. He loved the bones of me but we'd terrible arguments about my drinking and smoking and not looking after myself. I loved the gargle. He'd make sure I was left out of the team, but I played most of the time.'

Fortuna Koln's first ever match in the Bundesliga was away at Borussia Monchengladbach in August 1973. Monchengladbach had Allan Simonsen on the bench; Fortuna had Noel Campbell in midfield.

What does Campbell remember? 'We never got a fucking kick, I remember that. They beat us 3-1 and they beat us easy. I didn't play well. They'd players like Rainer Bonhof, Jupp Heynckes, they finished second that season. We knew we were in a different league.'

Fortuna were to stay in it for just one season, relegated on the last day on goal difference. They lost their city derby twice, which did not help. The two Cologne clubs were also sharing the Radrennbahn ground for that one season.

'It was a great little stadium, an old outdoor cycling place. FC Koln had a great team then, all internationals, they'd Heinz Flohe. We were decent but we were penny-ha'penny compared to them. I mean, they'd Wolfgang Overath, he kept Gunter Netzer out of the West Germany team in the '74 World Cup final.'

Following relegation, Fortuna almost won promotion, and Campbell stayed. He signed a second contract, then a third and were it not for a knee injury which forced him to retire at 28, he says: 'I'd have stayed for my whole career. I'd cartilage trouble, I'd three operations.

'If I'd one regret in all my time in Germany I would have been a better profes-sional – by a million miles. I liked the good time. I was living in the moment. Yeah, I'd be 100% better as a pro. There were some very good professionals there – well, compared to me.'

He won eleven Republic of Ireland caps in total, the first in 1971 against Austria, the last in 1977 in Sofia against Bulgaria when Campbell was sent off in bizarre circumstances three minutes after replacing Gerry Daly. Out of the public eye, Campbell was, as he puts it: 'In the chorus – when John [Giles] didn't want to play, I got a game. But I wouldn't have gone out of my way to seek attention.'

He had made enough money – just – in Germany to buy a house in Drumcondra. But Campbell needed a job and 'did every bit of scrappy work going'.

In late 1970s Dublin: 'Jobs were few and far between. Ireland was fucking de-pressed. But where else could I go? I played a bit for Shamrock Rovers and I helped John Giles doing a bit of training. But my knee was crippled, I simply couldn't do it. It was not for me.'

Noel Campbell had done enough and he had done something different. He has that Muller-Beckenbauer photograph to show the company he kept in Germany. In return, the annual invitations to Cologne show that Fortuna remember him.

LIAM BRADY – ITALY CALLING

'He's obsessed with Liam Brady and Arsenal. He always wears his scarf and on the way to every session he goes and stands in the middle of Highbury and pays the cab to wait for him.'
Guy Stevens, record producer on seminal album 'London Calling', as recalled by Mick Jones of The Clash.

GUY STEVENS ONCE POURED BEER INTO A PIANO 'TO MAKE IT SOUND better'. Guy Stevens once said: 'There are only two Phil Spectors in the world and I'm one of them.' Guy Stevens adored music and acoustics. Guy Stevens worshipped Liam Brady.

It was Stevens who shaped the sound of 'London Calling'. That record's title track would later be played as Arsenal emerged from the tunnel at the ground which replaced Highbury, the Emirates Stadium.

Liam Brady didn't know this. Brady had never heard of Guy Stevens. Now Brady reads, mildly perplexed, of how 'London Calling' was recorded at Wessex studios near Highbury; of how Stevens would arrive at the stadium in a black cab every day, keep the meter running while he walked out into the centre circle and gazed up at the stands seeking inspiration; of Stevens' Liam Brady scarf; of The Clash's one-time manager, Bernie Rhodes, saying: 'We picked Guy Stevens because we wanted a nutcase.'

Brady looks up and says: 'They were a bit heavy for me, The Clash. Semi-punkish, weren't they?

'I quite like some punk.'

Brady attracted many lyrical descriptions during a bountiful 17-year playing career but given how he faced down two domineering institutions – the Catholic church and Arsenal Football Club – by the age of 23, Brady was some punk himself.

In 1979 as The Clash recorded a soundtrack for a generation, Brady had established himself as one of the greatest footballers in Europe. That year he came seventh in voting for the European Footballer of the Year – he was in the top ten three years in a row – and in England he was voted the PFA Footballer of the Year.

Brady was on the way to making over 300 appearances for Arsenal, having had a debut at 17. But in 1979 London was no longer calling him, he was on his way out of Arsenal. At 23, Brady informed the club he would leave at the end of the 1979/80 season.

He had seen Kevin Keegan move from England to Hamburg, Tony Woodcock move from England to Cologne, Brady wanted to join them in Germany. An island of independent thought on the pitch, Brady's self-determination off it meant that even in that era he had an agent. He was a rare footballer: 'Thinkers are the deadliest men,' he once said.

Brady's agent was in contact with Bayern Munich – 'So much so that I was learning German at home,' he says. 'I thought it was more or less a done deal.'

That 1979/80 season at Arsenal turned into a 68-game marathon. The club reached the quarter-final of the League Cup, the final of the FA Cup and the final of the European Cup Winners' Cup. Arsenal came fourth in the league.

Brady played in 58 of those games, two of which were against Juventus in the semi-final of the Cup Winners' Cup. Arsenal were victorious but in the space of five days in May 1980 Arsenal lost the FA Cup final to West Ham and the Cup Winners' Cup final to Valencia.

But that was not the end. Two outstanding fixtures in the old First Division remained, at Wolves and Middlesbrough. Brady played in both. As he did, Bayern Munich withdrew. Brady got married that same month. He and Sarah flew to America on honeymoon. Their futures were up in the air.

*

'WHEN I LANDED AT THE AIRPORT IT WAS SWARMING WITH JUVENTUS supporters. They were on the tarmac. [Giovanni] Trapattoni stood at the bottom of the plane's steps to meet me, there were reporters from the press, TV, it was like rolling news. I hadn't expected it. It was a bit daunting. Then they put me on their shoulders and carried me into the terminal – these are vivid memories coming back. We did a bit of a press conference at the airport, then there was a car to take me to their training camp – *ritiro*. I went in time for an evening meal with the players. The players all stood up in the restaurant when I walked in, shook hands with me. The captain, Giuseppe Furino, welcomed me. They had a translator and Furino said to me: 'We know you're going to do a great job for us,' and handed me the No. 10 shirt. That first night, they put me in a room with Roberto Bettega. They would have done the same for anyone. But what a welcome.'

Liam Brady is describing another flight and another airport – Turin's – which followed his return from America. This had not been part of the honeymoon plan. A life in Italy and a career in Italian football had not featured in Brady's discussions and he had even resumed pre-season training with Arsenal, the club still hopeful of a change of heart.

Stalled, Brady was adamant he was departing – 'I didn't want to be eating any humble pie.' The arrival of a man called Gigi Peronace changed Brady's direction.

'Peronace was an Italian 'Mr Fixit',' Brady explains. 'He was saying Italian clubs would be interested. But nothing materialised. So I went pre-season training with Arsenal. I was wanting to go, I'd told Arsenal a year before. But it was only then that Juventus said they wanted to sign me.'

July 1980: for Italy and for Juventus, as well as Brady, this was momentous. For 16 years Italian clubs had been barred from signing foreigners; from the age of 15 Brady had been with Arsenal. Suddenly he was essential to the ornate re-invention of Serie A.

'There was nobody over in Italy at the time, they'd closed their borders. They'd decided that World Cup failures were down to having too many foreigners in Italy. I didn't know that then. But in 1980 they decided to allow foreigners back in, they wanted to make their league more attractive and their top clubs weren't having much success at European level. Real Madrid always had foreign players, Barcelona had had [Johan] Cruyff. So I got signed.

'Juventus are a huge club, so I didn't hesitate. I spoke to Peronace, he was full of praise for the club and the Agnelli family who ran it. I knew it was a great club, I'd played against Juventus in the Cup Winners' Cup, I'd played against their players, and I knew them all from watching the World Cup and European Championships.'

Italy's self-imposed high wall had been erected in response to the World Cups of 1958, when they lost out in qualification to Northern Ireland, and 1962 in Chile, when Italy did not get out of their group. Italian frustration was confirmed by the 1966 embarrassment of losing to North Korea at Ayresome Park.

This was a new era. Not since another former Arsenal man, Paddy Sloan from Lurgan, joined AC Milan had an Irishman played in Italy. And that was in 1948. Juve had Brady, Roma signed the brilliant Brazilian Falcao, Inter Milan brought the Austrian playmaker Herbert Prohaska to the San Siro. More would follow – Zbigniew

Boniek, Karl-Heinz Rummenigge and, dramatically for Brady, Michel Platini.

'This was just the start,' Brady says of the Serie A revival. He admits to 'a few butterflies, a few,' but this was a self-confessed 'cocky' young man. So there were no nerves in that first training session at Juve's *ritiro*?

'Nah, I wouldn't have had a problem in that area. I was always pretty confident.'

Such self-belief, added to the cocoon of professional football aided acclimatisation. But even if initially the language was a welcome barrier to the intense *calcio* culture all around Brady, he had an awareness of pressure and expectation. Juve had not won the Serie A title in the previous two seasons. They had never won the European Cup. Brady's mission in Turin was to rectify this.

He was the new No. 10, after all. At Arsenal Brady's left foot, vision and zip over five yards had seen him grow naturally into the team's creative director. In Italy he discovered this was a more formal status.

'It was the responsibility that was put on you. In England you weren't nominated as the most important player, or the playmaker. In Italy you were nominated. It was a bit like a quarterback in American football. It was emphasised. The recognition, even from your own teammates, was there. You had to do it. You're the No. 10, they give you the ball.

'It meant I was just purely focussed on being creative. As my teammates got to know me, they'd make runs for me to find them. [Marco] Tardelli was a bit like Terry McDermott, arriving late in that Liverpool team. We had [Pietro] Fanna up front who had speed and who could spin. And I had the ability to take people on.

'I played a completely different game. Trapattoni would say to me that he didn't want me running up and down the pitch. In England I would have been considered a Hoddle or a Brooking – who wasn't doing his work.

'But in Italy that was my role. *Trequartista*. No. 10. You were marked man for man, so you have to know what you are going to do with the ball before it comes to you. You have to be always thinking. When you're a playmaker, you can't get the ball, then decide what to do, you have to know. If you watch footage of Platini, you see him walking with the ball – a lot. I used to say that when I was coaching the kids at Arsenal: 'Walk with the ball, you've got more time to think.' Platini walked with it, head up, thinking: 'Right, who's going to move for me?' Like a quarterback. Then, 'pop', a pass. Those players have disappeared.'

First impressions were good. Brady took to Turin, and Juventus took to Brady. But he soon understood this was a gentle introduction to Italian domestic football, via the Coppa Italia. Juventus were top of a seeded group stage which preceded the Serie A season. Brady's real introduction, he felt, came on the league season's opening day, mid-September 1980, at Cagliari in Sardinia, an island more than 400 miles south of Turin. It was, Brady remembers, hotter than your average September day in north Dublin.

'We'd the early rounds of the Italian Cup. It was a group phase. The Cup was a bit of a nothing competition until the semi-final and final. The focus was on the league, the game at Cagliari. So I had about seven weeks before my debut. It was in Sardinia and it was fucking boiling. We'd been playing at night time in the Cup, this was the daytime, about 90 degrees. On the day I struggled. I really suffered, oh yeah.

'The reaction in the papers was that I was 'not impressive'. The critics had been favourable until then, but the real thing hadn't started. I was beginning to understand what people were saying, bits and pieces. We drew 1-1, we were expected to win, I wasn't happy with the way I'd played. Trapattoni was fine, he understood, he said to me: 'It was hot.''

There was more heat to come. If the temperature on the pitch got to a pale Irishman, there was a scene afterwards that pricked Brady and stayed with him.

He paints a picture: 'We were on the bus, ready to leave. I was sat on my own. One of the directors, a *dirigente*, asked somebody how Inter had got on, because they were the champions. The reply was: 'They won 4-0.' Something like that.

"And Prohaska?' – the *dirigente* asked. Prohaska had been signed by Inter.

"Yeah, he played well, scored."

Brady heard the Juventus director respond to this news with: 'Maybe we've got the wrong foreigner.'

Brady was not yet fluent in Italian but he had grasped the language quickly and he understood both the words and, more so, the sentiment. All these years later he repeats *sbagliato stranieri* – the wrong foreigner.

'I took note. I remembered it when he was kissing me at the end of the season. One game in … but then directors are like that.'

Presumably there was no such comment the following week when Juventus beat Como at home. This was Brady's first taste of the Stadio Comunale; he remembers nothing bar the outcome. It was all a happy blur, though it was not the beginning of a surge. Over the next five weeks, Juventus drew at Brescia, Ascoli and Perugia. They lost at home to Bologna and Torino. Mighty Juve were in the bottom half of the table and to some it seemed as if they had actually signed the wrong foreigner.

The Torino game was a city derby, though as Brady explains: 'It was not so big – like Man United v Man City years ago, when City weren't so good.'

But looming next were Inter Milan. This was *il Derby d'Italia* – Italy's derby. The scrutiny is always extreme but in 1980 Inter were champions at a time when AC

Milan had been relegated to Serie B in the *Totonero* match-fixing scandal. There was an even greater focus on Inter-Juve than normal.

'When we lost at home to Torino, I'd struggled,' Brady says. 'I was coming in for criticism – 'He hasn't made any difference', that sort of thing. We lost 2-1 to Torino and I think Bettega was sent off for something he said to the referee. Yeah, the first few games were a bit of a struggle for me. Then we played Inter.'

It might sound overly dramatic to a football realist like Brady, but this was the moment he truly landed in Italy.

'It was a big game for us and I was very good that day. They don't do Man of the Match, but I got star ratings. I scored a penalty and made the other goal, a long-range shot I hit smacked the crossbar and bounced down. [Gaetano] Scirea bundled it in. We were 2-0 up.

'Inter got a goal late on but we beat them. I was carried off shoulder-high by the players, because it was such a big game.'

To be chaired off on such an occasion is some image, some memory, even for someone as decorated as Brady.

'After that it was a breeze. As the season went on I was flying. We won 5-1 at Bologna, I scored two, at Pistoiese I scored a great individual goal. The consensus was that I was a great success and that Juventus had signed the right player – the right foreigner. We lost only one more match the rest of the season and that was at Inter.

'But during that time when I struggled, you'd get the newspaper ratings, they had a column: 'How the foreigners are doing'. The four sporting papers had ratings and they took the average. The press had power, for sure, but I think they were pretty objective. I always had confidence in myself, that I was going to do it. But if I'd known all that was being said out there, how mad it was, my bottle might have gone. Thankfully it didn't.'

Taking penalties helped Brady's assimilation. A fortnight earlier, Juve's troubled autumn also included elimination from the UEFA Cup.

Having drawn 4-4 on aggregate with Poland's Widzew Lodz, Juve lost the penalty shoot-out, at home, 4-1. Brady's penalty was Juve's only successful strike and from then he assumed the role held by Franco Causio. That task mattered against Inter – 'It gave me great confidence' – and it was to become more significant.

Elimination from Europe meant Juve's season became about re-taking the Serie A title. 'We were head to head with Roma for a long time and we played them with three games to go. It was a hugely controversial game – 0-0. They had a goal disallowed for offside. To this day, in Rome, they say that's a goal that should have stood.'

It did not. On the season's final afternoon, Juve met Fiorentina at a heaving

Comunale one point ahead of Roma. A 1-0 home win brought the title back to Turin and just as importantly brought back European Cup football the next season. For Brady it brought vindication.

'When we won the title I felt really, really proud,' he says. 'I scored eight goals, the top scorer in league for the team. It wasn't a lot, but Bettega had been banned for a while. A lot of people had said: 'What's he doing going to Italy? It's defensive, horrible.' I remember Keegan saying that he didn't want to go to Italy because his wife was frightened his children might be kidnapped. It was shite.

'There were a lot of people who said I was going to fail, that I'd made a mistake going abroad, maybe they saw me as being a bit of a bighead leaving English football.'

Eventually the Italians even stopped referring to Brady as *Inglese*.

'I had to keep correcting them. They assumed my culture was a London bowler hat and umbrella. I had to keep reminding them it wasn't. I suppose I'd come from England and English football. It wasn't until 1990, Italia 90 really, that Italians thought the Irish are an independent country with their own football team – I mean the masses.'

In Ireland, Brady's Italian progress received little attention. Via Sean Ryan at the *Irish Independent*, Brady was writing a weekly diary – 'So there was some awareness,' Brady says.

'But only because of Sean Ryan. You never saw TV footage in Ireland of what I was doing. And Ulick O'Connor, he was a feature writer for the *Sunday Times*. He came over to see me in Turin. Ireland's interest is the English league, isn't it?'

In turn, Brady felt a sense of removal from his previous life and times: 'There was no Internet then, no mobile phones. I used to go to get the Sunday papers on a Monday at Turin station. That's how I kept up with what was going on.

'But I was detached. One of the things I do remember from 1980 was being told John Lennon was shot. I was in a car with three teammates – I think we were going to get Christmas presents – and I heard them talking in the car. 'John Lennon e morto.' I was in shock.'

*

THAT 1980/81 SERIE A TITLE MEANT THE FOLLOWING SEASON JUVENTUS were back in the European Cup. And the first round draw meant Brady was back in the Irish, and British, public eye. It was Celtic versus Juventus.

'I couldn't wait to come back,' Brady says, 'to show myself playing in this team. It was great. I got an unbelievable reception in Glasgow when they read my name out in the team line-up. My folks were over from Ireland, relations, all that. Great. Celtic beat us 1-0.

'It was a night that certainly left a mark on me. When I was offered the Celtic job [a decade later], I remembered.'

In the return leg, Juve won 2-0. They met Anderlecht in the second round. Brady was confident prior to the first leg in Brussels: 'I was hoping we'd win the European Cup, we had the team to win it.

'But we were beaten by Anderlecht. I have no evidence but that was at a time when the Belgians were buying everything. I've a feeling that was fixed, that match. You look into the referee. He was English and he was struck off. Anderlecht beat us 3-1. I think that was fixed.'

The English referee was Clive White. At the end of that 1981/82 season White resigned from England's Football League referee list after admitting a charge of deception in court.

That is not proof of wrongdoing eight months earlier in Brussels, however, though Anderlecht were subsequently found to have bribed the referee of their 1984 UEFA Cup semi-final against Nottingham Forest. The Brussels club were banned from Europe for 12 months.

That Anderlecht '81 still rankles with Brady is obvious. 'Aston Villa went on to win it that year. We could have won it. That's another thing that would have counted against me with Agnelli.'

Agnelli was Gianni Agnelli, head of the family who owned Juventus. He was a billionaire, known as the uncrowned King of Italy, a sleek, Gatsby figure. His family's fortune stemmed in part from their ownership of car manufacturers Fiat. The 't' in Fiat is for Turin.

'Juventus had never won the European Cup, you see,' Brady says. 'That was the Holy Grail. They couldn't view themselves on a par with the likes of Real Madrid unless they won it. Inter and AC Milan had it over Juventus because they'd won it. That was a big thing for the Agnelli family.'

Agnelli's style was to suggest players to the Juventus manager, rather then dictate. But it amounted to the same thing.

Serie A's 1980 experiment had been a success and the foreigner quota was expanded to two per club, so Juve signed Boniek from Widzew Lodz. Brady and Boniek: all at Juve thought that was the future.

Giampiero Boniperti, club chairman and a Juve legend, even confirmed it officially. But Boniperti knew that Agnelli had already visited France to meet Michel Platini. There was a sensational transfer being kept under the radar.

It was now April 1982 and Juventus were three games away from sealing a second consecutive Serie A title, their twentieth in all. Fiorentina were pushing them hard. Their foreigner was Argentina's World Cup winner, Daniel Bertoni.

But when a flight control officer in Lyon leaked details of a private jet carrying Platini to Milan, the news broke. Brady was in anguish, undermined, shocked and angry. 'Devastated'.

He has been asked repeatedly down the decades since about this, because of what happened next. On the season's final day Fiorentina were above Juventus on goal difference. Both were away from home. Juve had to beat Fiorentina's result, and they did. While Fiorentina drew at Cagliari, Juve won 1-0 at Catanzaro. It was via a penalty-kick from Liam Brady.

'What happened at the end at Juventus was very hard for me to understand then, but I understand now,' he says. 'It was shocking to me at the time. But that's the way it is, there was a foreign player Agnelli wanted – Platini – and what Agnelli wants, he gets.'

Brady cannot regret something he had no control over. Unlike others, he did not run for home; he moved to just-promoted Sampdoria, then to Inter, then Ascoli.

'I probably played better football at Sampdoria than at Juventus. We won our first three games [Juve, Inter, Roma], we were top. We fell away to mid-table. It would have been a Leicester City story. I played well the following season as well, so much so that I'd Inter, Roma and AC Milan all wanting me.'

He moved to Inter in 1984: 'The regrets I have are that we didn't win the league with Inter when we had the team to do it. Rummenigge, Altobelli, Ferri, Zenga, Pepe Baresi, Bergomi. We had a real team. We should have won at least one title and we should have won the UEFA Cup – we were beaten by Real Madrid twice in two semi-finals.

'Then when I was leaving Inter I should have waited. But I went to Ascoli and that's my big regret. Not because of the place or the people, but the president was a rogue. Apart from Ascoli, it was brilliant. The first four years were particularly good, winning two league titles. I went on a bit of a wing and a prayer and it turned out great.'

Seven years Brady stayed in Italy. He was anything but the wrong foreigner.

LOUISE QUINN – SWEDEN

'WE WON 4-1 BUT, OH, I HAD A TERRIBLE GAME. THE BALL WAS *bouncing off me, going everywhere. Our coach didn't think that, he thought we were playing like the Harlem Globetrotters. But the nerves really got to me. Thankfully it turned out to be the start of a really successful season.'*

Louise Quinn is looking back at her debut for a club called Eskilstuna United in the second division of Swedish women's football. It was April 2013, Quinn was 22, and she felt a long way from Wicklow and Peamount United.

By the time she left, four seasons later, Eskilstuna had come a close second in the top division and played in the Champions League. Louise Quinn was described in Swedish newspapers as 'fundamental', 'a defensive rock' and 'a real servant who didn't miss a minute's play.' There were 324 locals at her home debut; two years later when Eskilstuna played Goteborg, there were 6,300 at the club's Tunavallen stadium.

The attendance spike is why in Sweden they refer to 'the phenomenon of Eskilstuna', a small city west of Stockholm where the women's football team is more popular than the men's. Quinn, who started out as a seven year-old playing for Blessington Boys, became a significant part of that. As they said, fundamental.

'It was exciting, it was the unknown, the second tier of Swedish football,' Quinn says. 'In the first couple of home games there were only two or three hundred people there but we kept grinding out wins and the club kept pushing it off the pitch, they were really good at promoting it. We'd be on social media, attending events around the town, going to schools, I've been standing in a thunderstorm at a shopping centre handing out leaflets. The people in the town felt we cared about them.'

The town responded, enabling a club formed in 2002 to sign and sustain players such as Quinn on full-time contracts. That in turn gave her a taste of professionalism and the knowledge that she could make a career, economically, from the growing interest in the women's game.

The thought had entered Quinn's mind seriously in 2011, when Peamount had made it to the Champions League and faced Paris St-Germain.

'Getting through to that stage was massive for Peamount,' Quinn says, 'but when you got there you saw the standard, where the rest of Europe was and where Ireland was. It was a bit of a reality check. It was about fitness and technique but also about the coaching structure around you. We did compete with PSG but in the end their fitness told. It was then that I started to think: 'Could I go abroad? Would I be good enough?"

*

THERE WERE COACHES IN IRELAND WHO WOULD HAVE ANSWERED Quinn in the affirmative. This after all was a defender capped at Under-17 level when she was 14. Or as Quinn puts it: '14 going-on 15 – I was a very large 14 year-old.' She became a full Ireland international at 17.

But Quinn had doubts. When asked if playing U-17 football at 14 was not a sign of talent, she answers: 'Well, Yes and No.' She had not been on the same school-system route that other girls in the international set-ups had come through. Plus, at 15, she fractured a hip and was out for ten months.

Furthermore, Quinn's mother Jacinta and father John, a Co. Wicklow Gaelic footballer, were eager for their third daughter of three sisters to complete her education. Quinn did that, getting a degree from University College Dublin in Sports and Exercise Management.

The emphasis on study, while playing for Peamount, meant that it was only when her degree was ending that Quinn used the video technology of FAI performance analyst Gerard Dunne at the course in Carlow to create a highlights package. A friend with an agent in the women's game had suggested this. That was, Quinn says, 'around November-December 2012'. By February 2013 she was signing a one-year full-time contract with Eskilstuna.

'Transfers aren't massive in women's football and there wasn't a lot of head-hunting five years ago,' she says. 'I was told Eskilstuna was a good club, an up-and-coming club that wanted to push on. They were in the second tier, but I thought that might be a good starting point for me. 'Will I like it?' 'Will I be good enough?'

'What helped was that a friend from Peamount, Vaila Barsley, was also joining.

She's a centre-back as well and we were thinking: 'Do they need two?' But she's similar, about 6ft, loves defending, heading the ball, we became a partnership. I was just very excited and my Mum and Dad were brilliant. My Dad always says: 'Any opportunity, take it."

A wage coming in, accommodation provided, Quinn endeavoured to settle into a full-time regime where a squad of 16-18 players trained every day. She was to make it work, but there were moments of hesitation along the way. The first day, for example.

'There was about a foot and a half of snow and I was thinking: 'Where am I? There were even some Swedes who hadn't heard of Eskilstuna United. And the first session was in the gym and I wasn't very educated in that, not like the Swedes who do some of that in school. Sweden is a very fit and healthy nation. It was a bit daunting all right and the snow stuck around for two or three months. But when we got on the pitch, I felt a lot more comfortable.'

Quinn experienced the long, deep, dark Swedish winter in which Eskilstuna would train in minus 18 temperatures – 'Oh, yeah, frozen eyelashes, frozen hair, and I still had that Irish reluctance to wear proper clothes.'

But something was coming together at Eskilstuna United. They won promotion in Quinn's first season and then finished a respectable seventh in the top flight in her second season. In her third, Eskilstuna finished just a point behind Rosengard, an established power in Sweden's women's game.

'When we were getting promoted people started coming and just clung onto it,' Quinn says of the effect on the population – around 70,000.

'It was the most successful team in Eskilstuna and people were enjoying what we were doing. As more fans came, the more we said: 'Let's keep this up.' The stadium was shared with two men's teams and had about 6,000 seats. We'd some great wins after promotion and we'd some local players, which helps. In the third season, when we finished second, we should have won it. But we didn't have the experience, nerves kicked in and we'd a tough run-in. We felt the pressure, even the coach. And Rosengard, on paper, they'd the bigger names.'

One of those Rosengard names was Marta, the Brazilian regarded as the greatest-ever female footballer.

Second place in 2015 meant Champions League football in 2016, however, and Eskilstuna beat Glasgow City, then faced Wolfsburg. Those were two different propositions, the Germans playing at a higher level altogether. The 3-0 defeat at Wolfsburg was Quinn's last game for Eskilstuna.

It was November 2016. She had signed one-year contracts and at the end of that fourth season, Quinn sat down to reflect on where she was in her career. She was 25 and could see money being invested in the French league, the English league. She had just seen the standard of German football.

There was an itch. She could speak some Swedish but found that when she tried to do so in social circles, the replies were in English. The coaching sessions were also held in English.

'I know the language but I'm not fluent in it. The club didn't make me learn it and I wasn't massive into languages at school because of the form of dyslexia I have. I found that tough, I'd have Swedes saying: 'Why don't you know the language yet?'

'I found it tough to make friends outside football and I do like to have that, so I'm not thinking about football all the time. I'd a good social circle in Ireland. And the Swedish winters are long and they're just dark and grey before the snow comes in January and February.'

Another unexpected thing Quinn noticed was that Swedes constantly called her British, not Irish. There would be media references to her and Barsely such as 'the two British centre-backs were dominant'. Barsley was unperturbed – she is English – but Quinn was bemused.

'I'm still educating them on Ireland. They always called me British and when I said: 'I'm Irish', they'd say, well, you come from the British Isles. I told them that was old-school geography.'

Quinn's personal geography was about to change. A 'homebird', she flew back to Ireland, then heard about an offer from Notts County in England's Women's Super League.

'Sweden definitely shaped me as a player. I was learning the whole time, new formations, training every day. I had given every ounce I had to the team but I needed a new challenge. I just took a chance on Notts Co.'

If Eskilstuna United was a risk that paid off, a new experience in another part of the world, Notts Co. was a blast of a different kind of reality. Two days before they were due to play Arsenal in the 2017 WSL season opener, the squad was called to Meadow Lane and informed the club had been liquidated.

'It was brutal,' Quinn says. 'I knew a little bit about the club, that there was a new owner and that they'd signed the likes of myself and re-signed the girls already there. But when we got a text to tell us to be at the ground the next day for 11, that training was cancelled – not re-scheduled, cancelled – then you fear the worst. And it was the worst. There was a lot of anger, tears, it was very confusing. Some girls even asked if we would still be playing on the Sunday. 'No, this is it.''

Because of what happened next, Quinn feels conflicted. She feels most for the players who had settled, arranged places to live and planned their lives around Notts

Co. But when she called her agent, she was told that Arsenal were looking for a centre-half and she was it. A week after Notts Co. folded Quinn was on the bench for Arsenal.

'I did have mixed emotions. I felt bad – I was with Arsenal and we were supposed to be playing them. I'm glad the majority of the Notts Co. girls got sorted.'

*

IT WAS NOT THE ONLY TIME IN 2017 THAT QUINN CAME ACROSS A major obstacle to progress in women's football, it is just that she and her Irish colleagues were not anticipating that it would come from the Football Association of Ireland.

But in April, the Irish squad was at their trade union offices in Dublin in a united display concerning the pay and conditions on offer from the FAI. At a time when the Association might have been expected to be promoting the women's game, there was inadequate provision of basics such as training kit and no compensation for loss of earnings. 'Fifth-class citizens', was how the solicitor representing the Professional Footballers' Association of Ireland put it.

The squad had addressed the FAI privately and Quinn says 'we thought it was sorted out without us having to go through the media'.

But it was not. So the Irish squad found themselves staging a press conference at the SIPTU HQ to air their grievances. They did not know what the public reaction would be, but it was positive.

Structurally, women's and girls' football in Ireland is young. It needs organizational assistance. Understandably, the women's national team think this should be offered, not something they have to coerce from the governing body with a public display in Liberty Hall.

'We thought people might think we were just moaning,' Quinn says. 'But it had an impact. We just felt far behind other countries and how they're treated, and we put in a lot of work to get to that day. There were specific issues but there is also the general feeling that the FAI don't utilise us and we are very willing to promote the game.

'There are some young girls coming through and they give you a real energy and we have a new manager in Colin Bell who is giving us a belief. There is some infrastructure. But we have to keep building. In no way will we accept a step backwards. The stuff I learned in Sweden about self-promotion, it's that you have to keep pushing.'

PART IV

INTERNATIONALISM

REPUBLIC OF IRELAND 1968-72
NORTHERN IRELAND 1971-75
REPUBLIC OF IRELAND 1986-96
LINFIELD 1988-1992

LOSING

'IN 1970 WE PLAYED POLAND IN A FRIENDLY IN POZNAN. THEY BEAT us 2-1. Three days later we play West Germany, as it was then, in West Berlin. We go by train. The best part of it was that we ended up sitting on our suitcases in the carriages where the post was. I'm not joking. And we're playing West Germany in the Olympic Stadium. The FAI expected us to adhere to that. We were either stupid or so much in love with football that we tried to make a laugh of it. You had to, otherwise you'd have jumped off the train in east Berlin and stayed there. That's how bad it was.'

Paddy Mulligan was unsurprised that after travelling in a Polish train's post-room, Ireland lost in west Berlin. Then again, losing was not something that shocked Irish players in 1970.

These defeats in Poznan and Berlin were the eleventh and twelfth games in a sequence of 20 – from 1968 to 1972 – when the Republic of Ireland failed to win any game anywhere, and anyone trying to assess where southern Irish football was approaching 50 years of independence, could have been persuaded that, collectively, it had stalled.

There were still good players at the best clubs in England, there was still talent coming through junior clubs and the League of Ireland, which was still popular, and in Jackie Carey there was a former hero player, who had been doing an excellent job as manager of Nottingham Forest. In 1965 Forest finished fifth in the First Division in England. Two years later they finished second and reached the FA Cup semi-final.

Since 1955 Carey had also been the 'manager' of the Republic of Ireland yet by 1967 when he stepped aside, there was no real sense of a 'Carey era'. In fact, certainly among the players, the sense was one of drift caused by bureaucratic amateurism, complacency and in the description of Eamon Dunphy: 'The age-old Irish trait of cronyism.'

There was, too, clearly a feeling that Carey, if he shared players' obvious disillusion, did not want to make a fight of it. But then he had other jobs, daily jobs such as managing Blackburn Rovers, Everton and Orient before Forest and when Carey landed in Dublin for internationals, it was not as a manager in the terms he recognised at club level.

Carey was in the Dalymount Park dressing room before kick-off giving instruction and on the touchline during games, but he did not select the squad or pick the team. He may have been consulted on personnel now and again but that selection process remained the remit of the FAI committee. As such, Carey's management was one of light-touch regulation and well before it ended, it both puzzled and frustrated many players.

Carey was not unaware of his limited input. Paid on a match-fee basis like the players, and paid the same amount, he turned down his fee for one of his first games, against West Germany in Hamburg, due to the lack of time he had been able to give to preparation.

The FAI, seeing the inspirational effect Peter Doherty was beginning to have north of the border – though it took time – had hoped for something similar. Instead there were heavy defeats in 1958 and 1962 World Cup qualifiers against England, Scotland and Czechoslovakia and facing Spain for a place at the 1966 World Cup, Dunphy said Carey forgot the name of a newly called-up player, Eric Barber of Shelbourne.

'Eh, eh, I'm sorry I've forgotten your name,' Dunphy recalled Carey saying to Barber. '"We'll call you Paddy." Again unsurprisingly, Dunphy added: 'A wave of embarrassment swept through the room.'

In *Boys in Green*, Sean Ryan quoted Shay Brennan on Carey: 'It was not what he said, it was what he did not say that disappointed me. I thought he was big enough in the game to have told the FAI that he was going to pick his own team.'

Noel Cantwell's observation was of the same tone: 'He [Carey] was a great father figure for the national team, but we probably needed a more aggressive coach and a stronger personality at the time. I wanted to change things and went to him with ideas, but he did not always back the players. Maybe he thought it was too much trouble. We couldn't even get a decent bus from the Gresham to Dalymount. That wouldn't bother him, but it bothered me.'

Ryan's dispassionate conclusion was that Carey was 'a passive servant of the FAI' and there seems to have been no awareness within the FAI that seemingly small-time details such as the state of the team bus actually affect players' keenness and professional pride.

For the first game after Carey left – Czechoslovakia in Dublin in May 1967 in a

European Championship qualifier – Charlie Hurley was appointed player-manager on an extra £20. The Czechs won 2-0 in front of an estimated 6,000. There would be no Irishmen going to Italy for the 1968 Euro finals. The Irish public were not being roused.

There was one group game left, that November in Prague. It was won, 2-1, Turlough O'Connor scoring a late winner. It was to be the last Irish winner for nearly five years.

Not until Don Givens scored in June 1972 against Iran in Brazil in the 'mini World Cup' would the Republic of Ireland win a match again.

Givens had made his debut in 1969. He was a 19 year-old striker with Manchester United and would go on to play for ten years in the First Division, mainly with QPR. An Old Trafford colleague, Tony Dunne, was in that Ireland team, as was Shay Brennan, the first player to use his parents' birthplace to play for the Republic of Ireland. Mick Meagan had won a League title with Everton in 1963 and was still playing. Joe Kinnear was a regular at Tottenham, Paddy Mulligan was to join Chelsea, Steve Heighway was coming through at Liverpool and John Giles was dictating the tempo at Leeds United. As Mulligan says: 'We'd decent players. There was nucleus of a decent team.'

But when, for example, 1970 World Cup qualifying Group 2 is reviewed, it is alarming. Fourth in a four-team group, Ireland lost five of six matches and drew one. They scored three goals. Nostalgia tempts every nation into sometimes florid reflection; here the facts counter that. This was the stuff of minnows.

'You must remember,' Mulligan adds, 'the team was being picked by committee people from the FAI. With respect to them, they had absolutely no idea of what a team should contain. We were completely disorganised. There was no manager. Johnny Carey had been there, but in name only.'

On his debut against the Czechs in 1969, Mulligan was told to play left back: 'I hadn't played left back in years. The Czechs loved it. I wanted so much to play for Ireland and then this. Total disorganization. I couldn't believe what I'd just gone through. It was at Dalymount and my Dad was there. Any player from that era will say the same thing. It wasn't doing any of us favours.'

Matches were organised for Sundays and players in England would often arrive on Saturday nights after playing for their club sides, or on Sunday morning. Then there was the League of Ireland quotient. There always seemed to be at least one local player chosen by the committee and if the theory behind this was well-meaning, the reality was that part-time players were being asked to step up into international football.

'I made my debut against Austria [in 1971],' says Noel Campbell. 'I was a St. Pat's player still. The League of Ireland season was over, over quite a while. I was working in Smithfield and I'd not been training for a couple of weeks and then I got a call to say I was selected. It wasn't from the FAI. Can you believe it?

'I got picked because Billy McCormack from St Pat's was a big shot in the FAI. God love him, he hadn't a clue. But that's the way it was.'

Eventually the frustration got to John Giles. Dropped by the committee for the qualifier in Denmark, Giles, Dunphy and a few other senior players sent a letter to the FAI seeking the appointment of a manager. This was 1969, not 1929.

Politically, Giles and the players were smart, saying the committee could still pick the squad but the manager would choose the team. The FAI agreed and Meagan was given the job. He is considered the first full-time Republic of Ireland manager.

But Meagan's impact was limited. He took charge of just twelve games and nine of them were lost, none won. In came Liam Tuohy. Tuohy requested matches be played on Wednesdays to allow for some squad preparation and he visited managers in England to try to persuade them to release players. In the past there had been repeated late 'injuries'.

Yet Tuohy's first match, October 1971, was on a Sunday in Austria. One player based in England was available – Mulligan. Austria won 6-0 and Noel Dunne of the *Irish Independent* wrote that the 'debacle marked Liam Tuohy's introduction to the unique horrors of Irish international football management.'

As Mulligan says: 'Some organization, eh? Lunacy. Liam Tuohy's first match. Thanks very much.'

If that was a low, this turned out to be the last in the losing sequence. Ireland were a late call-up to the mini World Cup In Brazil in 1972 and if overcoming Iran 2-1 is not the stuff of Irish dreams, after what the squad had been through in previous years, victory was greeted with gusto. A week later Ireland beat Ecuador.

'Iran and Ecuador, from where we were coming from, that was of paramount importance,' Mulligan says. 'We were acutely aware of the record, we knew as people. 'We've lost again.' That's all I needed to know. I didn't need to count the number.

'You're questioning your ability: are we good enough to compete at international level? You're questioning yourself. And you're representing the people of Ireland, not just yourself.

'I knew Liam Tuohy would be great, and he was. Tuohy makes a difference, no question. The FAI stumbled across it. In Brazil we were training on one side of the pitch and the blazers were over on the other side. Liam turned to us and said: 'We've a love-hate relationship. They love me and I hate them.' The lads creased up, this was the first time we'd heard it.

'There was no more cheating, which there was in my early Ireland days when there was no manager. Players wouldn't chase back, wouldn't make themselves available. Liam Tuohy, and Mick Meagan before him, they changed things. Irish football owes Liam Tuohy so much. Liam Tuohy owes Ireland nothing.'

Unfortunately for Tuohy, when qualifying began for the World Cup in 1974, Giles and Mulligan were injured and QPR refused permission for Givens to play against USSR. Terry Conroy, a Stoke City regular in the First Division, scored in a 2-1 loss, and Conroy scored in the next match. This was against France – it was a tough group – and for the first time since 1966 Ireland had won a game in Dublin.

It was 15 November 1972 – a Wednesday – and Sean Ryan writes of 'raised expectations', adding: 'so Tuohy's announcement on 1 December that he was resigning came as a bombshell. He had revived the team but he was also manager of Shamrock Rovers and a sales manager with HB Ice Cream and was over-committed.'

Ray Treacy said that Tuohy in his ten games in charge had at the very least 'set a pattern of play' and was the first to do so.

'Even in the midst of all this mayhem, the starting point of the next era was there,' says Mulligan.

Tuohy's departure ushered in the era of Giles, a new seriousness, coherence and near misses rather than apologies. In 1974, qualifying for Euro 76 began. In Dublin it brought a 3-0 victory over the USSR. There was a Givens hat-trick and a debut from 18 year-old Liam Brady.

It was, according to the great Irish sportswriter Con Houlihan: 'The Republic's greatest sporting occasion since the grey day at Cheltenham with nibs of snow in the wind when Arkle stormed past the 'invincible' Mill House and won his first Gold Cup … Ireland's albatross around the neck is the national sense of inferiority; at Dalymount yesterday the men in green shattered that.'

'John Giles had been brought up with managers saying: 'Let's keep the score down, lads,' a lot of the time,' says Brady. 'Giles said, no, if we're organized and play the way I know we can play, then there's no reason why we can't get good results. That game was a statement in itself. A lot of that Soviet team played for Dynamo Kiev then, who won the Cup Winners' Cup that season. Oleg Blokhin played in that game. He was European Footballer of the Year [1975]. They were top-notch.

'John was a real teacher, I loved playing with him and was so disappointed when he left. He was dealing with amateurs, the Football Association of Ireland. They got even more amateurish when Eoin Hand became manager because Eoin didn't have the same strong personality and knowledge as John.'

Instead of filing in fourth, the Republic of Ireland came second in that 1976 qualifying group, but while there were good players, and some very good, they were not there in the volume required when injuries or suspensions happen.

In this circumstance, organization on and off the pitch becomes even more important. But as Brady, Mulligan and the others all say, the casual, self-serving bureaucracy meant for the players there was often an energy-sapping struggle even before the first whistle blew. Players felt undone by the blazer culture of complacency and perks.

There have been times when Irish football, north and south, has been emasculated by the country around it; but there have also been times when the sheer folly of those allegedly governing the game have arrested its development. The FAI were creating a pool of player resentment that would ripple down the decades.

As Noel Campbell says: 'The players were well ahead of the organization, absolutely.'

LOSS

ON 23 OCTOBER 1971 GEORGE BEST STEPPED OUT ONTO THE PITCH at St. James' Park, Newcastle upon Tyne. One of football's standard phrases is 'target man' and, on this day, Best was one.

He was 24 and producing what turned out to be one of the last sustained bursts of his extraordinary talent. Manchester United were top of the First Division, freshly invigorated by the arrival that summer of 1971 of Corkman Frank O'Farrell as manager.

Best scored ten goals in United's first 13 league games. O'Farrell, not a man prone to exaggeration, would later say his brilliant, wayward lad from Belfast was a 'genius' who at Old Trafford was 'covering up a multitude of sins'.

On this afternoon on Tyneside it was Best who was exposed. The previous day a newspaper office in London had received a telephone call from someone purporting to be from the IRA. Their message was that if Best played at St. James' Park, he would be shot.

The police, Manchester United and Best had no option but to take the threat seriously. The background was that an hour from England, in Best's home city of Belfast a quasi civil war was in full bloody flow.

On the morning of the match at Newcastle, the news bulletins brought reports that two sisters, Dorothy Maguire and Maura Meehan, had been shot dead by the British Army on Cape Street off the Falls Road. The sisters, it transpired, were members of *Cumann na mBan*, and were the first female IRA members killed in the Troubles. Few knew that as the reports rumbled in.

Northern Ireland was unravelling. Later the same day three men were shot dead by the British Army in Newry while trying to rob a bank. October 1971 was a grim month; there were 33 murders across Northern Ireland.

Best was already concerned about his family's safety on the Cregagh estate in east Belfast. It had been rumoured that Best had contributed to Ian Paisley's new Democratic Unionist Party. It was a report Best scoffed at, but he knew others might think it was true.

The DUP had been formed on the last day of September 1971 following an IRA bomb which killed two men in the Four Step Inn on the Shankill Road in Belfast. Twenty-seven people were badly injured, some whom had just returned from Windsor Park where Linfield had lost 3-2 to Standard Liege in the first round of the European Cup.

Best denied any donation, and always denied it. He came from a Protestant background but he was no Unionist evangelist. 'Utter rubbish,' he wrote 30 years later, still indignant. But not even George Best could body-swerve the era gathering at home.

'The Troubles in Belfast had moved on from the drums-and-cakes marches which I had known as a kid,' he said, 'and before our game at Newcastle in October 1971 someone claiming to represent the IRA told police that I would be shot if I played. I was under enough pressure as it was.'

Best telephoned his father, Dickie. 'It's probably only a crank,' he said.

'You can't be sure of that,' Dickie replied.

O'Farrell offered Best a route out. Best's response was: 'I couldn't not play. Otherwise where would it all end? There could be death threats every week.'

So now Best was lying on the aisle of the Manchester United team bus as it travelled from the Swallow Hotel in Newcastle to St. James' Park. Best, with police outside his room, had eaten alone on the Friday evening and the mood in the camp was not improved when it was revealed the team bus had been broken into overnight. 'I suppose this is the work of one of your Irish mates,' one of the players said jokingly to Best.

It was decided that four plain clothes policemen should be on board the bus too. As Best got off at the ground the four gathered around him.

O'Farrell was quoted in the local paper, on the streets at lunchtime, saying: 'It is probably a hoax.' The headline read: 'Best gets bodyguard after threat'.

The report was below another about clashes in Newcastle that morning between 'gangs of skinheads' going to the match. The third front-page headline was: 'Sisters shot in Ulster'.

There must have been some atmosphere in Newcastle. The home team had played at St. James' the previous Saturday against Crystal Palace in front of 21,000; now there were 56,000 inside the ground. There were also forty extra police, some stationed on the rooftops of the buildings which overlooked the stadium in those days.

When the match kicked off, Best said: 'I couldn't really get it out of my head that maybe this time the whole thing was real. I was definitely nervous for a while. I never stopped moving on the field. Somehow I felt that I should not stand still. Even when there was someone on the floor injured I kept running around.'

This was not long after Best had moved from Manchester into his designer house in Blossoms Lane in leafy Cheshire and visiting him there the following week, Hugh McIlvanney wrote of the contrast between 'lungfuls of country air' and 'the lunacy of Ulster ... was like finding a piece of shrapnel in your cornflakes.'

At St. James' Park the game had finished 1-0 to Manchester United. The scorer was George Best. In the post-match press conference, Newcastle's manager Joe Harvey said: 'I wish they had shot the little bugger.'

*

TEN DAYS EARLIER, IN BELFAST, NORTHERN IRELAND HAD PLAYED A European Championship qualifier against the USSR. This was a game George Best was also due to play in, but he missed it. Terry Neill did not think this was coincidence.

Sitting in his London office 45 years after the match, Neill is still wary about going into detail.

'Belfast, then?' he asks, 'you wanted eyes in the back of your head going into the ground and coming away. It was a daily occurrence. My mother was blown over in a blast. She was frail. You were uncomfortable and you were unsure because you never knew where or when anything was going to come from. You felt OK in the compound of the ground because you knew there'd be a big security presence. But for George, George was the obvious target, more than the rest of us. Who knows what's going to happen?'

The game, an afternoon kick-off, ended 1-1. The point maintained the USSR's grip on Group 4 ahead of Spain. The Soviet team would go on to lose the final of Euro 1972 to West Germany in Brussels.

The significance for the Irish players, the Irish FA and the Irish fans was greater and longer though. This match marked the end of one era and the sombre beginnings of another. October 1971 was the last time Northern Ireland would play in Belfast until 1975. Not for the first time, or the last, Irish history wrapped itself around and smothered Windsor Park.

Terry Neill was 29 then. He had had eleven seasons with Arsenal plus one at Hull

City as player-manager. Even at 28 Hull thought Neill was management material.

So did Northern Ireland. Billy Bingham had two spells as manager of his country, with the first, 1967-71, remembered less frequently than the later World Cup period from 1980 to 1993.

In Bingham's first match in 1967 Neill was his captain. When Bingham left, becoming manager of Greece, Neill was offered the job. He took it: at 29 Terry Neill was player-manager of Hull City and player-manager of Northern Ireland.

'I think now, 'how did I get through it?" Neill says. 'Two jobs.'

In May 1971 Hull City finished fifth in the Second Division. Neill's opinion is that he got 'the tail-end of a good Hull team', but the task at Boothferry Park was straightforward compared to what confronted him at international level.

'It was all rumbling privately before the Soviet Union game,' he says. 'The IFA did the best it could, a lot of countries were starting to get worried, to rumble a bit, and we could understand it. The safety of other teams in Belfast could not be guaranteed. As players, we all realised we couldn't play in Belfast.

'The IFA worked closely with the security forces, but what could they guarantee? The Troubles loomed over us. We'd a couple of security men from the RUC with us, who travelled on the bus from the hotel to games. They integrated into the squad right away, just became part of it. It was tragic, but one, I won't give his name – he'd a young family – he was blown up leaving home.

'And you just … I'm so proud of Northern Ireland but this was so painful. It was heartbreaking. Everywhere we went people were asking us: 'What's happening over in your place? Have they all gone mad?' It was becoming regular, and you never get used to it. We've all known people who were involved in it – the victims.'

Northern Ireland had one last qualifier to play. It was home to Spain and scheduled for November. But Belfast was coming apart, and so the game was postponed. In the other seven Euro 72 groups all qualifiers were completed by November or early December, but in Belfast early December 1971 brought the McGurk's Bar atrocity in which 15 Catholics were killed by a loyalist bomb. The decision was made that Northern Ireland would fulfil their outstanding fixture somewhere else. It would be mid-February 1972 before it was played.

'Once we made the decision that we couldn't play home games at home,' Neill says, 'we just had to go on the road. We were the gypsies of international football. Then we had to start pulling in favours from people who were sympathetic to our situation.'

Neill's chairman at Hull City, Harold Needler, had been in discussions with the IFA's Harry Cavan over Neill's managerial positions. The two men had formed a working relationship. It was via this contact that Northern Ireland held their last 'home' Euro 72 qualifier at Boothferry Park, Hull. It was against Spain and Best did turn up for this one.

'George was late into Hull – late,' Neill says with emphasis. 'George had become *George* by then. But the strength of George Best showed in him still going out to play.'

Best's involvement was one consideration for Neill. Another was his reference to Northern Ireland as 'Ireland', commonplace among men of Neill's generation.

'I'd been quoted in the paper referring to ourselves as 'Ireland' and some nutcase – subsequently traced and arrested – started sending me little parcels with wire showing. It was amateur, but I'd to call the police in. There were wee notes too. They were directed to me at Boothferry Park. So for a month or so I had to have a reflector under the car and every now and again the coppers at the ground and at my home.

'You can dismiss it as 'just some nutter', but we'd just had our first two kids. It wasn't funny for my wife Sandra, with two young kids, one and three. But then, life goes on. They showed me how to activate the mirror.

'They found him, he was a sympathiser I think, but a bit off-key. A few others here and there said: 'We're gonna shoot you.' You become more aware of things – the word 'shoot'. You had to keep telling yourself that the world doesn't stop, my life doesn't stop. But it's there in your mind.'

*

NORTHERN IRELAND DREW 1-1 WITH SPAIN IN HULL. 'THE HULL PUBLIC were brilliant,' Neill says, 'it's not every day you get Spain playing at Boothferry Park, or George Best.'

The next game was due to be against Scotland in Belfast in the Home Championships, but the game was held in Glasgow. Northern Ireland were to play Scotland ten times in the 1970s and all bar the 1970 game were in Glasgow.

The draw for the 1974 World Cup qualifying campaign had the Irish in with Bulgaria, Portugal and Cyprus. Having played Bulgaria in Sofia and Cyprus in Nicosia, Northern Ireland hosted Portugal in March 1973 – in Coventry.

The first two matches had been lost but this was a 1-1, Martin O'Neill scoring his first Northern Ireland goal, Eusebio equalising with a late penalty. There were 11,000 at Highfield Road and when the next home qualifier came in May, there were 6,000 at Craven Cottage. Northern Ireland beat Cyprus 3-0 but this was a team on the margins of Europe. When the third home game in the four-team group was played that September, it was in front of the vast terraces of Hillsborough. There were only 6,000 at that game too. Isolated, needless to say, Northern Ireland did not qualify.

Neill had invited a special guest to address the squad before the Bulgaria game. Neill had first been called up in 1961, aged 18, to play Italy in Bologna. Neill had just swapped Bangor in the Irish League for Arsenal. Giovanni Trapattoni played for Italy. The Northern Ireland manager then, still, was Peter Doherty.

'We'd play occasional games and Peter was still the best player to my mind,' Neill says, and a dozen years on Neill had remained in touch. 'During our nomadic years I invited him to see us play, it was Bulgaria in Sheffield. I was thinking: 'What could I do?' I wrote to Peter and asked him to come and see us, stay for a couple of days. I've still got his letter back. Two or three pages. He thanked me – Peter Doherty thanking me.

'Peter being Peter, self-effacing, he came to the hotel and said a few words. It wasn't fire and brimstone, but he re-ignited the fire, he reminded people they were playing for their country. It was delivered in a level manner, but the message got through.'

A 0-0 draw in front of so few at Hillsborough will have saddened Doherty, just as it dismayed so many, although Neill stresses the help and goodwill received from clubs such as Sheffield Wednesday and Fulham: 'It has to be said these people couldn't have done more.

'That needs to be said. In all those games, the ovations we got were tremendous. The Coventry game, Eusebio said: 'I'm sorry we're not in Belfast.' The Spanish players were the same, and the Bulgaria players and the Cypriot players, they were all sympathetic. The football fans in all of those cities and grounds were brilliantly supportive. We were very welcome everywhere except home.

'The players, we were looking for a ray of sunshine in a tragic situation and the camaraderie was it. When we were the nomads, the togetherness got us through. It certainly felt an added bit of a burden to perform well. We'd always say: 'Give the people back at home something to cheer about.' That wasn't always easy. Well, maybe not a burden, but an extra responsibility.

'We were well aware of it. We'd all been through the euphoria of victory and the despair of defeat but this was not just a question of being happy with a win. What's going to happen to our country? Are things going to get better or go down the tubes?'

In the British Home Championships, there were Irish home games at Goodison Park against England and Wales and when qualification began for Euro 76, Northern Ireland's first two matches were arranged in Oslo and Stockholm.

The latter match in Sweden, won 2-0 by the Irish, was the eighteenth consecutive game staged away from home. It was October 1974. The next qualifier was scheduled for mid-April 1975 against Yugoslavia. The venue given to UEFA was Belfast.

'It was on a knife-edge all the time,' Neill says. 'The temperature was always being taken, the IFA were just trying to keep the door open, lobbying, no demands. They couldn't hold a pistol to anyone's head. We just didn't know when it would end.'

But against Yugoslavia, on a Wednesday afternoon, assured by the IFA, the British Army and the RUC, Northern Ireland's international isolation did end. Appointed manager of Tottenham, the victory in Sweden was Neill's last match in charge. He handed over to Dave Clements, who at 29 was playing for Everton.

What returning home meant to the players as well as the 26,000 at Windsor Park could be seen before kick-off. Northern Ireland's team came out first and formed a guard of honour for the Yugoslavs. In their green tracksuits, they applauded the visitors onto the pitch with the entire ground joining the reception. Yugoslavia were seen as brave men travelling to this Balkanised corner of Europe.

'That was emotional,' Neill says. 'I went because I just wanted to be there for the return. I didn't go to the team hotel or anything. The applause was mainly Dave's idea. He said: 'What do you think?' It was right and proper. I think there was a feeling all around beginning to creep in, fingers crossed, that as a society we were beginning to see some daylight. That was more important than winning football games. But football definitely helps, it definitely unites people and we were all beginning to hope.'

Bryan Hamilton's goal meant Northern Ireland defeated Yugoslavia and the team were back playing home games at home.

Four weeks later, England went to Windsor Park. It was one thing for the Yugoslavs to go to Belfast, it was another for England to take the risk. 'England wanted to make a statement,' Neill says. It was pithy: England flew in, played and flew back, all in the space of seven hours. One week on, Wales followed – Wales had been the first country to say they would return to Belfast.

Scotland made it over in 1980.

WINNING & CHANGE

'Ours is basically a hustling game. We play the ball in behind people, aiming to turn them all the time. We prefer to play the game in the other team's half of the field. If we get the ball behind full-backs, into the holes, one of our fellas will try to reach it first and if he does we'll support him wide and support him deep, creating productive triangles. Once we're in those hurtful positions there's nothing cut and dried – our fellas can be as imaginative as they like.'
Jack Charlton, The Observer, February 1990.

IT IS CALLED 'PRESSING' NOW. BACK THEN IAN RUSH HAD BEEN HAR-rying defenders for Liverpool for years. Jack Charlton called it hustling.

Charlton looked at the Republic of Ireland's last qualifier for the World Cup in 1986, a 4-1 loss at home to Denmark, and wondered how a team with players as gifted as Mark Lawrenson, Paul McGrath, Kevin Moran, David O'Leary, Liam Brady, Kevin Sheedy and Frank Stapleton could lose so heavily.

That was in November 1985. Charlton was an out-of-work manager. One month later, out of nowhere, the phone rang in his Northumberland home and four months on – late March 1986 – Charlton was at Lansdowne Road for a friendly against Wales in front of 16,500 half-curious, half-nervous, half-enthused people. 'Go Home Union Jack', read one banner.

It was only one, but it was evidence of a strand of opinion within Ireland. England, the English, had been in Dublin before and the Irish remembered.

By the end of his decade in Ireland, Charlton was credited with not only changing how Irish people felt about the Union Jack, but also about how Irish people felt about the Tricolour. John Givens, brother of Don, and a former League of Ireland player who became one of Charlton's advisors said: 'Nearly every house had one for Italia 90 and since then, if you have a flag in your house, no-one bats an eyelid. Before that, if you had the Irish flag outside your house, it had a totally different meaning. That was a significant change down to Jack.'

That is quite a claim – from someone close to Charlton. But it is not alone – authors such as Dermot Bolger and Roddy Doyle have written of their altered view of Ireland and Irishness prompted by Charlton's team. 'I was glad I was Irish, proud of it, I'd never felt that way before; I'd have been embarrassed to,' said Doyle of the draw against Holland at Italia 90. Others credit Charlton with a preparatory cultural role in the northern peace process; it is said, he was part of the origins of the Celtic Tiger. These are major extrapolations and some laugh at them, but what is generally accepted is that Charlton changed the atmosphere within southern Ireland between the GAA and soccer and he also changed the broad relationship between Ireland and England. Jack Charlton was more than a football manager.

Brian Kerr, one of those core Irish soccer men Charlton would look over the heads of, has reasons not to be generous about the Charlton era influence. But Kerr thinks it is a key period in the history of the Irish game and that qualification for Euro 88 was transformative.

'We were always struggling for acceptance, so it was very important for the credibility of soccer in Ireland,' Kerr says. 'We'd seen Northern Ireland in '82 and '86, but we'd never been to that top table. Now we were at the party and the Gaelic world understood where we were, the importance of it.

'It became acceptable for trenchant Gaelic people to be OK with supporting the soccer team. It was no longer the mortal sin. Before then there wasn't an understanding by the Gaelic people in Ireland of how Ireland might be seen abroad and that, actually, it might be negative and seen through the images coming out of the North.

'The fans travelling in large numbers and in good humour presented a different face. The football might not have been great, but this was different. Then you've the emergence of U2 as the biggest band in the world, you've Roddy Doyle, people like that. The football team is in there. Christy Moore – 'Joxer Goes to Stuttgart' – it summed up the emotion and the joy of it all. You don't know, maybe it did all help make doing business a little easier.

'Nah, it was very positive, and Houghton, Aldridge, Sheedy – there was an impact on the future. In France in 2016, look at the number of lads carrying Gaelic club bags, there to support the soccer.'

At the very least, as Niall Quinn says: 'The way Jack performed in the job and his public persona made us all feel better about ourselves.'

*

NONE OF THIS WAS ON CHARLTON'S AGENDA WHEN HE SUCCEEDED
Eoin Hand. Charlton's aim then was to re-organize a team that might at last qualify
for a tournament. Doubters were addressed with gruff conviction, there was energy,
drive and what John Giles called 'cussed determination'.

There was, simply, something new, even if in Jack Charlton, it seemed like
something old. After all, Giles had known Charlton a long time by 1986. The two
had been teammates at Leeds United in the 1960s and 1970s, a club Charlton had
joined as far back as 1950.

Charlton had something of that era about his appearance and spoke with the
experience and masculine authority of a man from that time. He had been part of
English football's world so long 'Big Jack' didn't require a surname. There was 1966
at Wembley, the 1970s impressing at Middlesbrough and by the mid-1980s he was
back in Newcastle upon Tyne, close to where he grew up in Ashington. He had
played with John Charles and managed Paul Gascoigne. Charlton had lived, no-one
questioned that.

He had walked away from St. James' Park four months earlier and if he never
worked again, people probably thought he had earned his rest. But Jack Charlton was
50, not 60, when the phone rang in Northumberland. He had plenty left.

He went to the World Cup in Mexico in the summer of 1986 as an FAI employee.
Belgium, Bulgaria and another opponent in the forthcoming Euro 88 group, Scotland,
were there. Charlton wanted to see the opposition but also observe international
football through the eyes of an international manager for the first time. And what
he saw was this: 'They all did exactly the same thing, all conformed to a pattern ...
everything went through midfield, every move had the primary objective of getting
the playmaker free.'

This was the international orthodoxy which on his return, Charlton wanted to
overturn. By being different, he thought, Ireland could join the gang.

His Irish squad had the capacity to play the accepted way – it had Liam Brady.
But in a country that had a lineage of Doherty, Carey, Blanchflower, Giles, Best,
O'Neill and Keane, as well as Brady, Charlton wanted their midfield/inside forward
territory bypassed. Kevin Sheedy protested, he wanted to play Evertonian football.
'This is not Everton,' he was told.

'We play the ball in behind people.'

It was a simplistic plan, but it was a plan. You could call it pragmatic – and people did; you could call it anti-football – and people did. It was the kind of football to make a Blanchflower wilt, but Charlton was honest about it – *'ours is basically a hustling game'* – and that bluntness, the refusal to be drawn into half-truth explanations, was part of his appeal. Especially as it worked.

It might have been by a narrow margin but when the Euro 88 draw was made, the Republic of Ireland were in Pot 3, behind Belgium and Bulgaria. When the group was done, Belgium and Bulgaria were behind the Republic of Ireland.

This had not been achieved before by this Ireland. Under an Englishman they had got to the finals, and it turned out that for swathes of the population who had not overly concerned themselves with Irish football, this was what it was about – getting there, being there. It wasn't about the football, or, to be more accurate, it wasn't just about the football.

*

IN THEIR FIRST-EVER GAME AT A TOURNAMENT, IRELAND PLAYED England. It was in Stuttgart in June 1988 and of the Irish starting XI, eight pre-dated Charlton. It would have been nine had Mark Lawrenson not been injured and it might have been ten if Liam Brady had not been injured. Both missed the tournament.

Ten men from previous eras – that would have been powerful evidence of Charlton's organizational and motivational abilities. As it was, he still had done more with the same resources, although he had added to those by recruiting second generation players and bringing them into the fold.

This was viewed sceptically at first, there was also hostility – and that was from within Ireland. But when Ray Houghton, the Glasgow-born son of a Donegal father, scored the goal that defeated England in Stuttgart, everyone agreed he was one of us and more.

Houghton plugged into one of the extra dimensions brought about by the Charlton era, 'the diaspora'. Diaspora joined Stuttgart in Irish soccer's new lexicon.

Niall Quinn was the youngest member of the squad and the most recent departure from Ireland. 'Stuttgart was a defining moment,' Quinn says, 'not only for the football team, but for the country. As players we started to believe we could hack it on the world stage and a bit of that belief, that feeling, made its way into Irish life.

'You could say the team was one of a few fuses that were all lit around the same time. In sport you'd Stephen Roche winning the Tour de France in '87, in politics there was a first woman President [Mary Robinson], and then there were cultural things such as U2, Roddy Doyle. Christy Moore had a hit with the song about Stuttgart.

'Sport, football paved the way. Jack Charlton was a seed, he changed a lot of Irish opinion about English people. At the start of the 1980s we'd the Hunger Strikes, that's an indelible moment. I was a teenager then and you wouldn't even tell people you had English cousins. A few years later an Englishman is idolised in the sitting rooms of Ireland.'

With hindsight, it seems like a process, but Quinn says there were no guarantees at the start – 'It wasn't straightforward. Before Jack really got going, lots of Irish people – and a lot of Irish football – weren't having him, at least not entirely.'

'It all changed when we beat Brazil in a friendly in Dublin [May 1987]. Liam Brady scored a great goal, Romario made his debut, and I know that changed how we felt in the squad but also on the street. Before then we'd be slagged by taxi drivers, now they were asking for autographs.'

After that result, 'our tolerance increased' Quinn says, 'and via television Jack entered Irish households with his blunt, humorous, at times passionate personality.'

The Charlton era was under way, and soon there was another social development presenting a different type of Irishness: the themed pub. In cities across Europe and beyond, themed Irishness took root. There are seven Irish bars in Stuttgart.

*

IN 1994 AS HOUGHTON SCORED ANOTHER CHARLTON-IRELAND milestone winner – against Italy in New Jersey at the World Cup – a young academic, Michael Holmes, was assessing the eight years and three finals of the Charlton era and writing about the beyond-soccer impact it had made.

Holmes had noticed 'a change in national identity' and that the Ireland around him was 'a more outward looking place. The isolation inherent in Gaelic games contrasts with the international outlook of football.'

Part of what Houghton, John Aldridge and Tony Cascarino represented was a shift in Irish understanding of that identity. They very word diaspora reflected that, conveying a larger image than the traditional term: emigration.

'In general, the football team's success has contributed to a far greater awareness and appreciation of the Irish diaspora,' Holmes said in 1994, and that this provided a picture that was 'more relevant and up to date than traditional Irish cultural depictions of emigration.'

Echoing what John Givens said about the Tricolour, Holmes also said: 'The team is the strongest symbol of a 26-county nation that has appeared.'

Twenty-two years on, Holmes had become a lecturer in History and Politics at

Hope University in Liverpool. How did 1994's view look from 2016?

'The debate starting in the 1980s is,' he says: 'Who are we? What are we? What is our place in the world?

'There was underlying social change taking place and sometimes the impact a cultural change can make is to re-enforce attitudes. What was happening with the whole Charlton era and the breakthrough of the football team into the national consciousness was a way of re-enforcing changing values and changing perceptions. What do we mean by a broader, outward-looking Ireland that could be successful? Oh, yeah, the football team.

'We now have more ways of celebrating our success internationally. We have a very successful rugby team – in that sense rugby has overtaken soccer. GAA has done a fantastic job of turning itself around from being inward-looking to trying to be as outward-looking as it can. So there's a different context. The soccer success in 1988, '90, was the first time we were putting ourselves on the world sporting stage. It was the breakthrough. Soccer has the global reach. It had a big impact within Ireland as well.

'Would we not have had a Celtic Tiger without Jackie Charlton? No, I think that's a bit too far. It's more in terms of social impact, attitude. Some of the Celtic Tiger boom was about being outward, open, expansive.

'The transformation to my mind is quite astonishing – divorce legislation, gay rights, the open, tolerant society, the tearing up of the implicit control of the Catholic church. You see a softening of the old intolerance. Pluralism is coming.

'Another part of changing Irish culture from the 80s going into the 90s is: 'We can't keep going around shooting each other.' That was reflected in the Good Friday referendum. The football team – and the fact it had to play Northern Ireland – was a reflection of a feeling that the reality is now: 'We still want a united Ireland but we need full consent.'

'I do think the Charlton era was significant in all this. But it wasn't the cause of it.'

What Holmes does believe Charlton changed, though, was the relationship the Irish Republic had with England.

'It doesn't change irrevocably but he changed how people felt about England, undoubtedly. There are others, it's broader than him, but I would struggle to think of any English person who's thought to have had the impact of Jack Charlton.

'His character suited the times, the context and the Irish people. There's a statue of him holding a salmon at Cork airport. For loads of Irish people he was a vision of an Englishman who wasn't stereo-typical – Army people, all out to get us.

'It is not that even the vast majority of people believed that, it's that they were not able to picture the alternative. Actually English people can be great craic. They like going for a pint, fishing, so do we. It normalised our approach.

'And it made us realise England's variety, that there's this great North-South thing in England. The Irish knew this in the back of our heads but Charlton made us think it consciously.'

*

IF NATIONAL IDENTITY IS A STATE OF MIND, THEN THAT MIND CAN be changed. Whether Jack Charlton was a catalyst, or one of several, is debated. Certainly his arrival coincides with changes in Irish society, of which the decline of the Catholic church, the rise of free market economics – the Celtic Tiger – and the IRA and Loyalist ceasefires, are the greatest.

To place a football man in this context can sound overblown but football is all part of society's weather and in Belfast there are two other footballers mentioned when the subject of Charlton's societal significance comes up: Tony Coly and Dessie Gorman.

Early in the summer of 1988 the Linfield manager Roy Coyle was at a trial match near Paris looking at possible future signings. Coyle saw two he liked and they would cost nothing in fees, just wages and accommodation. One was Antoine 'Tony' Coly from Senegal, the other was Abdeli 'Sam' Khammal from Morocco. Coyle spoke to the Linfield board. They gave him the go-ahead. He signed both.

Back in Belfast, Coyle went out to buy his morning paper when he saw a billboard: 'Linfield Sign Catholic'. He wondered who the board had been buying without his consent. It turned out to be Tony Coly.

'I didn't know he was a Catholic,' Coyle says. 'I was looking at a player in France, I was hardly going to ask him what school he went to in Senegal. People weren't bothered that he was black, it was that he was Catholic. I got abuse, oh yeah. But I still played him.'

Historically Linfield had signed Catholics – Waterford-born Davy Walsh joined Linfield from Limerick in the mid-1940s. But since Walsh, and with the onset of the religious division of Belfast by the Troubles, the possibility dwindled as attitudes hardened.

'To my knowledge,' says Coyle, 'in the Linfield constitution there is nothing that states you can't sign a Catholic. I was never told: 'You can't sign a Catholic.' But in this city, you'd a feeling you weren't going to be able to sign one.'

In 1988, Linfield pressed on. They found the two new signings, Coly and Khammal, houses. By the end of the season they had regained the Irish League title.

'Tony Coly sold himself,' Coyle says, 'he went back to Senegal with an Irish

League medal. Khammal went back to Casablanca with an Irish League medal. They played their part. More importantly they left that legacy for Linfield, the mould was broken. They changed attitudes, not so much on the board – I think it was quite liberal – but amongst the support.

'They didn't call Coly 'the black guy', they called him 'the Fenian' – and I was 'the Fenian-loving bastard.' But that broke the ice, that allowed Linfield to sign the Catholic players who followed. Tony Coly made the Dessie Gorman transfer possible.'

Dessie Gorman's name is microscopic compared to Jack Charlton's global fame. But Gorman occupies a memorable place cross-border place in Irish football.

Gorman joined Linfield from Shelbourne in 1992. He came from Dundalk and was a goalscorer: 'The Dundalk Hawk'.

To the *Belfast Telegraph* then, the transfer was 'sensational' and 'ground-breaking' and to Linfield follower and Queen's University lecturer, Daniel Brown, today: 'Dessie Gorman coming to Linfield was massive. Dessie always downplays it – 'just a bit of football' – but Dessie playing for Linfield in red, white and blue was of course significant.

'Whereas with Tony Coly, no-one knew what religion he was, everyone knew Dessie Gorman was a southern Catholic. There was nothing accidental about it. That gets people talking about something new, which is probably the same with an Englishman, Jack Charlton, taking over the Republic of Ireland team.

'Conversations normalise things. If there's something perceived as strange happening, or something different, people start talking about it. Over time, that something new and different becomes normalised. You can have all the back-channels you want, but attitudes don't change unless there is talk. Social change happens because people talk.'

A conversation about Linfield's status had been started by Coyle's successor, Eric Bowyer, in an interview with a fanzine, *One Team in Ulster* in December 1991.

Bowyer lamented the club's inability to sign Catholics, saying he would like to have signed Cliftonville's Peter Murray. But, Bowyer said: 'It couldn't have worked because Peter Murray couldn't have lived in Northern Ireland society. Even if he'd wanted to come here ... the crowd mightn't have liked it, but the more important thing is that when he went back to live in north Belfast, his life would have been miserable. Getting shot would not be an impossibility.'

A year later, Bowyer's successor, Trevor Anderson, the former Manchester United and Linfield striker, signed Gorman. Part of that was a response to the conversations begun by Bowyer's interview, which caused something of a sensation itself. Part of it was football pragmatism.

Linfield had finished 17 points behind Glentoran in season 1991/92. In 1992/93, with Gorman, they win the Irish League. And again the following season.

'In terms of acceptance and attitude,' Brown says, 'what also matters is football reality: Dessie Gorman is a winner. People at Linfield weren't happy, because they weren't winning. That's the same with Jack Charlton – people were prepared to accept the style of football, bypassing the midfield, because it was effective.

'The other thing is money: Dessie Gorman, and Pat Fenlon after him, they didn't join Linfield because they said to themselves: 'Let's go up and help the peace process'. The reality is that Linfield, and other Irish League clubs, were spending big in the early to mid 90s, and of course that played a significant role in the changes that were taking place. The reality of the Troubles is that they were hardly going to change things on their own, but it made people talk.'

MARTIN O'NEILL: AN IRISH CAREER IN THREE MATCHES

INTENSE, INTELLIGENT AND QUICK, IN THE NORTHERN THINKER MOULD of McCracken, Doherty and Blanchflower, Martin O'Neill raced onto the landscape of Irish sport with a burst of boyhood energy in 1969 aged 17. He has been here ever since.

From Kilrea in rural Co. Derry, in less than 18 months, O'Neill went from teenage schoolboy scoring for Derry Minors in an All-Ireland final at Croke Park, to English First Division footballer with Nottingham Forest.

In between O'Neill moved to Belfast, sat his 'A' levels, left school and started a Law degree at Queen's University; he joined Distillery in the Irish League and won the Irish Cup, scoring two in the final; he won an amateur Northern Ireland cap against Scotland in February 1971, then a senior cap against the USSR eight months later.

In the midst of this O'Neill played for Distillery against Barcelona in the European Cup Winners' Cup – and scored. The first leg against Barcelona was in September 1971. By mid-November O'Neill was at Forest, where he scored on his debut, and by early December he was at Old Trafford facing League leaders Manchester United. Where he scored. This was a boy in a hurry.

O'Neill has been an effervescent presence in Irish football from his Distillery debut onwards. Having captained Northern Ireland at a World Cup and managed the Republic of Ireland at a European Championships, in an XI of the most influential men of all-time in Irish football, he would be a certain starter.

1. EUROPEAN CUP WINNERS' CUP, WINDSOR PARK, BELFAST, 15 SEPTEMBER 1971
DISTILLERY 1-3 BARCELONA

Distillery	Barcelona
Roy McDonald	Miguel Reina
Raymond White	Joaquim Rife
Derek Meldrum	Francisco Gallego
Peter Rafferty	Antoni Torres
Tommy Brannigan	Silvestre Eladio
Martin Donnelly	Quique Costas
Mervyn Law	Juan Carlos
Peter Watson	Pedro Zabalza
Jim Savage	Carles Rexach
Martin O'Neill	Ramon Alfonseda (Miguel Bustillo, 55)
Sean Quinn (Alan McCarroll)	Juan Asensi
Manager: Jimmy McAlinden	*Manager:* Rinus Michels

Goals: Alfonseda (45) Asensi (57) O'Neill (77) Asensi (86)

Referee: Antoine Queudeville (Luxemburg)

Distillery FC were formed in 1880 on Belfast's Grosvenor Road by workers from Dunville's whiskey distillery. They came to play in all-white and became known as 'the Whites'.

Martin O'Neill surveys the teamsheet and is immediately transported back over four decades to a different time and place. But O'Neill's remarks are not distant, they are familiar. His thoughts on Distillery 1971 and this group of people come with affection.

He runs a finger down the team and begins with the goalkeeper: 'Roy McDonald – the older brother of Alan, you know, of Queen's Park Rangers.

'Raymond White: he and I were in the same class together for five years in Derry, one of my best friends. A very smart and intelligent boy, going on to study medicine at Queen's, he played in the Irish Cup final for Derry against Distillery in 1971. Then he joined Distillery a few months later, which I was pleased about.

'Derek Meldrum, Tommy Brannigan, Peter Rafferty – you'll remember him.'

Peter Rafferty was known as the Bald Eagle. A flamboyant defender, Rafferty's bald head was offset by a distinctive gaucho moustache. After Distillery he became a huge figure for Linfield and won one Northern Ireland cap. It was in 1979 against England, who scored five. The press said of Rafferty: 'He looked like a Mexican desperado and he played like one.'

O'Neill continues: 'Martin Donnelly, an excellent player who gave the team courage and determination. He went on to forge a really good career in America. Mervyn Law; Peter Watson – Billy Bingham gave him a cap, and it was a record then for the shortest time on a pitch, about 78 seconds. A lovely footballer.

'Wee Jim Savage, centre-forward, about 5ft 9in, quick; Sean Quinn; big Alan McCarroll, he was very influential for us.

'There's a player missing from that line-up – Geordie Lennox. He broke his leg a few months earlier. He had incredible skill. Honestly, Geordie Lennox could easily have made the grade in England. Geordie had played in the Cup final.

'Distillery was a great club, a fantastic manager in Jimmy McAlinden and a great set of players, both Catholics and Protestants, half and half. That was the last season Distillery played at Grosvenor Park because of the Troubles, and the city council eventually ran a motorway through it.

'At that time the two best sides in the Irish League were Linfield and Glentoran, but we finished third in '71. We'd a good side. And of course we went on the Irish Cup run. In the final, I scored twice. That was late April '71.'

It was that victory which brought Barcelona to Belfast. Barcelona had won the Copa del Rey – or Copa del Generalisimo as it was then – under English coach Vic Buckingham. But in the summer of 1971 Buckingham was replaced by the legendary Rinus Michels of Ajax. This was Michels' third competitive match as Barcelona manager.

Not that O'Neill noticed.

'Rinus Michels!' he says when told. 'No? Extraordinary.

'Other than my own manager I was never interested in who managed the other team. I'm not just saying this, McAlinden was as clever a manager as any of them – could have made the grade anywhere. He'd played for Portsmouth way back, knew football, he'd seen it. Knew it inside out. Even though I only worked with him for about a year, McAlinden was brilliant, definitely a major influence.'

Jimmy McAlinden was a distinguished former Belfast Celtic player, who won the FA Cup with Portsmouth in 1939. He played for both both Irelands – North and South – and was revered locally.

And Barcelona?

'They had the same prestige as now, of course,' O'Neill says. 'It's Barcelona. They're coming to Belfast. Absolutely.

'I never knew until recently that the Reina in goal was Pepe Reina's father.'

Thirty seconds before half-time, with the game goalless, Ramon Alfonseda gave Barcelona the lead and 12 minutes into the second half, Juan Asensi made it 2-0.

But on 77 minutes O'Neill pulled one back, beating Miguel Reina at his near post with an audacious strike. O'Neill was an inside forward then and as the *Belfast Telegraph* reported, the pass he received was behind him: 'But somehow Martin dragged the ball forward and blasted it into the net in one swift, stunning movement, a real masterpiece.

'O'Neill is always liable to do something spectacular.'

Not many saw it. The attendance, estimated at 2,000, was described as 'pitiful'. Tickets ranged from 25p to £1.25 and the gate receipts left Distillery out of pocket. Worse, that night a fire gutted the main stand at their home Grosvenor Park. They were playing Barcelona but the club was teetering.

Roy McDonald received some criticism, particularly for conceding the late third, which came from a cross from future Barcelona manager Carles Rexach and which took some optimism from the return leg. But then like O'Neill, McDonald was a teenager. It was a young team and they pushed Barcelona.

'I remember the goal I scored. The game was moved to Windsor because of the Troubles. We moved to Crusaders' ground, Seaview, we weren't at Grosvenor Park. My last Distillery game was actually down at Seaview.'

Barcelona won the second leg 4-0. The teenage O'Neill got to play in the Nou Camp, which was different from Seaview. He was given a taste of the professional's life.

'In terms of experience – travelling, staying overnight in a hotel, having a couple of days' preparation – it was almost a pre-cursor of professional life. It gave me a taste. I don't think Barcelona's stadium has changed that much, though there were only about 25,000 there. We were non-entities. But it was a big moment for me.

'I was starting at Queen's University. I'd a bit of a name by then, lots of scouts were coming over. Anyway, I'm at university and I get a call to say that George Best and a couple of others were not playing against the Soviet Union: 'Would you join up with the squad?"

Terry Neill was Northern Ireland manager, a role he combined with managing Hull City.

'So I join up with them for a few days. Matt Gillies [Nottingham Forest manager] was over at the game, keeping an eye on Liam O'Kane. And Terry Neill, who was at Hull, said he would put an offer in but he'd like me to continue my studying. Funnily enough, my older sister Agatha had been at university at Hull, so Hull would have been interesting.

'Hull did put in a bid, for about ten grand, but Nottingham Forest put a bigger bid in. It was a Tuesday night. I left university and became a professional player. Just before leaving I went to the head of the Law department and he said he'd hold a place open for me if I came back. Remarkably, on my UCCA form, I'd Queen's as first choice but my second choice was Nottingham.'

Distillery's second leg against Barcelona was on 29 September, O'Neill's Northern Ireland debut was on 13 October– as substitute for Bryan Hamilton. 'Then, a week later, I'd signed for Nottingham Forest – 20th October 1971.'

O'Neill's Irish League career – brief, glorious – was over. He had never set foot in England bar a stopover at a London airport but on 13 November he ran on to the pitch at the City Ground with Forest drawing 1-1 with West Brom: 'I scored to make it 2-1; honestly, after about eleven minutes on the field, at the Bridgford End.'

Forest won 4-1 to leave the bottom of the First Division. O'Neill was up and running.

'The next week we played Newcastle away. Malcolm Macdonald scored two in the snow at St. James'. Uncovered, 54,000. The following week we played Leeds United. Robert 'Sammy' Chapman got sent off, Leeds were the best team in the country. And then, on 4th December, we played at Old Trafford. George Best, Bobby Charlton, Denis Law.

'I scored there. I came on as a sub for 'Robbo' [John Robertson]. I picked the ball up on the halfway line, Charlton or Denis Law came close to me but then stopped. So I go on and from outside the box I hit it, past Alex Stepney to make it 3-2 [from 3-1]. I hit the post after that. That night Man United went five points clear at top of the league, and it was two points for a win then. They finished about ninth.

'Best was mesmeric, so for me to score with him on the field – I remember thinking: 'George Best will have heard of me now.'

'A couple of months later, February '72, Northern Ireland played Spain in Hull. George came to the game, arrived late. He was having some trouble at Man United but there's no question that at that time he was the most famous footballer on the planet and as good as any footballer on the planet. I kind of got to know him a little bit. So it was all happening for me, in a short period of time.'

When O'Neill looks back on that change in his life, from schoolboy to student, from semi-professional to pro, the pace is rapid. But there is another moment, another match, when he stalls for a while. It is when he thinks of the amateur international between Northern Ireland and Scotland in February 1971.

'I did all right in the game,' he says, though that is not his primary recollection.

'We got our own shirt. I remember showing my younger brother Owen when

165

I came home. We were so pleased: with the shirt, the badge. We washed it the next day, got it ironed.

'Honestly, you know what – I'm going to say this – that cap, that amateur shirt, is as important to me as any of the shirts I've worn since. It represented a breakthrough. It was green, round neck, the IFA badge on it, a proper shirt. It felt heavy enough, not too heavy, just nice.'

2. WORLD CUP QUARTER-FINAL, VICENTE CALDERON STADIUM, MADRID, 4 JULY 1982
NORTHERN IRELAND 1-4 FRANCE

Northern Ireland	France
Pat Jennings	Jean-Luc Ettori
Jimmy Nicholl	Manuel Amoros
John McClelland	Marius Tresor
Chris Nicholl	Gerard Janvion
Mal Donaghy	Maxime Bossis
Martin O'Neill	Bernard Genghini
Sammy McIlroy	Alain Giresse
David McCreery (^ 86)	Michel Platini
Gerry Armstrong	Gerard Soler (^63)
Norman Whiteside	Jean Tigana
Billy Hamilton	Dominique Rocheteau (^83)
Substitutes	
John O'Neill (^86)	Patrick Battiston
Tommy Cassidy	Jean Casteneda (GK)
Tommy Finney	Alain Couriol (^83)
Jim Cleary	Didier Six (^63)
Jim Platt (GK)	Christian Lopez
Manager: Billy Bingham	Manager: Michel Hidalgo

Goals: Giresse (33) Rocheteau (46, 68) Armstrong (75) Giresse (80)
Referee: Alojzy Jarguz (Poland)

Along with Brazil and Italy, Northern Ireland were one of the stories of the 1982 World Cup. In defeating hosts Spain with ten men on a famous night in Valencia, the Irish caused a sensation. They won their group – ahead of Spain, Yugoslavia and Honduras.

This led to a second group stage: four groups of three. The four winners would become semi-finalists.

Northern Ireland were drawn with Austria and France. France defeated Austria in the first game. Northern Ireland then drew 2-2 with Austria with two goals from Billy Hamilton. Austria were eliminated.

This left Northern Ireland needing a win against France to make the semi-final of the World Cup. France required a draw. Just before the half hour Martin O'Neill put the Irish 1-0 ahead.

Then a highly dubious decision by the Polish referee saw the goal disallowed for offside. O'Neill was clearly onside. Five minutes later Alain Giresse gave France the lead. The French won 4-1 and met West Germany in the semi-final, the game where Harald Schumacher clattered into Patrick Battiston.

That incident is remembered rather more than Northern Ireland's ruled-out opener against France, though not by O'Neill.

'When I think about it now,' he says of his disallowed goal, 'I really feel it was a major point in the game.

'That's around 27, 28 minutes in; if we go in 1-0 at half-time ... look I'm not saying we'd have won, France were a really fine side. But they were getting panicky.

'It was 0-0 and one of the great strengths of that team was the ability to defend a lead – as was demonstrated in the Spanish match. It'd be true to say we probably weren't as strong if we'd to chase a lead, although not many teams are. But with a 1-0 lead and in extremely hot conditions, France's task would have been made much more difficult.

'It was Atletico Madrid's stadium. I got the pass from Gerry Armstrong and I hit it, left foot, into the net and I'm halfway around Madrid before I realise it's been ruled out.

'If you're well-beaten you can accept it, but that moment had a big bearing on the outcome of that game. I smile when people talk about some decision not influencing a game. Well, if it's the opening goal, it does.

'Back at the hotel the BBC must have been doing a highlights programme. David Coleman interviewed me and said: 'By the way, you're a yard onside.'

'I remember that. I didn't really know until then. I thought: 'Well, this makes it even worse.'

'When the dust had settled I started to realise we are not going to play in World Cups every four years – we're not Germany. Best didn't get to one World Cup. So to have scored a goal in a World Cup, one of importance, in what was effectively a quarter-final, a three-team quarter-final ... Who's to say what would have happened if the goal had stood?

'People say: 'France beat you well.' Well, that was after we'd a goal disallowed.

'And for purely personal reasons, to be able to say to your youngsters that you actually scored at a World Cup … you're talking about a goal that might have been, in the scheme of my life, really important. But I'm not sure I've even talked to my daughters about it.'

It was a disappointment, an injustice that rankles, but it would wrong to characterise O'Neill's playing career similarly.

By 1982 he was captain of this over-achieving Northern Ireland side. He was also a European Cup winner with Nottingham Forest – twice. There was the 1977/78 League title in England plus two League Cups and, in 1980, the British Home Championships triumph with Northern Ireland. Articulate with and without the ball, O'Neill had developed into a major player.

He was 30 at the World Cup and had left Forest a year earlier, first for Norwich City, then six months at Manchester City before returning to Norwich. They had just won promotion back to the First Division when O'Neill went to Spain with Billy Bingham's 22-man squad. He was a central, controlling midfielder by this time, though O'Neill still does not know why or how that came about.

'I played inside forward for Distillery and really I was signed as that type of player for Forest,' he says. 'But, you know what, to this day I'm hardly sure how I end up playing midfield. I really don't know.

'You just go along with where managers decide to put you for a year or two. So by the time Brian Clough arrived at Forest, I was a midfield player, or wide right-hand side.

'If you'd said to me at 19, that that's where I'd play for Nottingham Forest – don't get me wrong, I'd have put up with it – but I'd have found it really strange. I don't actually remember when or why that transition took place.'

A rather more significant change was the spiral of the Troubles. In 1972 the sectarian-related murder rate was at more than nine killings a week. By 1982 that had dropped to two per week. But there is a gap: from 18 June to 16 July, there were no killings. Northern Ireland's first match was 17 June. The France game was 4 July.

To claim football brought about a period of calm might be extrapolating too far, but it is a coincidence to consider.

O'Neill, a Catholic captain of a mixed team whose support was overwhelmingly Protestant, speaks of a comparison with the cross-community impact of boxer Barry McGuigan. McGuigan came from Co. Monaghan but filled the King's Hall in Belfast with fans and excitement.

'For that short spell both communities came together,' O'Neill says of '82. 'It was a bit like Barry McGuigan did. McGuigan did most, and over a longer period, but I think the Northern Ireland team had for a short period a similar effect.

'There was also a contrast with the Republic. They hadn't qualified, and they'd good players. We were showing a bit of spirit and for all that the Republic had really fine players like Liam Brady and Frank Stapleton, they couldn't get over the line.'

It was France who denied Brady and Stapleton in qualification – on goal difference.

The good memories of Spain '82 trump the frustration of France but O'Neill is correct: World Cup appearances are not guaranteed. The talent within Northern Ireland, however, was such that they did qualify for the next World Cup, in Mexico in 1986.

In between, there was an impressive campaign to reach the European Championships in 1984, held in France. Drawn with West Germany and Austria, the Irish won three of those four head-to-heads, beating the Germans home and away, two 1-0 victories courtesy of goals from Ian Stewart in Belfast and Norman Whiteside in Hamburg.

They finished joint top with West Germany, missing the finals on goal difference in the era when only one team qualified.

O'Neill played in both those West Germany matches and in the first three qualifiers of the 1986 World Cup campaign.

After 13 years of international football, his sixty-fourth and last cap came against Finland in November 1984, a 2-1 win. Three months later, shortly before his 33rd birthday and carrying a knee injury, O'Neill played his last club game, in the Second Division for Notts County.

3. EURO 2016, GROUP E, STADE PIERRE MAUROY, LILLE,
22 JUNE 2016
REPUBLIC OF IRELAND 1-0 ITALY

Republic of Ireland	Italy
Darren Randolph	Salvatore Sirigu
Seamus Coleman	Andrea Barzagli
Shane Duffy	Leonardo Bonucci
Richard Keogh	Angelo Ogbonna
Stephen Ward	Federico Bernardeschi (^60)
Jeff Hendrick	Stefano Sturaro
James McCarthy (^77)	Thiago Motta
James McClean	Alessandro Florenzi

Robbie Brady	Mattia De Sciglio (^82)
Daryl Murphy (^70)	Simone Zaza
Shane Long (^90)	Ciro Immobile (^74)
Substitutes	
Aiden McGeady (^70)	Matteo Darmian (^60)
Wes Hoolahan (^77)	Lorenzo Insigne (^74)
Stephen Quinn (^90)	Stephen El Shaarawy (^82)

Goal: Brady (85)

Referee: Ovidiu Hategan (Romania)

In an interview before the finals with journalist and former professional cyclist Paul Kimmage, O'Neill talks of Brian Clough and says: 'He got his credibility from winning.'

Usually the focus on Clough centres on his maverick tendencies, his unorthodox genius, but O'Neill brought it back to results on the pitch. Before facing Italy in the last group game of Euro 2016, a game the Irish had to win to progress to the knock-out phase, O'Neill felt that same sense of priority.

His team had drawn against Sweden and lost to Belgium. They just needed a win and a manager of 29 years' experience understood that afresh.

'Absolutely,' O'Neill says. 'Two elements: firstly, when I took over this job, I thought I'd to make it work, I'm not here for a jolly up. The games come so infrequently that the pressure on those individual games is every bit as intense, if not more so, than league games at club level. In the league you've more a chance to put it right. At international level I felt you have to win, you have to be competitive. Or why bother?

'Secondly, we were following on from poor results at the Euros in Poland and a disappointing World Cup campaign for Brazil. I felt we'd to restore confidence and a little self-belief. More importantly, we'd to qualify for the European Championships.

'We started with seven points from three matches, including a draw in Germany. Then we got beaten in Scotland and that was November – there's a long time to wait for the next game. It was a draw with Poland, then a draw with Scotland. With four games left we're two points behind Scotland with a worse head-to-head. So we'd to make up three points on Scotland.

'But not for one minute did I think it was over. It meant we'd probably have to beat Germany at home or win in Poland. And so it materialised. But I've said it before: don't call things early. But we had to do something.'

What O'Neill's Ireland did was beat Germany in Dublin in October 2015 via a

Shane Long wonderbolt. That brought a tricky play-off against Bosnia-Herzegovina, won 3-1 on aggregate. That meant qualification for France and as O'Neill says: 'Total vindication.

'When we beat Germany, to me, even though it was against the world champions, it didn't rank as highly as beating Bosnia. The reason being, that while it was fantastic to beat Germany, there was a finality to the result against Bosnia. We're there, we've qualified, your tenure as manager is vindicated.'

He had been appointed manager of the Republic of Ireland in November 2013, succeeding Giovanni Trapattoni. O'Neill's previous position at Sunderland had been terminated abruptly seven months earlier. He was 61; he had been a manger since taking over Grantham Town in 1987.

And yet just as O'Neill cannot pinpoint why and when he changed as a player, he cannot say there was a plan for him to move into a role in which he was to excel.

'During my playing days I wouldn't have given management two thoughts, not even at 30,' he says.

'It's only when I got injured at Notts County that I realised I better start thinking about my future. I was 32 at the time and if I'd not been injured I probably wouldn't have thought about it. Playing is the ultimate, let no-one tell you differently. These men who've never played who become managers and think it's all about them, it's not, it's about players and playing.'

His playing days meant O'Neill witnessed the merits of Bingham and Clough, as well as McAlinden and Gillies – 'I would have learned a lot.

'Internationally, Billy Bingham was very good. Billy was different to Brian Clough in many aspects, but Billy grasped international football. He knew he had only a number of days to work with the players and he would be more inclined to play lesser players who were physically fit than perhaps a better player who arrived with an injury. Clough might have taken more of risk – but both would have calculated the risk beforehand.'

There was also Danny Blanchflower, who managed Northern Ireland from 1976 to 1979. Blanchflower's vision and approach could not be described as pragmatic.

'Danny wanted the game played in a pure manner,' O'Neill says. 'He looked at football from a different perspective. It was about purity – and that wasn't what people were demanding. I sound disparaging, but far from it, I love Danny's idea of the game, his mentality.

'But it's to do with your players. Remember Danny had George Best available a few times.'

The Irish squad O'Neill inherited as manager had no Best. But it possessed other qualities, not least indefatigability. That had helped the team get to Euro 2016 and now, in the dying minutes in Lille, it kept the team in Euro 2016.

'When I saw who we were paired with in France, I thought: 'Oh'. But then you go, you start and we'd a great performance against Sweden, should've won but didn't. Then an underwhelming performance v Belgium – that's being kind.

'Now we needed re-energising. I was ready for the challenge, because you have to be. I've never felt the need for someone to re-energise me – that's my job as a manager. But the team needed new energy both mentally and physically.

'It was now beat Italy or go home. In a way that's a really good thing: it clears your mind. We played with great intensity that night and deep into the second half we were still strong. But it's getting closer and you know you have to win.

'Then Wes Hoolahan spurns a great chance. Honestly, did I think we'd get another? No. I thought we might get the ball in the box, but another clear-cut chance? Very doubtful.

'Then Brady makes the run, the cross comes in and you're thinking: 'Can he get there? Can he get there?'

'And he does. There was euphoria. There was a great story with the travelling fans and I knew it would have an effect in Ireland. There was the credibility that comes with victory, as Clough had demonstrated.'

Next it was France, once again in a knock-out. Robbie Brady scores to put the Irish ahead. France win 2-1.

'To me there were parallels with the Northern Ireland-France match way back in '82,' O'Neill says.

'We're leading 1-0, can we see it out? Stephen Ward has a shot that's deflected for a corner, we don't get the corner, they get a goal-kick. From the goal-kick they score. They score again. We start to chase the game, get beaten, Shane Duffy gets sent off. It's all over.'

O'Neill rifles through it. But he knew his team had left a mark on the tournament and at home – 'And that's what it's about.

'When Jack Charlton took over they qualified for the first time ever, then great moments under Mick McCarthy – qualified for 2002 – so you joined that line. You became part of those things and I mean that, I actually feel that, you're part of the history.'

O'Neill had crossed Irish football's border, he had made himself part of two histories. And the ultimate personal question concerns Irishness and change: how he has changed, if he has changed.

'If there's such a thing as separating moments, then drawing them together as part of a pattern,' he begins, before digressing.

'To start a European Cup final for Forest – against Hamburg – that was extraordinary. But that night in Valencia, beating Spain in Spain, was really, really special. To be captain of the side, to play in the game, to hold out for the last 20-odd minutes with Mal Donaghy sent off, the ten of us, with Gerry scoring the goal, to take us to a quarter-final, it was magical.

'I played for Northern Ireland. I was manager of Celtic. I loved that Celtic-Rangers rivalry – beautifully incongruous. I'm now manager of Ireland. I'm an Irishman, I'm northern. I'm very proud of my roots. I'm very proud of where I was born.'

MICHAEL O'NEILL: AN IRISH CAREER IN THREE MATCHES

MICHAEL O'NEILL WAS A 15 YEAR-OLD SCHOOLBOY WHEN HE MADE his debut for Coleraine in the Irish League in 1984. O'Neill was at St. Louis Grammar school in Ballymena where his O-Level results – 5 As, 4 Bs – made his parents insist their son did A-Levels rather than join Manchester City.

Along with Neil Lennon, Gerry Taggart and Michael Hughes, O'Neill had been travelling to City for trials. O'Neill heard those exam results while on a visit to Maine Road.

City offered trainee terms but O'Neill's situation had been complicated by Coleraine's smart decision to sign their young talent in an official capacity. That meant Coleraine would need to be consulted and compensated. He returned to school and the Irish League.

Coleraine had come second in the League for a third consecutive season in May 1987, qualifying once again for the UEFA Cup. They drew Dundee United.

By September, the Scottish club were one of two suitors following O'Neill. The previous season Dundee United had knocked out Barcelona en route to reaching the UEFA Cup final. The other interested club was Newcastle United, in England's First Division.

O'Neill, 18 and studying for his A-Levels, missed the first leg against Dundee United but he played in the return in Scotland. In a fortnight he had signed for Newcastle, to some annoyance in Dundee.

Within four months O'Neill had been called up by Billy Bingham to play for Northern Ireland. He would go on to win 31 caps and a circuitous club career would see O'Neill play for 13 teams in four countries.

He stopped at Ayr United, aged 35, in 2004. Two years later he became manager of Brechin City and then moved to Shamrock Rovers in the League of Ireland. O'Neill led Rovers into the group stage of the Europa League. He was then asked to manage Northern Ireland, his first game coming in February 2012. In 2015 he led Northern Ireland to Euro 2016, the first tournament for the team since the World Cup in Mexico in 1986 under Bingham.

1. UEFA CUP 1ST ROUND, 2ND LEG,
30 SEPTEMBER 1987
DUNDEE UNITED 3-1 COLERAINE

Dundee United	*Coleraine*
Billy Thomson	Jim Platt
Gary McGinnis	Marty Tabb
Paul Hegarty	Dean McCullough (75)
Dave Narey	Dessie Edgar
Maurice Malpas	Nigel Quigley (75)
John Clark	Paul Kee
Gordon McLeod	Ricky Wade
Ian McPhee (75)	Jeremy Robinson
Alan Irvine	Michael O'Neill
Kevin Gallacher	Paul McGurnaghan
Paul Sturrock	Barry McCreadie
Substitutes:	
Scott Thomson	William McCurdy (^75)
Dave Beaumont	Jeff Wright (^75)
Ian Redford (^75)	Kiernan Harding
Billy McKinlay	Dermot Doherty
Iain Ferguson	
Managers:	
Jim McClean	Jim Platt

Goals: Gallacher (28) Edgar (48) Sturrock (73) Clark (80)

Referee: Allan Gunn (England)

When the car set off for the port of Larne, there were four men inside. When the car returned to the port of Larne there was one man inside. And a greyhound.

What lies between is the beginning of Michael O'Neill's professional career.

The quartet leaving Larne were Jim Platt, player-manager of Coleraine, Nigel Quigley, a young Coleraine full-back, and Des and Michael O'Neill. They were bound for Tayside in Scotland, then Tyneside in England.

Platt was driving as a representative of Coleraine, who hoped to make some money selling two assets, Quigley and O'Neill. Both players had impressed Dundee United manager Jim McClean in the UEFA Cup. Des O'Neill was accompanying his son. Making sure.

Michael O'Neill had joined Coleraine three years earlier after a knock on the door.

'Bertie Peacock had come up to my house with Jim Platt after I played in the Milk Cup for a Ballymena district team,' O'Neill says. 'I was 15, playing with Coleraine's reserves, training two nights a week. Jim lived in Ballymena so he used to take me to Coleraine. That was the start of it for me.'

Peacock played for Celtic for more than a decade and was part of Northern Ireland's 1958 World Cup team; Platt played over 400 games for Middlesbrough and in 1983 returned to the Irish League. He won 23 Northern Ireland caps. It was something to have them at the door.

'My debut was against Distillery at the Showgrounds, we won 3-2,' O'Neill recalls. 'Felix Healy scored a hat-trick. I always remember the pitch was frozen solid. It should never have been played. I can't have been much more than eight stone. All the time I was at school.'

He had just had his 18th birthday at the beginning of the 1987-88 season and was considering his options.

'I was having to fill out my UCCA form. I didn't know what I wanted to do. Will I stay and go to Queen's [University]? Will I do Accountancy? Or Physiotherapy? I didn't know. I just knew I wanted to play football.

'I'd started that season really well for Coleraine, scored six or seven goals. I played up front with Willie Beggs. He was some player, Willie, he'd been at QPR but just hadn't made it.'

There had once been a buzz about Beggs, now it was around O'Neill, and Dundee United in the UEFA Cup loomed.

'But I got a bad tackle before the first leg. I had to get out of school to basically go and do a fitness test of my own up at the pitches on the end of the road. I couldn't play, I was gutted. There was talk that Alex Ferguson was going to the game.

'So I just watched it, we lost 1-0, Paul Sturrock scored. I remember Jim McClean came into our dressing room after the game and congratulated us. I thought it was an amazing gesture. Given the McClean I came to know, that gesture might have been to get at his own players.'

McClean was a famously ferocious man. He and O'Neill would meet again.

In the second leg at Tannadice, Kevin Gallacher put United 2-0 ahead on aggregate, but Coleraine were still in the tie when Dessie Edgar scored early in the second half. One more and Coleraine were through on away goals.

'We had chances,' O'Neill says. 'Jim Platt was clever, he played Paul Kee as a sweeper – Paul was a midfielder who didn't play regularly. I was fit and I remember playing well on the night.'

Sturrock scored the next goal, however, and Coleraine were out. But they had made a mark, notably O'Neill.

'After the game, people were saying 'well done'. The next day I woke up in a hotel in Dundee, right near the bridge as you cross the Tay. The radio was on, Radio Scotland I presume, and they were talking about the game and they talked about me. It was quite exciting. People had spoken about me before but it was that game, to go against that level of opposition, it was the final tick in the box. I think I only played one more game for Coleraine after that, Glentoran away. Then I was transferred.'

This was when the four climbed into Jim Platt's car. Quigley was going to Tannadice on trial while the O'Neills were speaking to McClean before being driven down to Newcastle United to meet their manager Willie McFaul, who by coincidence came from Coleraine.

'Jim Platt handled it. He said to me the club had two bids, both accepted. One was from Dundee United, one Newcastle.

'It was a big decision. There was quite a bit of publicity locally about me going over, me being a wide player and all the comparisons that go with it. We drove over to Dundee after the second leg. McClean thought he was going to sign me and he took Nigel Quigley on trial as well, based on Quigley's effort against them. He was a big, strong boy.

'After Dundee, where we left Nigel, Jim took us to Newcastle. He was picking up a greyhound – Jim was into greyhounds. He left me and my Dad with Willie and I warmed to him. We'd dinner and he started to tell us about this young player, Gascoigne, how good he was, but also how Willie was having to hang on to his wages and stuff.

'We went into the training ground at Benwell the next day, then Willie took us down to the stadium, we met Joe Harvey. I'd made my mind up.

'We flew home. Jim drove back with his dog. Nigel was in Dundee.

'My Dad was asking me what I wanted to do. Fourteen months earlier I was discussing YTS with Man City, here I was being offered three years pro, signing on fee, £250 a week, £100 appearance money – it was a wage. My Dad said: 'This is different from City.''

O'Neill signed for Newcastle United; Dundee United were not happy. Coleraine got £100,000.

'My Dad had to phone Jim McClean and I remember him coming back into the kitchen saying: 'That man's just torn strips off me.' McClean immediately sent Quigley back. The boys at Coleraine used to give me awful stick: 'Selfish bastard, ruined Quigley's career,' all of that. Amazing. Jim McClean.'

O'Neill was on his way to Tyneside. First, though, he had to leave school. 'On my last day at St. Louis, they did a nice thing, brought me up in front of assembly, presented me with a pen. About a week later I was sitting on the bench for a League Cup-tie at Wimbledon – Plough Lane. You were allowed two subs then. Paul Gascoigne was brilliant that night. I was sitting on the bench going: 'Oh, my God, this is mad.' That was it, no sort of introduction to professional football, just straight into it.'

There had, at least, been one Newcastle reserve game.

'Willie was under a bit of pressure, Newcastle was a soap opera, still is. My first game for the reserves, there were about 4,000 there and Ian Bogie said to me: 'They've come to see you.' I scored a first-half hat-trick. It was great for Willie, gave him vindication. It was great for me, oh yeah, I'd instant credibility with the players. From then I was with the first team. Within three weeks I'd made my debut.'

But Michael O'Neill's schooldays were not over. The club placed him in Newcastle's Gosforth High School to complete his Maths A-Level.

'My first day was probably about a week later. I used to go in on a Wednesday. Alan Shearer had gone to Gosforth High and I became friendly with two lads who were mates of his. Shearer had just left for Southampton. They put me in digs around the corner. I actually did that, but it becomes difficult going to school as a Newcastle United player.

'Listen, it was a whirlwind.'

2. EURO 96 QUALIFIER, 15 NOVEMBER 1995
NORTHERN IRELAND 5-3 AUSTRIA

Northern Ireland	Austria
Alan Fettis	Michael Konsel
Steve Lomas	Markus Schopp
Colin Hill	Walter Kogler
Barry Hunter	Anton Pfeffer
Nigel Worthington	Andreas Herzog (^h-t)
Keith Gillespie	Dietmar Kuhbauer (^h-t)
Michael O'Neill	Helmo Pfeifenberger
Neil Lennon	Markus Schopp
Michael Hughes	Peter Stoger

Phil Gray (^78)	Toni Polster
Iain Dowie (^81)	Stefan Masarek
Substitutes:	
Alan McDonald (^78)	Arnold Wetl (^h-t)
Jimmy Quinn (^81)	Christian Stumpf (^h-t)
Trevor Wood	Otto Konrad
Pat McGibbon	Dieter Ramusch
Keith Rowland	Peter Artner
Managers:	
Bryan Hamilton	Herbert Prohaska

Referee: Leif Sundell (Sweden)

Goals: O'Neill (27) Dowie (32) Hunter (53) Schopp (56) Gray (63) Stumpf (70) O'Neill (76) Wetl (80)

At Newcastle United, 18 year-old Michael O'Neill surged. He scored 12 goals in 19 starts in the First Division in 1987-88 as Newcastle finished eighth. He was top scorer – one goal more than Brazilian Mirandinha – and enjoyed/endured the 'next George Best' label.

Then Newcastle sold Paul Gascoigne, Willie McFaul was sacked and the club slumped to relegation. O'Neill was ill, injured then sold, with a measure of irony, to Dundee United for £350,000. Jim McClean still wanted the boy winger he had seen, but the relationship between the two was fractious.

In 1991 O'Neill declined to extend his contract at Tannadice yet so obstructive was McClean, it was to be 1993 before O'Neill was able to join Hibs. He played more football at Easter Road than at any other of his clubs. He was a 26 year-old Hibs player when he won his 27th cap against Austria and, over the problems at Dundee United, O'Neill felt he was in form and established: 'I thought I'd get 50 caps. Yet it was done within a year.'

Northern Ireland's manager was Bryan Hamilton and as with McClean, there was something in the air.

'I didn't have a bad relationship with Bryan, but I didn't have a good one either,' O'Neill says.

The previous summer, 1994, Hamilton had included O'Neill in a tour to America for two friendlies against Colombia and Mexico. Hamilton used 17 players in those two games but not O'Neill.

'I was raging,' O'Neill says.

By October he was back in the team as a substitute for a 2-1 win in Vienna that kept Northern Ireland in contention in a group with Portugal and the Republic of Ireland – the two Irish teams drawn together again after their World Cup '94 experience.

In the summer of 1995 Northern Ireland again had a mini-tour, to Canada, and O'Neill was again selected. 'I phoned up and said I wasn't going. It didn't go down great. I had the hump because I'd gone to America and hadn't played.'

O'Neill was omitted from the next two qualifiers by Hamilton.

The two Irish teams finished on 17 points, behind Portugal, with the Republic going into a play-off having a superior goal difference. Austria was Northern Ireland's last group game and had Austria got a draw, they would have finished second. It is regarded as O'Neill's best display in a green shirt, which he recalls for another reason.

'I remember being on the bus from the Chimney Corner [hotel] where we stayed, the weather was horrendous. We didn't have fitted strips then and mine was always big on me. In the rain it was hanging off me.

'It was a bit of a shame because we couldn't qualify, we were in the Republic's group and we could catch them on points but we couldn't overtake them. They ended up with a play-off against Holland, partly because we beat Austria home and away.

'In the game before we'd played Lichtenstein and I scored and this game I got the first and the fifth – a chip at the Kop end. We broke off a corner. By that stage my strip weighed a ton. Hughesy carried the ball and gave it to me. I just dinked it over the keeper. They got another one after that – 5-3. It was a great game. Wet, slippy, goals, tackles.

'We should have done better in that campaign. We'd a better squad than we showed.'

Despite being drawn with Germany, Portugal again and Ukraine, O'Neill says he was confident about qualification for the France World Cup in 1998. Then Sergei Rebrov scored the only goal at Windsor Park in the opening qualifier and the next, also in Belfast, was a draw with Armenia. He did not know it, but when O'Neill walked off the pitch that day, his international career was over. He was 27.

'I'd made my debut in 1988 – against Greece,' he says. 'Mal Donaghy, Norman Whiteside were playing, Alan McDonald, John McClelland. I was still at school in Gosforth and for the Malta game [three months later] I missed sitting my A-Level Maths. We won 3-0. I never sat the exam.

'A few years later – it was before we played the Republic in Belfast [November 1994] I went to Queen's and sat the Open University Maths exam. The game was on a Wednesday, I sat the exam on the Tuesday. I'd to go into a room with an adjudicator – the Open University set it up.

'I was Hibs then. After what had happened at Dundee United with McClean, I went back to studying.'

By the time of his last cap against Armenia in 1996, O'Neill was a Coventry City player – in name at least – in England's Premier League.

'I was injured for a while, then I was called up for a squad in 1997, but I never played and I was never called up again.

'Billy Bingham had brought me in as an 18 year-old, I'd been in the squad as long as anyone, so it felt a bit weird. But Bryan didn't view me like that. I thought after Austria I'd kick on. I say that to players now – I got my last cap at 27. I thought I'd be an international for the best part of the next ten years.'

Prepared to criticise McClean and Hamilton, O'Neill is also self-critical when he reflects on his playing days and his attitude. Ask him about regret and he replies: 'Oh, yeah.

'There were peaks and troughs. I'd the boy-wonder phase, then Dundee United, illness, injury, contract disputes with McClean. McClean wasted about 18 months of my career and at an important time. I still had a good reputation – Lennie Lawrence wanted to sign me for Middlesbrough and I went to see them. But they didn't want to go to a tribunal with a Scottish club.

'You look at the peaks and wonder why it didn't stay at that level. Ultimately you have to look at yourself – at the age I was. The Dundee United thing did damage me, kind of took away from me and it took me three years at Hibs to recover belief. I was nominated for Player of the Year in Scotland.

'So I do have regret. I regret Coventry because I was going into the Premier League, but once I got injured in October I never really got going. Gordon [Strachan] signed me, though Ron Atkinson was the manager. That was circumstance, not anyone's fault. I'd groin problems from Coventry that persisted for about four years. I'd five operations.

'I'd loads of offers to go back to Scotland but I just didn't want to and I went to Wigan. That was a decision based on needing to play – and finance. They were a club on the up but it wasn't something I'd envisaged. I went to Aberdeen on loan and in my head I hoped I could play myself back into England's Premier League. It was unrealistic.

'The two years at Wigan, I enjoyed, but I was never picked for the international squad. Now I'm consistently picking players from League One.

'I suppose the regret has helped me as a manager, dealing with players. I see signs of it in players. Football disappears very quickly, you've got to hold onto it. I've so much admiration for lads like Aaron Hughes, who's still a major part of it at 37. When

I look back on myself: could I have done more physically? There was an element of me taking my career for granted. It fuels my appreciation of being in football. It helps me understand players.'

3. EUROPEAN CHAMPIONSHIPS GROUP C, LYON, 16 JUNE 2016
NORTHERN IRELAND 2-0 UKRAINE

Northern Ireland	Ukraine
Michael McGovern	Andriy Pyatov
Aaron Hughes	Artem Fedetskiy
Craig Cathcart	Yevhen Khacheridi
Gareth McAuley	Yarolslav Rakitskiy
Jonny Evans	Vyacheslav Shevchuk
Jamie Ward (^69)	Taras Stepanenko
Corry Evans (^90)	Serhiy Sydorchuk (^76)
Steven Davis	Andriy Yarmolenko
Oliver Norwood	Viktor Kovaleko (^83)
Stuart Dallas	Yevhen Konoplyanka
Conor Washington (^84)	Yevhen Seleznyov (^71)
Substitutes:	
Niall McGinn (^69)	Roman Zozulya (^71)
Josh Magennis (^84)	Denys Garmash (^76)
Paddy McNair (^90)	Olexandr Zinchenko (^83)
Managers:	
Michael O'Neill	Mykhailo Fomenko

Goals: McAuley (49) McGinn (90+6)
Referee: Pavel Kralovec (Czech Republic)

Michael O'Neill's first day as a football manager ended in relegation. It was 8 April 2006 and O'Neill had agreed to take over Brechin City, a club that had won one of its 31 league games in Scotland's second tier yet somehow the drop had not yet been confirmed.

'The pay was all right, and I got a car,' O'Neill says of his decision-making.

The role was part-time, O'Neill worked 90 miles away in Edinburgh as a financial planner.

'Brechin were basically relegated,' he says, 'but they weren't officially relegated. There were five games to go and they'd to win them all. Their goal difference was horrendous. They'd won one game all season. Everyone knew they were going down.

'We played St. Johnstone, Owen Coyle was their manager. They'd a strong team, they beat us 2-0 at home. That was it, we were relegated. I was relegated in my first match.'

O'Neill had re-located to Scotland after a 20-year playing career culminated with two seasons back in the Irish League with Glentoran and then, in August 2004, two substitute appearances for Ayr United in Scotland's third tier. He was 35.

He had left Wigan Athletic four years earlier and signed for St. Johnstone and a zig-zag trajectory saw him move to Portland Timbers, then Clydebank in the third tier in Scotland where his debut was watched by 333 people. Of greater long-term significance, O'Neill began coaching.

'I came back up to Scotland and did this accelerated B Licence, at Largs. I enjoyed it, people said I was good at it. I did my A Licence quickly after that. That was 2002, 2003. I got my Financial Planning certificate from the Chartered Insurance Institute on the same date, so I could become a planner.'

O'Neill was out of football for a year. He re-appeared in the unlikely setting of Cowdenbeath as Mixu Paatelainen's unwaged assistant. Paatelainen was a friend from Tannadice. Then another friend informed O'Neill of Brechin City.

He stayed at Brechin two-and-a-half years and is grateful for the experience, even the first day. There was an indication of O'Neill's resolve and ability when three days after relegation Brechin won at Dundee, their second victory of the season.

'The players were buzzing,' he recalls, 'but the board wasn't happy, they'd to pay out a bonus. I inherited a Dad's Army, a lot of lads I'd played with. I'd to take a knife to the squad and if you think it's difficult with a player earning plenty, it's more difficult with a lad who's relying on £200 a week. When I left we were second in the division. We had a wage structure and a much younger team. Brechin was a great grounding.

'I only left really because the company I was working for was struggling. I'd come on Shamrock Rovers' radar, they wanted something different in the League of Ireland.

'I was linked with Dundee at the time, but Brechin refused Dundee permission to speak to me. What pushed me into taking Shamrock Rovers was that the financial company was going into liquidation. I went over to Dublin, thought: 'Why not?' It was full-time, I fancied it. We'd one young kid, and we'd never lived back at home, we wondered. It was feeding that curiosity. We stayed three years.'

O'Neill took Shamrock Rovers into the group stage of the Europa League, which broke new ground – the first League of Ireland club to get there. The IFA sought him out and on 29 February 2012 O'Neill became Nigel Worthington's successor, managing Northern Ireland to a 3-0 home defeat by Norway.

It was bleak. Northern Ireland had won two of their previous 24 matches and would win only one of the next 18. Three victories in 42 games. But O'Neill understood the scale of the task.

'You're inheriting a culture where losing, whilst it's never accepted, it's almost expected. I knew it was bad. But the job was offered, so I took it.

'If we'd other players, it was a job where you make big changes, but we didn't have the resources. So it was very important for me to hang on to players like McAuley, and Gareth was wavering a bit at that point. Chris Baird was contemplating retirement.

'The first thing I'd to do was talk Aaron Hughes out of retirement – I remember when he phoned me to say he was coming back. That was my first win, if you look at in a certain way. Those first few weeks were difficult; those were three players who came to the Euros.'

From that opening, O'Neill built what Hughes calls 'a culture of standards'. Losing repeatedly from 2009, Northern Ireland started winning again in 2014. A new professionalism and a new unity of purpose saw a team drawn from Pot 5 for the Euro 2016 qualifiers win the group.

The finals were expanded but Northern Ireland would have been present anyway as group winners, something that was forgotten when they turned up in France and lost meekly in their opening finals game to Poland 1-0 in Nice.

On the flight back to the Irish base near Lyon, O'Neill picked a team for the second game. There were to be five changes. That knifework at Brechin had sharpened him.

'I watched the Poland game on the flight back from Nice on my laptop. We needed more energy in the team. We always knew we'd change the team for the second game because we had to play four at the back to combat Yarmolenko and Konoplyanka. We couldn't go with a three because a three would become a five. We knew Jonny [Evans] would have to go to left back and we had conversations. He was brilliant, saying he'd do whatever was asked.'

Bringing in five new faces was the easy part; leaving five out, that was different.

'I told them individually; players don't disguise their disappointment. I was OK but I felt consumed by it all. The biggest call was to leave Kyle [Lafferty] out. I knew that would be a hard conversation with him but I'd rather go out of the tournament having picked the right team, than go out another way. And I believed in the team.'

Conor Washington replaced the talismanic Lafferty. Washington sprinted towards Ukraine from kick-off and forced a throw-in. In ten seconds, Northern Ireland had set a tone. It would not relent and four minutes after half-time, McAuley scored with an athletic header. Six minutes into injury-time, one substitute, Josh Magennis, passed to another substitute, Niall McGinn, who made it 2-0. O'Neill leapt onto the pitch.

'It was such a massive win. In the press conference the day before I'd asked the question: 'Do we belong here?' And the answer was: 'Yes'.

'As a team we covered 10km more than against Poland. That's a stat that matters to us.

'I'll always remember the emotion in the dressing room. It was such a dream to be there, to take part. Now we were in the competition.'

It had been 30 years since Northern Ireland had been at a tournament, so to question belonging was understandable. A defeat against Germany followed, but O'Neill's players had done enough to progress to the knock-out stage. They lost 1-0 to Wales, but hardly deserved to.

Gareth Bale delivered the cross from which McAuley scored an own goal and O'Neill considers Real Madrid Bale's presence: 'To me, what that match showed more than anything else, was: match-winner.

'Our team is our match-winner, our work ethic is our match-winner. We don't have an individual. Kyle scored the goals in qualification, but it was our team that got us to France.'

As a 12 year-old boy O'Neill was inspired by Billy Bingham's squad that played in the 1982 World Cup. He was then capped by Bingham and as a manager replicated Bingham's qualifying. But, when pushed, O'Neill is more interested in the future than the past.

'I don't really look at connecting it to 1982, I look at it more that there's a generation now who can talk about Northern Ireland 2016.

'You can only really talk about '82 if you saw it. If you're 30 or under, you don't really feel 1982. It's like me with 1958, I know the names but I don't feel it the same way. 1982 means everything to me because I sat and watched it. Hopefully there's young people engulfed by this the way I was by '82. It fuelled me.

'There's a photograph of the crowd after McAuley scores, so many Northern Ireland fans having such a good time, brilliant atmosphere. It was like being invited to the best party and going there and enjoying it. That's what it felt like. It's whet the appetite.'

WES HOOLAHAN – THE CHANCE

'AND THEN I GET THE CHANCE,' HE SAYS.

For a few moments Wes Hoolahan is back in France, back in Lille, back at Euro 2016 and back in the last six minutes of an enthralling, decisive match in Group E that will determine whether he and his fellow Irishmen fly home the next day or live to play another match in the tournament. It's all or nothing time.

Hoolahan – quiet, reserved, not one to blow a trumpet – is recalling how he looked destined to be the man who would put the Republic of Ireland through to the knock-out stage. But as Hoolahan knows all too well, looks can deceive. He is 34.

He has been on the pitch for seven minutes when the chance arrives. Italy are the opposition. They have qualified from the group already. Antonio Conte has changed his team. Some key men are rested, but that means the new faces are fresh, so you can see it two ways.

But the Irish players know only one outcome will do: they must win. Now, 84 minutes in, it is goalless. Martin O'Neill's players are pushing, they have pushed all night. And it appears at last as if the Italians have cracked, the defence opens and Hoolahan is there. He has Aiden McGeady and Shane Long nearby. This is what the whole team has fought for.

'I see the fella slip and me and Aiden are closest to the ball,' Hoolahan says. 'I seemed to pick up the ball and run through.

'I think I'd too much time to think about it. 'Should I pass it to Shane?' 'Should I let on to shoot and go around the defender?'

'In the end I kind-of placed it in the corner and the keeper guessed right, got his body on it.

186

'I thought that was it.

'The chance was gone.'

*

THERE ARE THOSE WHO WOULD HAVE BEEN UNSURPRISED THAT THE
Chance became The Miss. Wes Hoolahan has always collected naysayers among a
throng of personal support that has grown year-on-year.

There is a perception that Hoolahan needs to prove himself in every minute of
every game in a way that other players do not. Essentially, this is a failure of trust.
Unfortunately for Hoolahan, some managers have shared this perception, or at least
have been partial to it.

Whole chunks of Hoolahan's career have been accompanied by an undeserved
question mark. Even when he erases it, such as playing three consecutive seasons in
the Premier League for Norwich City, there seems to have been doubt over Hoolahan's
pedigree.

This stems from the Dubliner's physique. He is 5ft 6in, he is not muscular. Those
were factors in why he did not leave Ireland until he was 23 and this detail has since
been employed as a reason to query the true quality of Wes Hoolahan.

As a teenager he went over to Millwall, Sunderland and Ipswich Town on trial,
and then returned to Dublin.

'Ipswich were the only ones who showed real interest, they asked me back,' he says.
'At the time I thought I was a bit too young, so I decided not to. I was 16. Physically
I was small, lots of lads my age stronger than me, I hadn't filled out yet.'

Hoolahan was playing for Belvedere boys club then, moving to Shelbourne in
the League of Ireland when he was 18. He was to stay nearly five years, picking up
compliments as Shelbourne won the League of Ireland three seasons in a row from
2002.

Shels got into Europe and in 2004 eliminated KR Reykjavik and Hajduk Split
in the Champions League qualifiers before meeting Deportivo La Coruna in the
third qualifying round. The first leg was moved to Lansdowne Road and 24,000
saw Shelbourne draw 0-0 with a team that had just finished third in La Liga, a place
ahead of Real Madrid.

'It was on the telly,' Hoolahan says, 'and lots of people who would never go to a
Shelbourne game were there, a lot of Irish followers went because it was an occasion.
I think people from the outside took notice. In the tie before we'd to beat Hadjuk
Split. That was at Tolka Park, Dave Rogers scored a brilliant goal – and let us know

about it. That was fantastic. We played well at Deportivo too.'

The second leg ended 3-0 to Deportivo but the breakthrough took an hour and there was an 88th minute third. Shelbourne, organised and professional, knew what they were doing.

As Hoolahan says: 'We were full-time, we'd a good squad of players, a few coming back from England. You can do it in the League of Ireland if you're full-time. Look at Dundalk, what they're doing is brilliant.'

Hoolahan was content. Around him other Irish players travelled across to Britain, some returning, some not. He had done that; he was not overly anxious about doing it again.

'I never actually thought about going to England after that, it wasn't something that nibbled at me. I just kept playing. I was thinking: 'I'm here at Shelbourne, this is my job, I'll probably be here ten years.' Then I'll do something else.'

It was late 2005 when Shelbourne's colourful chairman Ollie Byrne called to say that Livingston, then in the SPL, were interested. They were managed by Paul Lambert. Shelbourne could do with the money, but it was up to Hoolahan.

'I said I'd think about it. My wife said: 'What are you thinking about?' So then I said: 'OK, I'll go.' She was right. It's worked out.

'Paul Lambert had watched me in a game at Drogheda, which I didn't know. He only told me when I'd signed. My Livingston debut was at Alloa Athletic in the Cup [January 2006]. We'd Paul Lambert and Robert Snodgrass in midfield, I came on on the left, and Graham Dorrans was on the bench as well. It was interesting.

'Paul Lambert was player-manager and in training the stuff he did was amazing, he could find you anywhere, amazing to play with him. The training ground was lovely, the facilities were better than Shelbourne, but I was only there five months and we got relegated. Paul had brought me over and after six weeks he got sacked.'

This was the real, sometimes brutal world of professional football and Hoolahan was on his own. Then Simon Grayson, managing Blackpool in League One, got in touch. Wes was invited down, he thought it was a loan deal but he discovered it was 'not a loan as we know it – I'd to go and train and prove myself.

'I felt quite nervous because I thought I was going there on loan and I'd sign. But I was going there just to see. Simon Grayson then invited me to Latvia, where they had another week's training planned. They still could have sent me back.'

It was fragile, but Hoolahan stuck at it. Grayson saw enough. When the League One season started in England, Hoolahan was on Blackpool's bench. By the fourth game he was starting and at the end of a season which climaxed with a play-off victory at Wembley, Hoolahan had played 49 times for Blackpool.

'It was my first taste of big English games, getting to Wembley. It was brilliant.'

He was now in England's Championship. Blackpool stayed up, they had 51 games in all that 2007/08 season and Hoolahan played in 50 of them. He was a delicate-looking left-winger with a sure touch and often under-appreciated stamina and those qualities brought Norwich City to the door of Bloomfield Road with £250,000.

On the opening day of 2008/09 Hoolahan was in Glenn Roeder's XI that lost at Coventry City. It was a bad start to a season that ended in relegation. Along the way Roeder was replaced by Bryan Gunn and Hoolahan was back in England's third tier.

On the opening day of the next season, in League One, Norwich hosted Colchester United. The score was 1-7 and Hoolahan played. It was a dramatically bad result and a week later Gunn was sacked. Colchester's manager just happened to be Paul Lambert. Norwich took note and appointed Lambert as Gunn's successor.

It appeared a rekindling of the Lambert-Hoolahan Livingston relationship was on, only for Hoolahan to find himself out of the team.

'I wasn't playing under Paul when he first came in. Then there was a reserve game against Peterborough, Paul said he'd play me in the middle. I did well, made a goal, scored a good goal. On the Friday he said he put me in behind Grant Holt.'

Holt and Hoolahan both scored in the game the next day against Charlton: 'And from then on I played virtually every game for the three or four years with Paul Lambert. I felt comfortable. I thought: 'This feels like my position.'

'You learn, you get more of the ball and you become a bit more clever on the ball. As a left-winger I probably didn't have lightning pace, in the middle I'd more options, I could see things, see a pass. So your confidence grows, you're scoring goals, setting them up, winning games. Winning games is big. And I became more professional, that dedication. You want to stay in the game longer and you keep to a strict regime.'

Under Lambert Norwich won League One, then in 2010/11 they immediately won another promotion, coming second in the Championship. Hoolahan played 42 times in Lambert's first season, 44 in the second. In August 2011 he lined up as a Premier League player five-and-a-half years after leaving Shelbourne and scored Norwich's first goal of the season at Wigan.

Norwich stayed up, as they did the next season. Wes Hoolahan had become an established top-flight player and though Norwich have been down, up and down again since, he is still at Carrow Road almost a decade on.

He is not Lionel Messi, despite the nickname 'Wessi', but there are obvious attributes: skill, vision. What is less appreciated is the perseverance he has shown in his career and shows over 90 minutes.

Which is why around 2011, when he was among a decreased number of Irishmen in the Premier League, more and more wondered why Hoolahan was not a regular international.

Fourteen years before Euro 2016, Hoolahan, 20, was called up by Don Givens for a friendly against Greece. Givens was standing in as Irish manager, between Mick McCarthy and Brian Kerr. Glen Crowe, another League of Ireland player, was also called in. Crowe played, Hoolahan didn't.

That was November 2002 and Hoolahan made his Ireland debut in May 2008. When it came, it was a two-minute sub for Andy Keogh in a friendly at Fulham. Giovanni Trapattoni was the new international manager; he did not select Hoolahan again for four years. All the while, there was a Wes debate.

'I'm an Ireland fan, so I'd be watching the game, I'd know what's going on,' he says. 'Obviously some people were calling for me to be called up. It never happened, so you just concentrate on your club football. You get on with things, keep going, work hard, just hope the penny will drop.

'Don Givens took over for a game against Greece and I got called up, me and Glen Crowe. Glen started, did well, I didn't manage to get on. Four or five years later I get called up by Trapattoni and he gives me a cap against Colombia at Craven Cottage – I got two minutes. I didn't get another cap for a while, got one or two caps, then Martin [O'Neill] took over.'

Hoolahan started O'Neill's first match as Trapattoni's successor. While he has not been an ever-present 90-minute man since, Hoolahan was on the pitch in the Euro 2016 qualifiers when John O'Shea scored in injury-time in Germany and when Shane Long scored in injury-time against Poland – from a Hoolahan header.

He also started the two play-off games against Bosnia-Herzegovina and when O'Neill named his team for Ireland's opening game at Euro 2016, Wes was there. And then, two minutes after half-time, he scored with a sweet volley.

'The Bosnia night was great,' he says, 'that was the first time I'd experienced qualifying from a campaign. The fans cheered us off the pitch and that night we went out and had a good shindig. Everyone was buzzing in the dressing room, everybody happy, it's great to experience. It's a moment you cherish.

'Then the Euros: I think we got the hardest group, the Group of Death. The Italians had one of the best qualifications, Sweden had Zlatan [Ibrahimovic] and Belgium were one of the favourites to win it. I just thought: 'You never know.' If we could get a point or win in the first game then we'd have a chance. It worked out.'

Before meeting Sweden in Paris, Hoolahan says he was: 'Quite relaxed. I was more nervous before Norwich's play-off final at Wembley – you know, against Middles-brough? That was really nerve-wracking for some reason. Sweden, I was fine.'

He was better than that when Seamus Coleman entered the Swedish box and delivered a cross.

'Seamus cut it back for me and it seemed to fall nicely. I just concentrated on getting my foot on it. It hit the back of the net. All my family were there. When I scored I ran to the left and they were up there. Sweden equalised to make it one-all but it was a good start to the group.'

Hoolahan knew what his goal would mean back in Dublin and across Ireland, because he had been that fan.

'I've been at home watching the tournament so I know what it's like. I remember Euros, World Cups, Ray Houghton scoring, Robbie Keane scoring. You're roaring at the telly, jumping up and down, your Mam's asking: 'What's going on?

"*Ireland scored!*'

'So to do it, to take it all in, the magnitude of it, it's massive. Maybe in 20 years I'll look back. Then I might realise how massive it is, that you're part of it, part of the history. Brilliant.'

Against Belgium five days later in Bordeaux, O'Neill again selected Hoolahan. Belgium had been beaten 2-0 by Italy and needed to get themselves into the tournament. In a rapid burst after half-time they did so, scoring three.

'We went into the game a bit flat, I don't know whether we put so much energy into the Sweden game. We started the second half well and we should have had a penalty when the fella kicked Shane Long in the head. Then they go up the pitch and score, three goals in 20 minutes, it just killed us.'

Italy had beaten Sweden 1-0, Belgium were expected to do the same to the Swedes but in the expanded format, three teams from the group might go through. But the Irish had to beat Italy and Hoolahan was on the bench.

'The gaffer made the changes for the Italy game to freshen it up. That worked a treat. You could see in the dressing room that we were up for this game. You could see the mentality, the attitude.

'I didn't know if I'd start, Martin keeps things close to his chest. Everybody has to be on their toes and you have to expect to play or expect to be involved at some stage. You're looking to see if you'll get on. And then he calls your name.'

After 77 minutes, with the game goalless, Hoolahan heard O'Neill's call. He went on for James McCarthy.

'You just think: 'I've got to do something.' You do what you can. We were all over them but we needed one goal.

'And then I get the chance.'

*

WHEN THE CHANCE HAS GONE, A NATION SLUMPS AGAIN. THIS IS Italy the Irish are facing, Italy, who haven't conceded a goal since March. It's now 22 June and it's getting late.

'At the time I thought I've just got to get on with it, there's minutes to go. Maybe I'll get another chance; to redeem this. If we didn't score and it's nil-all and we're out of the tournament, I think it would have haunted me forever.'

The enormity of the situation – that Wes's chance had become Wes's miss – had just enough time to become a fact, just enough time for the old question about Hoolahan to rise anew. But the game was still flowing and as he has done from the beginning at Belvedere, so was Wes.

'Luckily enough, about 25 seconds later, Robbie Brady has passed the ball to Aiden and Aiden's passed it to me. Robbie's continued his run . . .'

Hoolahan had received the ball on his right foot, he switched instinctively to his left, his head was up and he could see Brady running. This was the quarterback moment, the delivery had to be clean so the man in motion would connect without checking his run.

' . . and I've managed to find him in the penalty area. His header was great.'

Brady's header was brave and accurate, Ireland were through and Wes Hoolahan, the man who had missed one chance, had created the winning chance.

'The stadium went electric! People were running around, jumping, crying. They're the things you remember, how much it means to fans.'

Ireland were through to meet the hosts France in Lyon. That could wait, on the long bus journey back to Paris, there was celebration and reviews and then, after a while, a comment for Hoolahan's ears.

'There was a bit of craic on the bus, everyone enjoying it, the boys didn't mention the chance. But then someone said: 'No-one's said anything about Wes's miss, have they?'

'I was: 'Sorry, boys."

There was no need. There was the chance, and then there was the second chance, and Hoolahan made it.

GARETH MCAULEY – THE LADDER

CONSIDER GARETH MCAULEY AS HE APPROACHES HIS 38TH BIRTHDAY: here he is, the oldest player appearing regularly in the Premier League, in possession of the same physique he had as a teenager with Ballyclare Comrades almost two decades ago. McAuley has the wiry strength of a scaffolder and the spatial perception of the 6ft 3in draughtsman he was once. Both are appropriate, because when he surveys his route through football, he does so from the top step of a career ladder he has made for himself.

At its peak, in the summer of 2016 in Lyon, McAuley rose higher than any Ukrainian defender to head in a soaring Northern Ireland goal that launched them into Euro 2016 properly and McAuley into a hundred thousand photographs. It was a moment in Irish football history.

The high point of his career?

'So far,' he deadpans.

McAuley is only half-joking. Self-improvement to him is no mere mantra, it is his daily work. He has been urging himself upwards from not going 'across the water' as a boy, from not making it at Linfield, to doing so at Crusaders, then Coleraine and leaving the Irish League for Lincoln City in League Two, aged 24. From there he moved up to Leicester City and Ipswich Town in the Championship and from there up to West Bromwich Albion in the Premier League. Always up.

He was 31 when he made that West Brom step in 2011 and says of his Premier League debut: 'Walking out there, it was like the first time I'd been to New York, seeing all the buildings.

'I'd only seen the Premier League from TV. To be on the pitch, that's completely different, a real experience. It was just that first time. After that, I was comfortable.'

And here was another step up, an international tournament. Again he looked at it, took it in and – Northern Ireland 2-0 Ukraine – again Gareth McAuley felt comfortable.

'Loads of people gave us no chance,' he says. 'It was annoying and disrespectful. It wound me up. We won our qualifying group. Had the tournament not been expanded, we'd still have been there. We play with great intensity, especially at home.

'Yeah, I scored a goal and it's something I'm very, very proud of. Obviously being in a major tournament, the significance of it, it still hasn't really sunk in. It was 30 years since the last tournament, I hope it's not 30 years to the next one.

'But for me it was the team performance I was delighted with. I was also delighted that Niall McGinn scored. He started in local football too and worked his way up to that stage. He scored on that stage as well. It is incredible that both of us started in the local game. Yeah, that's the highlight so far. Now I've got to try to do it at a World Cup. That would beat it.'

*

GARETH MCAULEY WAS NOT THINKING OF WORLD CUP APPEAR-
ances when he was assessing his chances at Linfield aged 18. He had had his rugby difficulties at Larne Grammar and, while he was on the same Lisburn Youth team as future internationals David Healy, Aaron Hughes and Grant McCann, they had joined Manchester United, Newcastle United and West Ham United. McAuley could not break into the Linfield first team.

'I never had the chance to go across and I didn't think about a career,' he says. 'I was playing football just because I enjoyed it.'

Aaron Hughes's 1997 debut for Newcastle, which was against Barcelona, altered McAuley's thinking. He wondered how he could have the same career, the same experiences. By the time he was 19, he had moved to Crusaders – 'a big decision', he says.

McAuley justified it, winning Young Player of the Year. Then the award was taken off him: 'I was told I was too old. I've been told that a few times.'

But, as he says: 'I just got my head down. I loved it at Crusaders, loved it. At times it was tough but I got to play with the likes of Alan Dornan, Glenn Dunlop, who was way too good for local football. I went to Coleraine because [manager] Marty Quinn twisted my arm. He sold it to me with the players they had. It was massive for me to leave Crusaders but I saw it as a step up and every time I have moved, I always felt it was a progression. We won the Irish Cup against Glentoran, I played against Michael [O'Neill]. It was at Windsor Park – interesting.

'I was proud as you could be going back to Coleraine, I'd my medal around my neck. Then when we pulled up, Harry Gregg – he was at the front of the bus – stopped me and took the medal off. I wasn't thinking, if I'd have got off with that I'd have lost it. Big Harry was looking after me. Harry's such a dominant figure of a man, you listen. Manchester United, Munich, Northern Ireland, you learn what he did.'

It was 2003, May, and McAuley was 23. He won a Northern Ireland B cap against Scotland and Sammy McIlroy, who had just left the post of Northern Ireland manager for Stockport County, invited McAuley over to Edgeley Park.

'I'd three weeks over there but they were in trouble and I came back,' McAuley says. There were other rumours about other clubs but McAuley had no agent or advisor to filter these.

'I didn't have anyone looking after me. To me it was hearsay. I was on my own trying to work out who to speak to. It turned out Lincoln were watching.'

Many players' careers have unforeseen connections and for McAuley one in the background was that Marty Quinn knew the late Keith Alexander, who had an unlikely loan spell at Cliftonville as a player. Alexander was managing Lincoln.

'Marty knew him,' McAuley says. 'So I went over to Lincoln, played in a behind-closed-doors friendly against Peterborough and I stayed. That was midweek before the season started. At the weekend I travelled with the team. I'd left with a bag, that was it. I was well-supported by my family but I think they were a bit shocked when I said: 'Right, that's me off.' I had to go for it.'

But there he was at Shrewsbury Town versus Lincoln City in August 2004, about to climb a step. McAuley's next birthday, his twenty-fifth, was four months off. He was on Lincoln's bench; on Shrewsbury's was a 17 year-old Joe Hart.

There were 20 minutes left: 'Keith threw me on up front – he did that a few times before I got established. It was boiling. It was 20 minutes and it felt like two days. I didn't score.'

But McAuley had got across the water, set down a foot and crucially did not feel out of his depth. Football had been part-time in the Irish League, he had a day job and trained at night. This was professionalism.

'I had done a full pre-season at Stockport so I was fitter than the other lads at Lincoln who were coming back. That gave me a load of confidence. Coming from part-time to full-time football, you think you're going to be behind fitness-wise, but I'd worked hard for a long time to be as fit as possible.

'The biggest thing I found was that my days used to be long – working, travelling three nights a week to Coleraine to train, getting back home late, getting up and going again. So finishing at midday took a bit of getting used to. I'd stay around the club, do fitness work with a few of the lads.

'I signed a two-year contract. For a few years I'd been fixated on this – it was when [Aaron] Hughesy made his debut for Newcastle. That was the point when I thought: 'I used to play with him and he's got a career in football.' Although I was happy, it just wasn't enough. That was the click that made me think.'

Keith Alexander picked McAuley 44 times that season, 40 the next, and halfway through McAuley's second season, Leicester City showed interest. It was January 2006 and Craig Levein was Leicester manager. Then Levein was sacked, Rob Kelly took over.

Leicester's interest stood despite the change of manager and in June 2006 McAuley moved as a free agent. He was in the Championship and says: 'Concentration is the thing, you've to make decisions more quickly as you go up levels.'

That was on the pitch and in a way that was the easy part. Off it, McAuley was learning other, hard lessons.

'It was a real eye-opener for me, Leicester, it showed me how ruthless football can be.

'That season Leicester had something like 55 pros. Managers changed, [chairman] Milan Mandaric kept bringing players in. It was so draining, the level of chaos behind the scenes, the chopping and changing of managers, I just kept on doing what I'd to do and even as the managers changed I kept on being picked. Mentally it gave me a toughness.

'Leicester was bittersweet – I'd reached the Championship but the chaos at the club was mad. Mandaric appointed an agent to sell me, and not just me. You don't think about this kind of thing – at that stage I'm just about playing football. There was all sorts going on. You're learning on your feet.'

Ultimately, McAuley says: 'It was a good experience, though it ended badly.' By badly he means relegation in May 2008, the end of his second season at Leicester.

'We were relegated on the last day at Stoke. I hit the inside of the post at 0-0. A goal then would have been enough to keep us in the Championship. That affected me. Walking past our fans was terrible. There was a pitch invasion and I'd my shirt ripped off me. About two years later a guy came up to me at an Ipswich game, we were at Plymouth, and asked if I wanted the top back. He'd sell it to me.'

McAuley felt able to decline that offer and he was also able to decline dropping a division with Leicester. Ipswich, where former Northern Ireland midfielder Jim Magilton had become manager in 2006, were keen.

'I felt comfortable in the Championship,' McAuley says. 'Leicester were relegated, so they were going to League One. Having been in League Two, I didn't want to take a step down.

'I felt a little guilty leaving Leicester and it took me a bit to settle at Ipswich. Jim

Magilton, who I didn't have a relationship with before, took me there, believed in me, made me captain. It was a big responsibility – I didn't know a great deal about their history until I got there. You go behind the scenes and you see the size of the club. John Wark's walking about – he's been in Escape To Victory!

'It's a fantastic club. That's all there is in that part of east Anglia. Everywhere you go, everyone is an Ipswich fan, it's the first time I'd experienced a bit of a goldfish bowl. The expectation probably got Jim in the end.'

After twice narrowly missing out on the play-offs and with a new owner, Marcus Evans, Magilton left Portman Road in April 2009. And as one former Irish midfielder departed, another walked in. Roy Keane had a quick look around and McAuley was no longer captain.

'At the time I thought he was trying to get rid of me. I'd actually arranged to leave, for Middlesbrough, but he turned around and asked me not to. Roy, he's someone who challenges you, all the time. He wants people with him who will always challenge themselves. All the time. That's the one thing I learned from him that's really stuck with me.

'He used to say there were too many at the club who were comfortable in the Championship. He thought they had more to give. He could be abrasive, just as he was as a player, and he was a straight talker. It was a difficult time for the club but when you look at it now, you can understand what he was trying to do.'

By January 2011 Keane was gone and McAuley left soon after. At 31 he was off to the Premier League with West Brom and a different kind of Roy – Hodgson.

'I was desperate to play in the Premier League, desperate to get on the pitch. Then I got sick after my medical, I'd a virus, had a horrific pre-season. I'd to give up training for a couple of weeks.'

Then, at home to Fulham, McAuley had his New York moment and another like it three months later: 'We were at Newcastle, at St. James' Park under the lights, a midweek game, and Shane Long came up to me before the game and said: 'This is what's it's about.' That atmosphere they create there. I scored that night, my first goal for West Brom.'

Six years on, McAuley is the oldest outfield player in the Premier League, averaging 36 games a season for West Brom and in 2016/17, scored seven goals. Nor is he stopping. There is a new one-year contract.

'I do believe that it is something to do with coming over later,' he says of his longevity and freshness. 'In terms of my body, my body was fully developed through playing games on grass, rather than training on artificial surfaces – boys shouldn't be on those pitches.

'Another thing about the Premier League is that going into games, you feel good. The Championship has so many games, you don't feel that way in the majority of games. In the Premier League, during the week you can actually do fitness work, rather than recovering all the time. Even now I'm still trying to better my match velocity or how high I can jump. You keep on challenging – if I wasn't able to play in the Premier League, it would show in my figures, they'd be tailing off.

'So, yeah, I'm a better player than I was – significantly. You learn the game, you learn what you're good at and the big thing I've found is trust – players' trust, managers' trust, coaches' trust. If you've got that, you can go a long way.'

*

'AFTER THE GAME IN FINLAND, WE WERE WALKING OFF AND HE SAID to me that I'd easily one, maybe two more campaigns in me. I was laughing, we've had a few jokes since.'

Michael O'Neill trusts Gareth McAuley. This is McAuley relating the pair's conversation as they walked off the pitch in Helsinki having won Group F of the Euro 2016 qualifiers. O'Neill was already putting the World Cup of 2018 in McAuley's mind.

It is easier to excite players about the future when you are winning of course. McAuley understands, because he was with Northern Ireland when they were losing. He was there when he would not play.

Lawrie Sanchez had given McAuley his debut in 2005, at the end of that first season with Lincoln. But pride at that turned to dissatisfaction and McAuley talked of not continuing with Northern Ireland.

'My biggest frustration was not feeling part of it when Lawrie Sanchez was there, not just me, probably five or six of us. He gave me my debut, but I felt like a spare part. The boys used to call us the 'mushrooms' because we'd to go and stand in the corner of the pitch while Lawrie did his stuff. You just felt like an outcast, you'd do all the travel and never get a kick. That's why toward the end of Lawrie I spoke about stopping. You just couldn't be bothered. I'd get back on a Thursday and Leicester were struggling in the Championship. I just thought 'it's not fair'. Pure frustration.'

He had only five caps then. 'I was about to stop and then Nigel Worthington came in and put me on standby. I got called up, started away at Sweden [2007] and have been around ever since.'

He was at right back that night in Stockholm. By Euro 2016 no-one thought of McAuley as anything other than a centre-half. By midway through the 2018 World Cup qualifiers, his cap tally was 72.

Scoring against Ukraine, when Northern Ireland needed it most after the disappointment against Poland, is the high point and even though McAuley then scored the own goal that decided the knock-out game with Wales, it is the Ukraine photograph brought which is always brought over for him to sign.

'I've not carried it with me,' he says of Wales. 'Scoring an own goal is not like missing a penalty in a shoot-out, I can live with it, it's part of football. I've signed loads of pictures of me scoring against Ukraine but none of that goal against Wales. People come from all over to West Brom games to get it signed, stuff is sent to the club for me to sign, loads from German fans now we're in the same World Cup group.'

Russia 2018 is in his sights, not that Euro 2016 will be forgotten.

'When you come home now and get in a taxi at the airport and the driver says: 'Thanks for what you've done', you get a bit embarrassed. It's nice. As a footballer it's incredible to think what you do affects people so much.'

PART V

DOMESTIC AFFAIRS (2017)

LEAGUE OF IRELAND
DUNDALK V SHAMROCK ROVERS,
24 FEBRUARY, 2017

'IT WAS THE SHORTEST OF WINTERS.'

With this small sentence, large in its novelistic possibilities, the Dundalk manager Stephen Kenny began his programme notes for the first match of the 2017 League of Ireland season.

Six words: six words to preface one season and link it back to the one just gone, when Kenny's club had been Irish champions for a third consecutive season. More than that, Dundalk had reached the third round of Champions League qualification and 30,000 went to see them play Legia Warsaw in Dublin's Aviva Stadium.

They lost on the night and on aggregate, but being at that stage meant an automatic place in the group stage of the Europa League. And more than that, they started the group with a draw at AZ Alkmaar and then a victory in Dublin against Maccabi Tel Aviv.

From having 'more or less nothing' when he walked into Oriel Park four years earlier, where crowds could dip to the hundreds in the really bad times, Kenny had fashioned something. It was something others wanted to emulate.

So while the winter may have been short, Dundalk could enjoy it and tonight, a Friday, the 2017 League of Ireland season begins with smiles and handshakes at Oriel Park.

For 14 years the League of Ireland has been a summer league – March to October – though some in Ireland call it a 'two winters' league. This late-February start is to accommodate a mid-July break, although while it will be greeted by the rest of the League it does not apply to Dundalk, who face Rosenborg in Champions League qualifiers then.

Against richer, larger, European establishment opposition, Dundalk go down 3-2 on aggregate to Rosenborg, having been ahead twice. The second leg in Norway goes to extra-time and the close nature of the games leaves Kenny so frustrated he refers to Dundalk's home ground, as 'bloody Oriel Park.' It is a significant comment.

'There is nothing between the teams and yet we are playing in bloody Oriel Park, very limited facilities, and we are coming to grounds like this,' Kenny said in the modern, 21,000-capacity stadium in Trondheim.

'The players deserve to be playing on stages like this. They showed that last year and they showed it over two legs. To go through wouldn't have flattered us.'

Kenny mentioned 'margins', as managers do. But he knows. At 45 he is hardly old, but he has been around Irish football long enough to have gone over to Oxford United in the late 1980s with Paul Byrne – later of Arsenal and Celtic – and then sign Byrne's son Kurtis for Dundalk.

In 2006 Kenny's Derry City team knocked out Gothenburg in the UEFA Cup, on the way to losing narrowly to Paris St-Germain. In 2016 Dundalk's four defeats in the Europa League group were all by a single goal. Oriel Park had not met UEFA's stadium criteria, so 'home' games were played in Dublin.

And over two days north and south of the Irish border, facilities, infrastructure and finance become the overriding theme. The domestic game needs help. Externally, it needs attention from government, local and national; internally, it needs it from those who run the leagues on a daily basis. It also requires imagination.

Dundalk's 2016 success – not just reaching the group stage of the Europa League, but being competitive – raised the profile of the League of Ireland. Two of the team's stand-out players, Daryl Horgan and Andy Boyle, were sold to Preston North End in the Championship when it was over.

Tonight, facing Shamrock Rovers, the only other Irish club to reach the Europa League group stage – under Michael O'Neill in 2011 – Oriel Park is alive. There are almost 5,000 here, with the main stand full and the shed stand opposite packed and colourful. They are singing: 'Champions of Ireland, we know what we are.'

Behind both nets it is open-air and standing on the grassy knoll behind the goal Dundalk attacked in the second half was to be surrounded by running groups of young boys and girls having a fine time. The atmosphere was happy, old-fashioned Ireland, and with Rovers bringing 600 followers from Dublin, this was an occasion. More folk attended it than saw Peterborough United face Rochdale in League One in England that weekend.

Yet on a wall in the main stand tea-room is an aerial picture of Oriel Park from 1953. It has not changed much in over 60 years and in that same room three months later, Kenny talks about where Dundalk FC are and where the League of Ireland is in 2017.

'Results in Europe give you credibility,' he says of the Europa League run. 'Dundalk captured the imagination of the wider public. I got a lot of letters from people I don't know saying: 'This is brilliant, different, this is what we believe in.' Others just liked the idea of a small-town club competing with Zenit St. Petersburg.'

When Kenny was appointed in November 2012, the club had just won a relegation play-off against Waterford. Dundalk would have been relegated already had Monaghan United not folded mid-season, itself a comment on the state of the League. 'I'd been offered the job three times previously and in better circumstances,' Kenny says.

But Dundalk had new directors and they wanted the Dubliner who had settled in in Derry. 'They came up to the house, said there was no shortlist. I made them soup. They slag me now: 'What did you put in that soup?'

'They said they'd do it properly – which means the wages are paid, not some grand investment. They said they'd make sure. They're fans. They stand on the terraces. It was a blank canvas but it wasn't an easy sell – none of the top players in the League would come here, we couldn't pay them and they wouldn't commute. We moulded a team from more or less nothing. I didn't envisage it would go this well.'

In Kenny's first season, 2013, Dundalk finished second; in his second season, Dundalk finished first, claiming the club's first League of Ireland title since 1995.

'For the players it was a first league title,' he says, 'it wasn't like they'd won it before. It was fresh and people connected with it, there was a lot of passion. It's raw, Dundalk, a border town, gets a negative press. But it's a good place. Facilities are limited but the rawness of the support helped us. Dundalk won the League in 1995 but in the 19 years after they'd never finished in the top four and had been in the First Division [second tier] for seven years. They could get 700 then.'

League titles followed in 2015 and 2016, players were coveted - Richie Towell preceded Horgan and Boyle, moving to Brighton & Hove Albion. More and more took notice of Kenny and Dundalk and they played on grander stages, but the driving force behind progress in football – money – remained and remains tight.

League of Ireland prize money is low, unsustainably low. Dundalk received just €110,000 for winning the league in 2015. For coming second Cork City received just €55,000. Given that clubs have to pay a registration fee to participate in the League, it is no surprise that the 2017 season saw Bray Wanderers in financial peril, with both Bohemians and Finn Harps needing to ask fans for an injection of cash to tide them over.

The FAI oversee the League and it is pointed out regularly that chief executive John

Delaney earns more than three times the amount the champions receive. Delaney has described the League of Ireland as a 'difficult child'. The Republic of Ireland manager Giovanni Trapattoni, appointed by Delaney, said in 2013 that 'there is no league in Ireland'. What Trapattoni may have meant was that there is no full-time professional league in Ireland but the players, managers, fans and so many volunteers involved felt aggrieved, understandably so. Neither remark helps sell the league. Neither remark showed respect.

Reports are commissioned and read but little seems to change and there is a pronounced disconnection between the avid fans and the administration. There have been experiments: in 1981/82 the League introduced a new points system – 4 for an away win, 3 for a home win, 2 for an away draw and 1 for a home draw. There were the fewest number of 0-0 draws in 45 years, but the economics were unchanged and Cork United went bankrupt.

It is the longstanding issue. As Kenny says: 'There's a lack of money invested in the game, a lack of promotion. There's only one or two employees at the FAI designated to the League. We don't get any TV money. From that side we need concerted effort, put manpower into it. Can we promote it? Can we get the players to connect with the public? These things aren't really considered in a major way.

'We need to be more creative: 'How do we make it better?' We have poor stadiums, poor facilities. In European cities, the local government build a lot of the stadiums.'

Post-recession, post-Celtic Tiger, the idea of municipal investment in sport is not a priority despite the known benefits. Dundalk brought in around €4m from their UEFA 2016 run, and are looking at building a new ground, but local government interest would give plans impetus.

Kenny's loss of players to England shows there is talent. There is something to watch. To illustrate the benefit of infrastructure, he offers an example of a previous player he sold, Niall McGinn, when they were at Derry City. McGinn impressed at the FAI Cup final in 2008, which was held at the RDS Arena, capacity 18,000.

'It was a proper match in a proper stadium and Niall had a good game,' Kenny says. 'Swansea bid £200,000 for him. Roberto Martinez said he would put Niall straight into his team in the Championship. Celtic came in and matched it and he chose to go to Celtic. The point is about presentation. The same with Daryl Horgan and Andy Boyle, they played good matches in good stadiums and got their move.

'The big problem as I see it is infrastructure. People want to come to good stadiums, they want to come to nice places. And the games look better aesthetically in nice stadiums. I think that's a huge thing. Facilities.

'Pitches – the move to a summer league has meant they're better. But it's the stadiums. If we compare them to other parts of Europe, they're not impressive. Oriel Park isn't.'

*

IN DECEMBER 1972, CRYSTAL PALACE BEAT MANCHESTER UNITED 5-0 at Selhurst Park. According to Paddy Mulligan 'it had a huge impact'.

Mulligan was the Palace captain and he scored the opening two goals, but the impact he was referring to was not in south London, it was in the south of Ireland.

Mulligan had been a Shamrock Rovers player for six years in late 1969 when he signed for Chelsea, joining Palace in '72.

'The League that I was leaving was in great shape,' he says. 'But then around 1970, they started showing *The Big Match* in Ireland. All of a sudden at 2.30 on a Sunday afternoon people were watching The Big Match on TV and not going to matches. It was very significant, that's what I feel. Games like the Palace-Man United one would have had a huge impact on crowds in the League of Ireland. That was the sad part.'

The Big Match was ITV's response to BBC's *Match of the Day*. It was broadcast at 2.30 on a Sunday, at a time when the League of Ireland staged its games. Not all of Ireland received the ITV signal, but enough of it did.

'From a Shamrock Rovers perspective I also felt that [the owners] the Cunningham family had maybe done as much as they could,' Mulligan adds. 'Perhaps the energy levels weren't what they were.

'With due respect to the rest of the clubs, the League needed a winning Shamrock Rovers. We played Glasheen, a local Cork team, in 1965 in the Cup and Turner's Cross was full. The decline of Rovers spread to the rest of the League. Games on English television meant that people here were following, I mean really following, English clubs. They were going over on a Saturday. To a degree that was happening in the 1960s but people would make sure they were on the boat home to be at Milltown or wherever on the Sunday. The English game became more attractive.'

After ten years in England, Mulligan returned to Shamrock Rovers and the League of Ireland. What he discovered was a League 'withered'.

'It was completely different. I couldn't believe how different it was in ten years. There was an awful lot of apathy, that bounce that you would have going into Milltown wasn't there and it's very difficult to bring back when it's gone. Sligo Rovers v Shamrock Rovers in 1966 and Sligo Rovers v Galway in 1984, these are two different planets. You wouldn't have been able to get into the Showgrounds in 1966; in 1984 you could walk in any time, a few hundred there.'

Officially Milltown stadium's biggest crowd was the 28,000 who saw Shamrock Rovers play Waterford in 1968, but unofficially, it is said there were quite a few days when that attendance was surpassed.

In 1945, a figure of 44,000 was recorded for the Shamrock Rovers-Bohemians Cup final at Dalymount Park. In 1960, it was 32,000 for Shelbourne v Cork Hibernians and in 1968, 39,000 for Shamrock Rovers v Waterford. Yet by 1973 it was down to 12,500 for Cork v Shelbourne and by 1985 just 7,000 were turning up to see Rovers play Galway United.

A year earlier Ryanair began operating a Waterford to London flight that would in time transform low-cost aviation and enable many more Irish people to make many more journeys to England. The goalposts had shifted. In 1987 Milltown, Rovers' much-loved home, became a housing estate.

*

BACK IN THE TEA-ROOM AT ORIEL PARK 30 YEARS ON, STEPHEN KENNY says players' agents are now advising them to sign one-year deals so that if there is English or Scottish interest, the signing club is less likely to have to pay a transfer fee.

In pessimistic moments he thinks how hard it is to build a team when he has to keep replacing players and acknowledges there is a large section of the Irish public who would agree with the Trapattoni viewpoint.

At his most optimistic, though, Kenny says that the effect of the game in a city such as Derry should be measured in more than crowd figures. And there is scope for optimism: at the last two Cup finals, which involved the best two sides in the country – Dundalk and Cork City – attendances have been over 25,000.

Then there is the all-Ireland, one-League proposal, which was put forward in 2008 by Derry City chairman Jim Roddy and businessman Fintan Drury.

'I did like the idea of an All-Ireland League that was proposed by Jim Roddy,' Kenny says. 'It was based on the population centres: Belfast, Cork, Limerick, Derry, Dublin – you'd get TV money.

'But there wasn't the appetite for it in the North; there was here. Then the financial crisis hit and clubs had to get their house in order. To me that was the way it could work – they've an all-Ireland League in rugby, in GAA, in hockey, why haven't we got it? Obviously there's the two Associations, but if you focussed on the population centres, get proper crowds, proper matches, rivalry, that's the way I see it.'

On the pitch that Friday night, Dundalk won 2-1. As the season developed Cork City emerged from their second-place finishes to overtake the champions, with striker

Sean Maguire in prolific form until Preston came calling on the League of Ireland once again. Preston also signed Cork's Kevin O'Connor.

It can feel like a League of two halves at times. Cork, Dundalk and Shamrock Rovers – with a new academy and Damien Duff on the coaching staff – are looking forward. Some of the others are just looking around, trying to pay the bills.

IRISH LEAGUE

GLENTORAN V LINFIELD, 25 FEBRUARY, 2017

TOM CLARKE WAS THE SON OF A BRITISH SOLDIER WHO WAS EXecuted by his father's army for his pivotal role in the Easter Rising. On the 50th anniversary of his death, Dundalk train station was named after Clarke. You notice these things waiting for a train.

It is the same the next day, waiting for a crowd. In east Belfast you stand on the corner of Dee Street awaiting swarms of Glentoran and Linfield fans heading towards the Oval for the latest meeting of the Irish League's 'Big Two'. You wait and wait, standing beneath a threatening mural of three UVF gunmen in balaclavas encircled by the phrase: 'We are the pilgrims, master; we shall go always a little further.'

The words were taken from the Golden Journey to Samarkand, and were adopted as an unofficial motto by the SAS. The image sends out a clear message about the turf you are on and who controls it. It is hard not to be struck by it and other paramilitary imagery in the surrounding streets.

In part this is because there is so little contrast. Were thousands assembling on the Newtownards Road or Mersey Street as they did once, anticipation in their step and football on the tongue, it would be different. But the wait for a crowd, for a buzz, was forlorn.

Glentoran versus Linfield in the most played senior football match in the world. They have been facing each other since 1887 and this was the 455th meeting. Few, if any, of those matches can have been so depressed.

As a club, Glentoran are in decline and in debt. The future of the crumbling Oval is in question, they have not been Irish League champions since 2009 and were on their way to finish ninth in a 12-team League where the biggest crowd of the season was 7,500 and lowest was under 200.

The largest attendance was for Linfield-Glentoran at Windsor Park on Boxing Day, but when the reverse fixture came in February, Linfield fans were staging a boycott. It was due to allegations of sectarianism at the previous game, which some said were, quietly and unofficially, made by Glentoran. Linfield had played the banned song "The Billy Boys' over the Tannoy, which the club said later was an accident. It apologised but fingers had been pointed. In Belfast it is called 'what-aboutery' – as in 'what about what you said first'.

If there were more than 1,000 at the vast Oval, it cannot have been by many and none can have left impressed. It was a dreadful game. 'Crap,' said David Healy, Linfield's manager of 16 months. And his team won.

It was slow football. A fixture known for the depth of its feeling was drained of it. Some might consider that a good thing, but it sounded and looked strange.

Both sets of supporters come from working class Protestant backgrounds but they do not like each other. It was on this ground in 1985 when the Irish Cup final saw a pig painted blue released onto the pitch by Glentoran fans to antagonise their rivals – the Blues.

'My name was written on it,' says Roy Coyle. Coyle, born nearby, played for Glentoran before becoming the highly successful manager of Linfield. He knows both sides. 'I found out that the pig had been kept overnight at the Oval. I don't know who kept it, but my name was scrawled on it.'

Later Coyle returned to Glentoran as manager and won a match at Linfield. The players were celebrating in the dressing room when an irate Linfield 'fan' burst in. He may have been one of the city's known-knowns. As Coyle remembers: 'He put his finger to my temple and said: 'You're a lucky boy I didn't have a gun with me.' The players grabbed him and threw him out. It was scary. That was the worst. While hatred is a strong word to use, Linfield and Glentoran certainly don't get on. No question.'

Given such incidents, and there have been plenty of others, to lament an absence of tension might seem perverse. Maybe it was the nothingness of the afternoon in a stadium that looks like a relic.

Still attached to Glentoran, Coyle, 71, has strong opinions on this. 'Our game is going down,' he says, before echoing Stephen Kenny at Dundalk – 'The biggest problem we have in Irish football today are the stadiums. They're frozen in time, they're a millstone. We didn't get the grants from the Taylor Report.

'Years ago you'd turn up at 2.45, the queues were long and then you'd leave after the final whistle. Nowadays football's a day out – people leave this little island of ours to go to England or Scotland and they're prepared to spend money at clubs where there are restaurants, shops, comfort. There's no comfort here, no memorabilia, no shops, no museums.

'This is our national sport, and we're just left. Our game has been completely ignored. We took kids off the streets – training, playing, watching. This game of ours has been going on the whole way through the Troubles and what help have we ever got? I've spoken to politicians, you may as well talk to the wall. But I guarantee the government are helping out rugby, the Belfast Giants [ice hockey]. To me our game is near intensive care because of the stadia. We need emergency surgery.'

In June 2017 the IFA produced a document for the next five years, part of which includes the aim to 'rebuild the football estate'. There is £36m available from local government.

The Association is at least starting to address the issue but those long in the tooth feel like they have heard this before. The dates and numbers are different but this is reminiscent of the 1970s when the bible of the UK game, Rothmans Football Yearbook, began its 1973 Irish review like this: 'Another season of crisis.'

It reflected on Derry City's withdrawal due to other clubs' refusal to play at the Brandywell and on the ongoing 'isolation' of the League and the turmoil around it: 'To complete the programme within the specific period was in itself a feat.'

The next year the stand-out remark was that the Irish League 'battled through a virtual civil war' and with less than 6,000 attending the Irish Cup final, in 1976 Rothmans view was: 'You could say it is a fight for survival.'

This was how it felt there and then, as if the Irish League was operating under curfew. Yet optimism was found whenever possible: in 1977 a grant of £50,000 from government for ground improvements and a 12,000 crowd at the Cup final brought the comment: 'Happy days are here again.'

It was a clutching at straws. Between 1970 and 1998 Cliftonville were unable to host Linfield due to security precautions. The two clubs are three-and-a-half miles apart, but for 28 years the fixture was not allowed by the RUC to be played on Cliftonville's turf. This is the street-by-street reality the Irish League had to face.

*

DARKO PANCEV WAS SITTING IN THE FOYER OF A HOTEL IN DUNMURRY flicking through *The Sun*. It was October 1991 and Pancev's club, Red Star Belgrade, were European champions. They had drawn Portadown, Irish League champions, in the first round of their defence of the European Cup.

The first leg was in Belgrade, won 4-0 by Red Star, and the second leg was to finish the same. It was comfortable but Shamrock Park in Portadown was busy to see players like Pancev and Sinisa Mihajlovic. There was income, prestige and participation.

The next season, Glentoran drew Marseilles in the first round. They again lost heavily but the Oval was bouncing the night Marseilles and their fans arrived. The French saw east Belfast and the Glens fans saw Basile Boli, Rudi Voller and Abedi Pele.

But that was the beginning of the Champions League and soon that format would expand to push clubs from leagues such as the Irish League and League of Ireland to the edges. The days and nights of Red Star Belgrade and Marseilles were coming to a close. Instead of Crusaders drawing Liverpool, as they did in the 1976/77 European Cup, there would be anxious first round qualifiers against equally desperate clubs from Bulgaria or Georgia or Finland.

As Dundalk's Oriel Park experience in 2016 highlighted, UEFA also increased the number of criteria required to even host a match. Year on year economic life got harder for struggling clubs in small Leagues.

Yet today across in north Belfast at Crusaders, Europe and UEFA is now seen differently to that view from the 1990s and 2000s.

'The only significant source of income for Irish League football is if you qualify for Europe,' says Mark Langhammer, a Crusaders director. 'That money, which used to be relatively low, is now life-changing. If you get it.

'For kicking a ball in the Champions League we get €400,000. That's the first qualifying round. We got into the second round [in 2015], we beat an Estonian team. That broke the back of all the debt we had. We got €650,000 at a time when the pound was dropping in value.'

Fan-owned, with an average crowd of 1,500, Crusaders won the Irish League in 2014-15 and 2015-16.

'For winning the League the season before last, we got £21,000 – for coming first,' Langhammer says. 'Three years before that when Cliftonville won, they got £50,000. Prize money is going down radically.'

The club is punching above its weight on the pitch but Langhammer is realistic about economics – the club needed a bond scheme in 2008 to prevent liquidation. If things continue to go well, Crusaders hope that their part-time players can become 'what we call three-quarters professional.

'We've seen what Dundalk have done. The League of Ireland is ahead of us in terms of having four or five clubs almost totally pro. I saw Dundalk play Zenit St. Petersburg last season and there wasn't a huge difference. We've started a conversation with Dundalk about how they moved up. It wasn't rocket science, they appointed a manager with commitment and bought the right players. Three years ago, Dundalk had our budget.

'Three or four Irish League clubs have the capability to go three-quarters professional, and if we changed the calendar, within five years one of those teams would reach the group stage of the Europa League. That's do-able. It's what Dundalk have done.'

The IFA say the calendar will change so that clubs involved in Europe in early July will have had matches in May and June to get players match-fit.

'We are starting our richest game of the year having played one friendly, one pre-season match and then you're playing FC Copenhagen,' Langhammer says. 'They blew us away in the end. The aim of the Irish League should be that some club – Crusaders, Ballymena United, Linfield, whoever – gets into the group stage of the Europa League. To do that, we've to shift the season, so we've eight to ten weeks before you go into those qualifiers.

'An argument against is that you'd miss Boxing Day, New Year's Day, big fixtures. But you needn't necessarily, you could start our League in May and finish in January. It's a no-brainer.'

*

EVEN IN VICTORY, DAVID HEALY ACCEPTED THE STANDARD OF FOOT-ball was poor. As it transpired, Linfield went on to win the League and then landed an old-style European Cup windfall by drawing Celtic in the Champions League qualifiers. It brought a date-change – from 12 July– it brought tension and bottle-throwing, it brought defeats in both legs and a fine from UEFA, but it brought Linfield money.

Already the biggest club in the best stadium, the Blues should dominate. But Healy is circumspect. Although he said: 'I'd love to be in at nine o'clock in the morning, training full time,' he added: 'The finance isn't there in the Irish League. These players have jobs. Unless the finance is there, it's probably never going to happen.'

While that is the case it is hard to foresee an Irish League club making the same European progress Dundalk and Shamrock Rovers have made recently. Another League of Ireland club, Bohemians, have beaten Aberdeen, while Derry City got past Gothenburg.

The Northern Ireland manager Michael O'Neill is concerned. This is where his football began and he says: 'The saddest thing for me is that the Irish League is still functioning as it had when I started. Train Tuesday-Thursday, game on Saturday, it hasn't progressed.

'And it's one of the things that as an international manager I harp on about: the Irish League has to produce players for the international team. Four months after playing for Coleraine, Billy Bingham called me in to international football. I came from nowhere to be a player for him and you need players to come down that route.'

At the 1982 World Cup Bingham included four Irish League players – Felix Healy of Coleraine, Johnny Jameson and Jimmy Cleary of Glentoran and George Dunlop of Linfield. In 1986 Linfield's Mark Caughey was in the squad with Jim Platt, who had moved home by then.

A promising feature for both the domestic leagues is that the Euro 2016 squads Michael and Martin O'Neill took to France contained prominent players who had begun in the League of Ireland or Irish League, though both international managers, and others, might debate the contribution to the development of those players' talent made by Irish domestic football.

The bulk of both squads was made of players who had gone 'across the water' as young teenagers, joined a professional club there and stayed.

One aim of the domestic leagues is to delay that emigration by giving players a platform at home. For that to happen there needs to be more care and attention paid to the Leagues and there possibly needs to be an honest discussion about how many clubs a population of 6.5 million on the island can sustain in a sporting culture which, uniquely, includes GAA and which is under increasing pressure from rugby's expansion.

The League of Ireland has 20 clubs in two divisions; the Irish League has 24 clubs across two divisions. There are 44 clubs, some professional, some semi-professional, some amateur and all with eager volunteers and fanbases large and small. Of these perhaps half could be considered 'senior' in terms of history and current scale.

Talent still emerges. Glentoran gave a debut in 2016 to 15 year-old Ethan Warnock, who promptly signed for Everton. That traffic across the water will never cease.

*

WALKING AWAY FROM THE OVAL, BACK ONTO THE NEWTOWNARDS Road, and after a bad match in a dead stadium, all it needed was some late-February sleet. It is quiet, oppressive, more paramilitary graffiti, a few hundred yards away Madrid Street is cut in two by one of Belfast's multitude of so-called peace walls.

Paul Theroux saw this area in 1983 and wrote of 'a sort of nightmare charm'. A generation earlier Louis MacNeice saw 'the hard cold fire of the northerner ... down there at the end of the melancholy lough.'

MacNiece was from these parts, so too CS Lewis and up the road now stands a series of bold bronze statues, particularly the lion and the wardrobe. Lewis's memoir of his time here was called *Surprised By Joy* and you walk along thinking of how Joe Bambrick, Peter Doherty, Con Martin and Danny Blanchflower had been launched from here, so many others; of how we had seen in a packed Oval in 1977 Glentoran push the Juventus of Zoff, Gentile and Causio in the European Cup. A 1-0 defeat, a penalty-kick missed. William McCrum's legacy.

The sleet never comes. Instead winter sun breaks out and above one of those pretend shopfronts councils use to disguise the absence of economic activity, a familiar face appears at an upstairs window. He is wearing his old Wolverhampton Wanderers kit. He sports that big Mexican bandit moustache. He is painted on and, maybe surprised by joy, Derek Dougan is smiling.

EPILOGUE

ACROSS THE WATER. SOMETIMES IT SEEMS LIKE IT ALWAYS COMES comes back to George.

Twenty-four hours later at the Queen's Film Theatre on broad University Street they are showing the latest re-telling of the George Best story – *All By Himself*. It is a cold night and a sobering film. Best is portrayed as risen, fallen, misunderstood, tragic as well as glorious. And it is on a screen two miles from the house on narrow Burren Way where he grew up.

That was where the greatest Irish across-the-water story began and ended and began again. It was all those summers ago, 1961, when Best returned home from Manchester after just 48 hours away, when he should have been on trial at Old Trafford. It was No. 16 and standing in the front room one day in 1996, George's father Dickie went over the story while, incidentally, dropping in how good Peter Doherty was.

'I thought: 'It can't be George, he's only been away a day," Dickie said. 'When he walked through the door I said: 'What are you doing here?' He said he was homesick. I said: That's all right, son, grown men get homesick."

It is an emotion so many Irish families have been through. Don Givens ran home from Manchester United after a month, Seamus Coleman was delighted when his first flight to England to join Everton was cancelled. He was in Derry and could have gone to Belfast to get a different connection. Instead he raced back to Killybegs for another last night in the house.

Best was the same, he returned for another few nights on Burren Way. Departure for him and Eric McMordie had been by boat to Liverpool followed by a train to Manchester. The second time Best went was by plane and this time he stayed. Soon he would be sending home letters jokily signed 'Garrincha George', which was not too far off.

Best had never before worn long trousers and there were quiet years before his balletic storm washed across England and Europe. He made his Northern Ireland debut with Pat Jennings in 1964 in Swansea. Best was 17, Jennings was 18 and after an Irish away win captain Terry Neill said: 'George plays a game with which I am unfamiliar.'

Today Neill says: 'I must have been listening too long to Danny Blanchflower to speak like that.'

Neill recalls how the shy teenagers roomed together and how the senior players would mimic their presumed conversation:

'Cup of tea, Pat?'

'Yes, George, thanks.'

Pause.

'Another cup of tea, George?'

'Yes, Pat, thanks.'

George Best wasn't a Beatle then. Harry Gregg remembers Best putting on that front-page sombrero on the way home from Benfica and telling Best on the aeroplane: 'George, great players don't need gimmicks.'

Tonight, on screen, Gregg repeats the story in *All By Himself*. Gregg saw Best from the start and must wonder more than half a century on what new there is to say. But the documentary places Best in a different frame. There is much familiar footage but there is also a respectful analysis of Best's decline from hero to alcoholic. He is portrayed as someone falling from a height in plain sight with people just watching transfixed, unable to help or feeling unable to help. He was so physically tough and brave people didn't notice how fragile he was. But Best needed help and the film pulls that out.

Germaine Greer recognised that. She worked in Manchester in the late 60s and knew Best well enough for him to leave her match tickets. When Best died, Greer wrote of the lack of care, real care, he received from the elders at Manchester United. But also, 'it's typical of George that he never blamed anyone but himself.

'George was a genuinely hard man, but hardness results in fragility. His working-class Ulster-Scots upbringing afforded him no way of coming to terms with that fragility, except to deny it and order another round of drinks.'

In *All By Himself* Best's American wife Angie sees another tension, between talent and fame: 'If 70,000 men wanted to have a drink with George, that's one drink for them and 70,000 for George.'

And of course 70,000 men wanted to have a drink with George Best. It is why another film was made more than a decade after his death, why his house is a tourist site where you can see those letters, why there is a George Best walking tour, why there will soon be in the centre of Belfast a George Best-themed hotel, why they named the airport after him. At 20 in 1966 Best was a one-man industry; he is still and the orders keep coming.

But those letters home are a reminder that at first George Best was just a boy who loved football. He became the ultimate. *All By Himself* shows that, it shows the tragedy, too. It shows he left but never left. Good, bad and at times ugly, creative and destructive, gifted and flawed, fierce and fragile, as the cinema lights go on, you cannot help thinking that so much of 140 years of Irish football was captured in this once-in-a-lifetime figure, George Best.

ACKNOWLEDGEMENTS

THIS BOOK COULD NOT HAVE BEEN WRITTEN WITHOUT THE CON-
siderable help of my sisters, Rosemary and Patricia in Belfast, and my brother Johnny.
They gave constant encouragement and information and I cannot thank them enough.
Were they still here, I would say the same of my parents Tommy and Ella.

Other family members who deserve my gratitude are George Walker and Elizabeth
and John Walker. George knew Johnny Brown as his uncle and found him that bleak
day on Roslyn Street in 1963. George's recollections are clear and emotional. Johnny
Brown was not just someone George had heard or read about, he was someone George
knew intimately. It was sad listening to him, but it also felt necessary.

Beyond family, the most important help came from the footballers and managers
who agreed to speak, sometimes about sensitive and personal subjects; reporting
colleagues; and the librarians of Belfast, Coventry and London.

My thanks go to Liam Brady, Noel Campbell, Roy Coyle, Johnny 'Jobby' Crossan,
Lenny Fletcher at Ipswich Town, Harry Gregg, Wes Hoolahan, Stephen Kenny, Mark
Langhammer, Mick Martin, Gareth McAuley, Jimmy McIlroy, Alan McLoughlin,
Paddy Mulligan, Terry Neill, Martin O'Neill, Michael O'Neill, Jimmy Quinn, Louise
Quinn and Niall Quinn. I would particularly like to thank Brian Kerr for generously
re-telling the Joe Bambrick story of his father Frank.

Historically, belated thanks go to Dickie Best, Jimmy Jones, Harry Walker and
Con Martin for interviews done in the 1990s which I have returned to.

Hugh McIlvanney was kind enough to provide memories of Charlie Tully. In
Belfast, Stephen Looney and Mark McIntosh gave generous assistance. In Dublin,
Neil O'Riordan, Sean Ryan, Sean Creedon, Philip Quinn and Emmet Malone did

the same. Many other colleagues have given help: Steven Beacom, Marshall Gillespie, Paul Lennon, George Caulkin, Dan McDonnell and Jonathan Wilson among them. At Euro 2016 thanks to all covering Northern Ireland near Lyon – too numerous to list, but in particular Andy Dillon and Andy Hunter. In Paris thanks to Paul Hayward and Oliver Holt. Martin Hardy has provided much consideration throughout.

Searching for information from clubs led to Pat Quirke and David Instone (Wolves); Jim Brown (Coventry City); Jeff McInery and Ian Garland (Barry Town); Colin Adwent (Ipswich); Rick Glanvill (Chelsea); Noa Bachner (Eskilstuna); Darren Crawley (Dundalk) and in Belfast, Stephen Henderson (Glentoran) and Padraig Coyle (Belfast Celtic).

Alex Jackson at the National Football Museum in Manchester was of great help, as were Daniel Brown at Queen's University, Belfast, and Michael Holmes and Bryce Evans at Hope University, Liverpool.

Fergus Dowd and Alan McLean have been formidable in researching Patrick O'Connell and Mike Bolam was vital in helping with Bill McCracken.

The dedicated and professional staff of Belfast Central Library deserve huge gratitude, as do the staff at the British Library at St. Pancras in London, Newcastle Central Library and Central Library, Coventry.

At the Football Association of Ireland, thanks go to Gareth Maher and Mark MacNamee and, previously, to Sarah O'Shea for the FAI archive at University College Dublin. Visiting it to view documents from 1937 and discovering the archive jumps from 1936 to 1938 was a memorable day.

At the Irish Football Association, thanks to Neil Brittain and Nigel Tilson and to the staff at PRONI for access to the IFA archive and also their excellent day of lectures: New Perspectives on Association Football in Irish History. All the speakers were fascinating.

Thanks to James Corbett, Simon Hughes, Jack Gordon-Brown, Zoran Lucic, Sabahat Muhammad and Megan Pollard at deCoubertin.

Apparently it is advisable to have companion books on a project such as this and Sean Ryan's *Boys In Green* and Cormac Moore's *The Irish Soccer Split* have been invaluable works of reference. So too all those *Rothmans Football Yearbooks* – thanks again Tony Richardsdon. One other has been Gary Imlach's *My Father and Other Working-Class Football Heroes* – my father's copy.

Finally, love and thanks to Sue, Pearl & Irene, as always.

BIBLIOGRAPHY

BOOKS

Best, Barbara – *Our George* (2007)

Best, George – *The Good, The Bad & The Bubbly* (1990)

— *Blessed* (2001)

Blanchflower, Danny – *Danny Blanchflower's Soccer Book* (1959)

— *The Double and Before* (1961)

Bolger, Dermot – *In High Germany* (1999)

Boll, Heinrich – *Irish Journal* (2011)

Bowler, Dave – *Danny Blanchflower* (1997)

Brady, Liam – *So Far, So Good* (1981)

Brodie, Malcolm – *History of Irish Soccer* (1963)

Brown, Daniel – *Every Other Saturday* (2016)

Buchan, Charles – *A Lifetime in Football* (1955)

Busby, Matt – *Soccer At The Top* (1973)

Byrne, Peter – *Green is the Colour* (2012)

Camkin, John – *World Cup 1958* (1959)

Campbell, Tom – *Charlie Tully, Celtic's Cheeky Chappie* (2008)

Carter, Raich – *Footballer's Progress* (1950)

Charlton, Jack – *The Autobiography* (1996)

— *The Authorised Biography* (2016)

Corbett, James – *The Everton Encyclopedia* (2012)

Coyle, Padraig – *Paradise Lost And Found* (1999)

Cox, Jack – *Don Davies, An Old International* (1962)

Craig, Patricia (ed) – *The Belfast Anthology* (1999)

Cullen, Donal – *Freestaters* (2007)

Doherty, Peter – *Spotlight On Soccer* (1948)

Dougan, Derek – *The Sash He Never Wore* (1972)

— *The Sash He Never Wore, 25 Years On* (1997)

— *How Not To Run Football!* (1981)

Dunne & Ryan – *Bass Book of Irish Soccer* (1975)

Dunphy, Eamon – *The Rocky Road* (2013)

Eastham, George – *Determined To Win* (1966)

Edelston & Delaney – *Masters of Soccer* (1962)

Finney, Tom – *Football Round The World* (1953)

Flynn, Barry – *Political Football, The Life & Death of Belfast Celtic* (2009)

Foy & Barton – *The Easter Rising* (2011 ed)

Galvin, Robert – *The Football Hall of Fame* (2011)

Garnham, Neal – *Association Football and society in pre-partition Ireland* (2004)

Giles, John – *A Football Man* (2010)

Gray, Marcus – *Route 19 Revisited, The Clash and the Making of London Calling* (2009)

Gregg, Harry – *Harry's Game* (2002)

Hannigan, Dave – *The Garrison Game* (1998)

Hazelwood, Nick – *In The Way!* (1996)

Hornby, Nick (ed) – *My Favourite Year* (1993)

Houlihan, Con – *More Than A Game* (2003)

Humphries, Tom – *The Legend of Jack Charlton* (1994)

Jack, David – *Soccer* (1934)

Jennings, Pat – *An Autobiography* (1984)

Joannou, Paul – *Newcastle United: Ultimate Who's Who* (2014)

Kennedy, John – *Belfast Celtic* (1989)

Kilbane, Kevin – *Killa* (2013)

Langhammer, Mark – *We're Red, We're Black* (2016)

Lennon, Neil – *Man and Bhoy* (2006)

Lovejoy, Joe – *Bestie* (1998)

Luscombe, William (ed) – *Park Drive Book of Football* (1969)

Marshall, Evan – *Spirit Of '58* (2016)

Matthews, Stanley – *The Way It Was* (2000)

Mercer, Joe – *The Great Ones* (1966)

Meisl, Willy – *Soccer Revolution* (1956)

Miller, Clark – *He Always Puts It To The Right* (1998)

Moore, Cormac – *The Irish Soccer Split* (2015)

Mortensen, Stan – *Football Is My Game* (1949)

Murray, Charles Shaar – *Shots From The Hip* (1991)

McIlroy, Jimmy – *Right Inside Soccer* (1961)

McIlvanney, Hugh – *McIlvanney on Football* (1994)

McKittrick, Kelters, Feeney, Thornton – *Lost Lives* (1999)

McLoughlin, Alan – *A Different Shade of Green* (2014)

O'Connell, Sue – *The Man Who Saved FC Barcelona* (2016)

Quinn, Niall – *The Autobiography* (2002)

Rothmans – *Football Yearbook* (1970 -)

Rouse, Paul – *Sport & Ireland* (2015)

Rowland, George – *Coventry City 100 Greats* (2001)

Ryan, Sean – *The Boys In Green* (1997)

Shankly, Bill – *My Story* (2009)

Simpson, Dawson – *The Whites: A History of Distillery FC* (2004)

Tully, Charlie – *Passed To You* (1958)

West, Patrick – *Beating Them At Their Own Game* (2006)

Williams, Richard (ed) – *George Best, A Life in the News* (2006)

Wilson, Jonathan – *Inverting The Pyramid* (2008)

Younger, Dylan – *Newcastle United Cult Heroes* (2012)

NEWSPAPERS

Belfast Telegraph

Birmingham Mail

Daily Mail

Daily Telegraph

Derry Journal

Dublin Evening Herald

East Anglian Daily Times

Glasgow Herald

The Guardian

The Independent

Ipswich Evening Star

Irish Independent

Irish News

Irish Times

News Letter

Midland Daily Telegraph

The Observer

The Sheffield Star

The Sheffield Telegraph

Sunday World

Sunday Life

Thomson's Weekly

WEBSITES

Balls.ie

BBC

Guardian

NIFG

RTE

Wikipedia

11 v 11

INDEX